"If you are a concerned citizen, a nonprofit, an educator, or an activist, and you want to know how to connect digital natives to civic life and politics, Ben Rigby's excellent book—full of real-life examples and step-by-step how-to (and equally important, *why*-to) instructions—is a great place to start."

> —Howard Rheingold, author, *Smart Mobs*

"While there has been a lot of talk about Web 2.0, there have been few attempts to clarify what that means, its potential for civic engagement, and most importantly, how it works in real life. This guide fills that gap by providing concrete information about a wide range of new technological tools that can and do provide people, especially young people, the power and opportunity to make their voices heard and participate more meaningfully in the issues they care about."

> —Cynthia Gibson, Cynthesis Consulting, and author, *From Inspiration to Participation: Strategies for Youth Civic Engagement* and *Citizens at the Center: A New Approach to Civic Engagement*

"This book is an invaluable resource for any organization seeking to successfully engage youth using emerging web technologies."

> —Anthony S. Jennings, web site specialist, Service Employees International Union

"*Mobilizing Generation 2.0* deftly chronicles the ways in which techno-powered 'digital natives' are changing political communications in the United States, democratizing the process along the way. Attention politicos: don't miss an opportunity to engage young voters in 2008."

> —Julie Germany, director, Institute for Politics, Democracy, and the Internet

"Ben Rigby understands the mind-set of those of us in the nonprofit world: we do not have enough time, money, or human resources to experiment with each Web 2.0 technology, but we understand how critically important it is for us to learn these tools to attract a new generation of donors, activists, and staff. This book clearly explains new technologies, best practices, and common challenges to help us evaluate their effectiveness when appealing to our constituents."

> —Rebecca Hankin, director of marketing, International Rescue Committee

"Whether you're a for-profit, a nonprofit, a one-person show, or a multi-national corporation, there's something in this book for you. Ben Rigby neatly unpicks the family of Web 2.0 technologies and guides the reader through the many ways they can be applied in a range of activities on the ground. This book is long overdue."

 —Ken Banks, founder, kiwanja.net

"Anyone interested in learning the *who, what, where,* and *how* of mobilizing youth for social and political change needs to read this book. Web 2.0 is where it's at, and this book will get you there in a clear, practical, and user-friendly way providing the tools to engage, interact, and empower young people to change the world."

 —Meredith Blake, founder and CEO, Cause and Affect, and former
  executive vice president, Participant Productions

"Young voters, in increasing numbers, are tuning in and taking charge. This book is a great look at how to reach them more effectively."

 —Congressman George Miller, chairman of the House Education
  and Labor Committee

"Ben Rigby has pulled together the ultimate up-to-date guide to using social media for political organizing. How to blog, why to wiki, and when to social network—it's all here."

 —Micah Sifry, cofounder, Personal Democracy Forum and techPresident

"Ben Rigby helps the people working hard to create change—no matter where they work—to make sense of the vast array of technologies available to actually connect to youth in ways that will engage them, involve them, and help to get things done."

 —Marnie Webb, coCEO, TechSoup/NetSquared.org/*ext337.org*

"The next generation is online and waiting for their chance to make the world a better place. *Mobilizing Generation 2.0* is an outstanding field manual for all nonprofits who want to engage tomorrow's citizens today and create change in their communities."

 —Holly Ross, executive director, NTEN: The Nonprofit Technology Network

Mobilizing Generation 2.0

Visit the Web site **www.mobilizingyouth.org** to find more useful information on and relevant to the topics discussed in this book. Here you will be able to experience the technologies covered in *Mobilizing Generation 2.0* as well as stay current with new developments in the world of technology, new media, and youth. The site includes:

- links to Web sites, organizations, and resources mentioned in the book

- additional tips and practical how-to's

- more screenshots and examples, as well as videos

- ongoing commentary about the state of Internet technology and social change

- and up-to-date information about the latest trends in new media and Web 2.0

Mobilizing Generation 2.0

A Practical Guide to Using Web 2.0 Technologies to Recruit, Organize, and Engage Youth

BEN RIGBY

Foreword by Rock the Vote

JOSSEY-BASS
A Wiley Imprint
www.josseybass.com

Published by Jossey-Bass
A Wiley Imprint
989 Market Street, San Francisco, CA 94103-1741—www.josseybass.com

Jossey-Bass books and products are available through most bookstores. To contact Jossey-Bass directly call our Customer Care Department within the U.S. at 800-956-7739, outside the U.S. at 317-572-3986, or fax 317-572-4002.

Jossey-Bass also publishes its books in a variety of electronic formats. Some content that appears in print may not be available in electronic books.

978-0-470-22744-2

Cataloging-in-Publication data on file with the Library of Congress.

Printed in the United States of America
FIRST EDITION
PB Printing   10   9   8   7   6   5   4   3   2   1

CONTENTS

LIST OF FIGURES

FOREWORD

Rock the Vote

n 2008, the question shouldn't be whether or not organizations and campaigns use new media and technologies to engage new members and supporters. It should be *how* they will use them.

Eighty-eight percent of adults under age thirty are online (as well as 71 percent of all adults). Most kids today were surfing the Internet before they learned to ride a bike. Text messaging and social networks are a ubiquitous part of nearly every young person's daily life.

The possibilities for using Web 2.0 technologies to engage young people are endless, which is one of the reasons they can be so overwhelming.

This book is a must-read for any organization, political campaign, or organizer that wants to engage new members, turn out voters, or educate the general public. It is targeted toward reaching young adults, but its lessons have much wider applications for the social sector. In short, if you want to grow your cause in the short and long term, read this book.

In particular, *Mobilizing Generation 2.0* can help you find and target young supporters, volunteers, members, voters, and donors. Although young adults respond to traditional outreach tactics—phone calls, campus organizing, door-to-door canvassing—as well as anyone does, new technologies hold enormous potential for increasing and energizing that response. Using social networks, the Internet, e-mail, text messages, and other new media, campaigns can reach and engage a broad and diverse audience at the click of a button.

Figuring out how to use these new media effectively, however, takes some savvy—and we're all still learning. To get in the game, though, read this book; if you're wondering why you should use Facebook, how a wiki works, or what on earth a video blog is, this book is an excellent primer. You'll find out how young people use the Internet and how it can help you enlist them in your cause. This book will give you practical advice and real-world examples—showing you what works, what *doesn't* work—and what we haven't yet figured out. This is your guide to mobilizing young people in a new online arena.

Today's teens and young adults, labeled the Millennial Generation because they began to come of age around the year 2000, are a major force in politics and society today. At 75 million strong, and including 44 million people in the eighteen- to twenty-nine-year-old youth vote bloc in 2008, this generation is not the future—it's the *here and now.*

And this generation is looking for campaigns and causes to join. Today's teens and young adults are volunteering at record rates, voting in growing numbers, and engaging with news and current events as their older brothers and sisters of Generation X never did.

They're online, texting, video blogging, and Facebook messaging. Learn how to do the same, and you can mobilize what promises to be a world-changing generation.

Rock the Vote has boundless confidence in the Millennial Generation. We've polled, tracked, and watched the young adults of this country, and we know some things for certain: they're engaged in their communities and following key issues, and every year more and more of them are turning out to vote. Young people have the potential to change the world, which is why organizations and campaigns of all shapes and sizes can and should incorporate them into their efforts.

But be forewarned: young people today use the Internet unlike anyone else. This makes a solid knowledge of Web 2.0 technologies essential for anyone mobilizing the Millennial Generation.

ACKNOWLEDGMENTS

Foremost, I thank the hundreds of people working at nonprofits and political campaigns who have documented their efforts on the Web. I also thank the people and organizations who aggregate, organize, and analyze their combined efforts, such as Beth Kanter (beth.typepad.com), Nten (nten.org), MobileActive.org, and Net Squared (netsquared.org). The Web sites developed by these people are troves of valuable information about the use of Internet technology in the social sector. I relied on them extensively in the writing of this book.

I give much thanks to the book team for their tireless efforts. The researchers were Jen Cohn, Lewis Eichle, Elizabeth Kotin, Emma Rodgers, and Lena Zuniga; the reviewers were Tate Hausman, Michael Stein, and Katrin Verclas. A special thanks goes out to Katrin, who spent hours on the phone with me dispensing advice, debating the future of the Internet, and connecting me with numerous people in the field. You are the best board member ever! To my editor, Jesse Wiley, thanks for making the process so easy and giving all kinds of support to make this book happen. To Mickey Butts, thank you for bringing structure, logic, and style to my inchoate drafts. And my appreciation goes to those who assisted with various reviewing, research, advice, and information: Nino Walker, Christian Nold, Rebecca Hankin, Dale Larson, Beka Economopoulos, and all the Big Picture contributors.

I also acknowledge those who supported Mobile Voter throughout the last several years. This includes mobile industry folks: Jed Alpert, Dan Weaver, Doug Busk, Kathie Legg, Michael Silberman, and Justin Oberman; Aron Goldman; Kid Beyond; Becky Bond, for endless support and advice; Richard Schlackman, who was the spark that got Mobile Voter moving in San Francisco; Chris Wright, Baha Hariri, and Nathan Nayman at SFJobs; and Jerry Huang at MacArthur. Thank you to Gunner for always inviting me to meet the smartest activists around; to Bart Cheever, founding partner of Mobile Voter and current board member; to Jordan Snodgrass, Tom Arthurs, and Chris Purvis, for long nights building out the software. And to my partner and coexecutive director, Grace Stanat, for his incredible smarts, quick wit, and willingness to dive in.

Mobile Voter got a tremendous kick-start in 2006 with a grant from the Pew Charitable Trusts, coordinated by Young Voter Strategies (YVS) at George Washington University's School of Political Science. Led by Heather Smith, YVS coordinated a national youth voter registration campaign of which we were fortunate to be a part. The YVS team went on to take leading positions at Rock the Vote, and it's through that relationship that this book was born. Thanks to Heather, Kat Barr, Lindsey Berman, and Mary McClelland—without your support, editing, and enthusiasm, this book would not be. A special thanks to Heather, who believed in and supported what must have seemed like harebrained projects upon my initial proposals.

And finally, thank you to my family—Helen, Gerry, Theo, and Jess Rigby—for boundless support and love. To my new dog, Elf Rigby-Son: it's amazing how much perspective you can gain in the five minutes it takes to rescue something dangerous from the mouth of a puppy . . . thirty times a day. And to my love, Charlene Son.

This book was made possible in part by a grant from the MacArthur Foundation.

ABOUT THE AUTHOR

Ben Rigby has spent the last twelve years developing youth-focused Web and mobile phone strategies for nonprofit organizations and some of the world's top businesses.

Rigby began his career in high tech in 1995 as "webmaster" for a startup named the Main Quad, which launched one of the first online communities for college students. At the Main Quad, Rigby invented an application that allowed students to publish personal profiles online, and he innovated what may have been the first-ever Internet greeting card system. The Main Quad was acquired by Student Advantage in 1997.

Next, Rigby cofounded and became CEO of a Web development firm called Akimbo Design. Here Rigby explored the convergence of design and Internet technology, creating high-end Web sites for top-tier brands. Akimbo achieved international renown and a world-class client list that included such companies as The North Face, Beringer Vineyards, California Pizza Kitchen, Nokia, Sony Pictures, MGM, and Macromedia. His work won dozens of awards and has been featured in many publications, such as *Newsweek*, the *New York Times*, the *Washington Post*, and *USA Today*.

While at Akimbo, Rigby developed an affinity for a client doing innovative work with young people and digital filmmaking. Rigby joined

DFILM.com as CTO and guided the development of the DFILM MovieMaker—a Web application that allowed people to create and share online films. It was an instant hit, attracting millions of young filmmakers in its first two months and subsequently licensed by Yahoo!, Sam Adams, Hyundai, IBM, the Sierra Club, and Old Navy. It was at DFILM that Rigby began to explore mobile phone technology. He developed one of the first-ever text-messaging games for Calvin Klein in 2000 and a platform for cartoon-based mobile messaging, which launched on KPN's iMode network in the Netherlands.

Rigby then became president of 415 Inc, a Web development firm with a nonprofit focus, based in San Francisco. 415 developed Web sites and software for such clients as the International Fund for Animal Welfare, the Women's Funding Network, Bay Area Rapid Transit, KQED, the Library of Congress, McGraw-Hill, Peninsula Open Space Trust, San Francisco Ballet, and the San Francisco Symphony. In this role, Rigby worked closely with organizations to develop strategies to further stretch chronically stretched nonprofit budgets.

In 2004, Rigby founded Mobile Voter, a nonpartisan nonprofit organization dedicated to using Internet technology to empower young people's participation in civic life and politics. Mobile Voter conducted innovative voter registration drives from 2004 to 2006 using mobile phones and text messaging. The organization's mobile software has been used by over two hundred nonprofits in the United States. In 2005, the organization won the Wireless Innovation Award at CTIA (the premier wireless conference). Rigby is a frequent speaker on the conference circuit and is an active participant in the community of organizations using new media for social change.

Rigby earned his BA in Anthropology from Stanford University in addition to Honors with Distinction in Science, Technology, and Society. He was also elected to Stanford's Phi Beta Kappa chapter. Rigby currently resides in San Francisco, where he enjoys frequent trips to the area's many taquerias.

ABOUT ROCK THE VOTE

R ock the Vote's mission is to build the political clout and engagement of young people in order to achieve progressive change in our country. We use music, popular culture, and new technologies to engage and incite young people to register and vote in every election, and we give young people the tools to identify, learn about, and take action on the issues that affect their lives and to leverage their power in the political process.

Founded in 1990 in response to a wave of attacks on freedom of speech and artistic expression, Rock the Vote (RTV) has over the past eighteen years become a name nearly ubiquitous with youth political engagement. And for good reason.

The Early Years: Gen Xers Rock the Vote

In 1990, RTV launched our first national campaign, "Censorship Is UnAmerican," with Iggy Pop, the Red Hot Chili Peppers, and Woody Harrelson as spokespeople. In 1991, with RTV's support, including public service announcements (PSAs) and a "Dear Senator" postcard campaign, the U.S. Congress passed the National Voter Registration Act, more commonly known as Motor Voter.

In 1992, RTV and our partner organizations registered 350,000 young people to vote and helped lead over two million new young voters to the polls. In 1993, RTV successfully worked with other organizations to pass the National and Community Service Trust Act, a bill to encourage volunteerism.

The Middle Years: RTV Hits the Road and the Net

In 1996, RTV's reach expanded exponentially through a partnership with MTV's "Choose or Lose" bus campaign. RTV and MTV registered over five hundred thousand new voters through the partnership.

In the same year, RTV launched an innovative program that allowed voters to request voter information and absentee ballots by calling 1-800-ROCK-VOTE, and, with MCI, developed the first online voter registration, dubbed NetVote '96.

In 2000, RTV continued to expand and innovate. During the 2000 election cycle, RTV registered more than five hundred thousand voters online and all over the country. Programs that year included a brand-new online voter registration application and absentee ballot request system; a twenty-five-city bus tour with members of the *West Wing* cast, Rah Digga, Outkast, and Hootie & the Blowfish; and the launch of Rap the Vote 2000 with Russell Simmons's 360HipHop.

In 2002, RTV expanded our work to include Community Street Teams, and built on our previous work with online voter registration, concerts, a bus tour, and more. Partner artists and PSA features included Dilated Peoples, Eve, Chris Rock, Russell Simmons, Kelly Osbourne, Ozzfest, the Warped Tour, and more. During this midterm election cycle, RTV registered two hundred thousand people to vote.

The Recent Years: The Millennial Generation Rocks the Vote

In 2004, RTV ran a nationwide campaign that registered more than eight hundred thousand people to vote, partnering with BET and MTV and with celebrities, musicians, and activists from every walk of life.

And on Election Day 2004, RTV helped contribute to an historical 4.3 million voter increase in eighteen- to twenty-nine-year-olds' turnout—a turnout jump that signified the arrival of a new, engaged, and politically active group of young adults: the Millennial Generation.

Building on our work in 2004 and on the energy of the Millennial Generation, in 2006 RTV partnered with such new media outlets as Facebook, and entered the Web 2.0 scene with a bang. Registering more than fifty thousand voters, RTV helped make 2006 another huge year for young voters: nearly two million more eighteen- to twenty-nine-year-olds went to the polls than in the previous midterm election.

o   o   o

From street teams to entertainment partnerships to innovative online efforts, Rock the Vote has been a leader in the movement to make young people a more permanent part of the American political process. Rock the Vote is creative, effective, and controlled by nobody's agenda but our own. We tell it like it is and pride ourselves on being a trusted source for information on politics.

In the decades to come, Rock the Vote will continue to use the microphones of music, technology, and youth culture to empower the forty-five million young people in America who want to step up, claim their voice in the political process, and change the way politics is done.

Rock the Vote edited this book, arranged financial support, and will spread the word to political campaigns and nonprofits that this is a must-read manual for engaging young people with Web 2.0 technologies in 2008 and for years to come.

INTRODUCTION

Sweat flies from the bald pate of Andrew Chaikin, aka Kid Beyond, as he leaps from one side of the stage to the other at club Studio Z in San Francisco. The sounds coming out of his mouth—drums, trumpets, guitar, keyboards—are unbelievable. Kid Beyond is an elite beatboxer, a musician who uses his mouth and body as his only instruments. He ends his set with a spectacular series of drumbeats, and the young crowd explodes into cheers. Then Kid does something unexpected. He stops the show and steps under the center spotlight. Still catching his breath, he says,

> "Listen everybody. There's an election coming up, and you've only got two weeks left to register to vote. Pull out your mobile phone and send your name and address to me by text message right now. I'm at 415-341-5015. I'll make sure you get the forms you need and a reminder to vote on Election Day."[1]

My heart was racing as I watched this scene backstage. I had been working to make this moment happen for almost year—developing the software to receive and automatically record incoming text messages, researching voter registration, and setting up the relationship with Kid Beyond—and it was all coming together before my eyes. By the end of the night, about 16 percent of the audience had used text messaging to

1

sign up for our voter registration service. At the time, I was disappointed, as I had hoped for a bigger response. Little did I know that this would be one of our most enthusiastic response rates for the next three years.

From 2004 to 2006, the nonprofit I ran, Mobile Voter, worked with hundreds of nonprofits to roll out this voter registration service, the first of its kind in the world. We learned when text messaging worked and when it didn't. Unfortunately, in the vast majority of cases, response rates hovered at a lackluster 1 percent. It made more sense to send out a few volunteers with clipboards than to use our text-messaging system. In rare instances, though, response rates were much stronger. Things clicked when one of our partner nonprofit organizations teamed with a dynamic performer like Kid Beyond and got the message out right before an upcoming registration deadline.

After the 2006 election, I reflected on the experience of the past three years and pondered how to continue fulfilling my nonprofit's mission of using Internet technology to facilitate civic participation, particularly among youth.

I thought about our text-messaging campaign: although we didn't register as many voters as we'd hoped, we'd developed a trove of information about how to use this technology to recruit, engage, and mobilize youth. Our results would be tremendously valuable to any organization considering using text messaging as a tactic. And any organization working with youth would want to know about text messaging.

I considered that nonprofits and political campaigns could learn from our mistakes and benefit from our hard-earned strategic knowledge. And, in fact, there were dozens of organizations just like Mobile Voter that had developed expertise using the technologies becoming central to young lives, such as blogging, social networking, video, and virtual worlds.

Here's where the inspiration for this book took shape. I envisioned a handbook for nonprofits and political campaigns about these emerging technologies. It would describe them in plain language so that readers could quickly get a sense of the range of possibilities. And it would show how real organizations were using these new tools, bringing together their stories and strategic lessons. I pitched the idea to folks at Rock the Vote, with whom we had worked closely on our text-messaging campaign, and our book project was born.

Why This Book, and Why Now?

Even if you only casually follow the news, you can't help but notice that something big is happening with young people and the Internet. The media buzzes with stories about MySpace, Facebook, YouTube, blogging, virtual worlds, text messaging, and many other technologies that seem to be reshaping young lives. The trouble is, most nonprofits and political campaigns are so cash-strapped and underresourced that they just don't have the time to investigate all these trends or terms. They'd like to know what they could do with the latest technologies, but the demands of day-to-day operations create more than enough work.

Without good information with which to formulate a strategy, some organizations jump in blind. They hear that the social networking site MySpace is a great place to reach youth, for example, so they quickly set up an outpost there. Several months later, after many hours of labor, the results disappoint. A contrary tendency toward inaction abounds as well: without good data, many organizations take a wait-and-see approach.

In both cases, organizations and campaigns miss out on the real opportunity that these technologies offer both to supplement existing tactics and to open new avenues for recruiting, engaging, and mobilizing supporters. The tools have the potential to increase effectiveness and lower costs, but for you to reap these rewards, you have to understand how young people are using technology, and you need to be able to weigh one tool against another so that you invest your resources wisely.

Unlike such time-tested tactics as leafleting, phone-banking, and even e-mail marketing, new technologies haven't been the subject of many scientific studies that evaluate their effectiveness. You can't purchase a report about social networking that tells you exactly what to do and how much it's going to cost. Nonprofits and campaigns are still experimenting, and there are no proven formulas.

However, a trove of anecdotal experience is accumulating. This book brings together stories and strategic lessons to identify trends and opportunities for engaging youth in politics and social causes. If you want to know how nonprofits and politicians are using the latest tools to connect with young people, you'll find it here.

You should read this book if you want to

- Understand the technologies—how they work, what they can do, how people are using them, and what we still have to learn about them.

- Learn how nonprofits and politicians are using new tools to recruit and mobilize supporters and achieve real results.

- Engage young people on their own terms, using the technologies they use and understanding their subtle cultural nuances.

- Harness the energies of your supporters and develop deeper and more personal relationships with them.

- Get a sense for the range of possibilities, so as to choose technologies that are appropriate for your organization's objectives and to make more informed strategic decisions.

- Understand common pitfalls and mistakes.

- Peer into the future and see the big picture from the perspective of some of the world's smartest technology thinkers and activists.

Why Focus on Young People?

Mobilizing Generation 2.0 focuses on the passion and power of *young* individuals. Generally, today's youth—those born between 1977 and 1997—are known as the Millennial Generation. This group shines as one of the most dynamic, concerned, and civic-minded generations in history. They can help politicians get elected, help nonprofits fulfill their mission, and work with both to change the world for the better. The Millennials are

Politically Involved Perhaps it's the war, the crisis in Darfur, global warming, or 9/11—whatever the reason, Millennials are reporting high levels of interest in politics. A recent poll cosponsored by Rock the Vote found that more than 77 percent of Millennials are paying "a great deal" of attention to the 2008 presidential election, and 87 percent report that they plan to vote.[2] With a voting population projected to hit more than fifty million in 2008, Millennials rival the Baby Boomers in size. If the last several elections are any indication, they will continue to vote in increasing numbers.[3]

Civically Active Young people are also deeply involved in their communities. In 2005, an all-time high of 83 percent of college freshmen reported that they volunteered at least occasionally during their high school senior year, and 71 percent volunteered weekly.[4] The number of applicants for careers in service—AmeriCorps, Peace Corps, Teach for America—has skyrocketed in recent years.

Tech Savvy This generation is also extremely familiar with technology. It's how they communicate with friends, do their work, and learn in school—and it's also how they keep up on politics, international issues, elections, and the news. For youth, interacting with technology is not a distinct activity; it's integrated into their lives.

Influential In 2006, young voters helped propel Jim Webb in Virginia and Jon Tester in Montana to Senate victories through their avid use of YouTube, the online video-sharing Web site, and energetic grassroots action.[5] In less than two years, students formed a coalition of more than three hundred colleges and two hundred high schools, raised over $250,000, and galvanized thousands of their peers to take action against genocide in Darfur.[6] A nineteen-year-old started Facebook in 2004, and it's now valued at about $15 billion and plays a central role in the social lives of more than thirty-seven million of his peers.[7]

o o o

In short, young people are becoming a major civic, political, and economic force. Nonprofits and politicians have the opportunity to take a leadership role that recognizes the newfound powers of youth, while offering avenues for participation and involvement. Organizations willing to invest the time will benefit from young people's energy, enthusiasm, and intelligence. Those who seek to understand how we'll use the Internet for years to come can start by learning from youth.

What Is Web 2.0?

The tools discussed in each chapter are generally referred to as *Web 2.0 technologies.*[8] The term refers to a group of popular technologies that survived the dot-com bust, so-called 2.0 because they pick up from the previous generation of technologies invented during the last wave of Internet innovation (circa 1995–2001).

If you've been keeping up with political, nonprofit, or business news, you've probably seen the term attached to just about everything. By now it's a buzzword that people use when they want to demonstrate that they really know what's going on with technology. It's used to describe Web sites, businesses, and (gasp) even books.

Despite its sometimes indiscriminate use, the term Web 2.0 remains a useful one because it describes not only a set of popular Internet technologies but also the phenomenon of a group of people who believe that we are entering a new era. Seeking a more descriptive label for Web 2.0, some people call it the "social web" or "live web," but regardless of the wording, there is a general sense among technologists, legal scholars, economists, and sociologists that tremendous societal shifts are under way—and that recent Internet technology has a lot to do with it.

For the purposes of this book, I'll use the term to describe the technologies and software applications that are empowering these changes. Each chapter of the book covers one or more core technologies. I'll also use Web 2.0 to refer to the broader *movement* defined by shifts in the ways that technology is developed and used. The following list broadly outlines trends and attributes that characterize the Web 2.0 era.[9]

- **A massively connected world.** Over one billion people have access to the Internet. More than 50 percent of U.S. citizens have broadband access. Most Web 2.0 software applications rely on there being a vast number of people connected to each other via the Internet.

- **The network effect.** One of the practical effects of a massively connected world is that as more people use a software product or service, it becomes more valuable. Some software has been specifically designed to harness the "collective intelligence" of its many users.

- **Users as cocreators.** People are no longer simply readers of online materials; they are also writers and creators. Their contributions enhance the value of the software and services they use.

- **Decentralization.** Despite the fact that people who use the Internet are located all over the globe, when they act together, either intentionally or unintentionally, the combined force of their actions can have a tremendous effect and influence. This same trend is observed *within organizations* as individuals gain avenues to lend their expertise without need for strict workflow and hierarchical management.

- **Openness.** Many parts of the Internet, such as data and software, are becoming available to people who want to make use of them, at little or no cost. Using nonproprietary standards, it's easier than ever for organizations to share their wealth.

- **Remixability.** Because so much of the technology is free and open, software developers assemble new software by using bits and pieces of other people's work. These new creations are typically called *mashups.*

- **Emergent.** In the past, software consisted of predefined sets of actions, processes, and behaviors. Its designers decided how you would use it. Web 2.0 software offers looser structures and relies on its *users,* rather than its designers, to come up with ways to use it.

- **Rich experiences.** Web sites are full of video, photos, and vibrant visual environments. They're coming ever closer to approximating real-life experiences.

- **The Web as a platform.** In earlier years, using software that ran in a Web browser (in other words, any Web site) was a slow and stilted experience, whereas software that ran on your desktop was much smoother and more reliable. This gap is closing as Web sites run more like desktop software, and more software makers are choosing to launch their applications on the Web.

Why Focus on Campaigns?

I use the term *campaign* throughout this book to refer to any activity that is intended to fulfill an organizational objective. Traditionally, the term is used in the phrase "political campaign," which specifically refers to an effort by an organization to elect a candidate. Although this book discusses political campaigns, I also use the term more generally as in "a campaign to raise funds for fighting cancer" or a "campaign to stop the seal hunt."

Typically, an organization will use Internet technology to support some part of a campaign. For example, Rock the Vote sends a text-message reminder to vote on Election Day. It also makes phone calls, organizes street teams, and runs public service announcements on the radio. Text messaging is one part of its broader *get out the vote campaign*.

I'm assuming that your organization structures its strategy and activity around something approximating my definition of a campaign. You may call them initiatives or programs, but whatever the term, these efforts are the core work of your organization.

Who Should Read This Book?

Mobilizing Generation 2.0 describes the intersection of Internet technology, social change, and young people. If you're curious about any one of these areas, this book offers a rich set of practical information. And if you're working with or leading an organization that intersects with all three of these areas, this guide should help you do your work more effectively. Although many others may find it valuable, including for-profit companies, the book is oriented toward the following people:

Nonprofit and Political Leaders   If you're leading a nonprofit organization or running for or holding public office, this book explains what you need to know about young people's use of the latest Internet technologies. For a quick overview, read the beginning of each chapter for a succinct description of the technology and how organizations are using it, then turn to the "Strategic Considerations" section for guidance about how to use the technology to fulfill your organization's mission, recruit new supporters, engage constituents, or win more votes.

Nonprofit and Campaign Staff Members   If you're in the trenches working for a cause or a candidate, this book gives you the know-how to get started with the latest tools. You might focus on the How It Works and How to Get Started sections in each chapter to begin putting the technology into practice in your organization; read the entire chapter for fresh new ideas.

Those Who Work with Youth   The entire book is invaluable for understanding young people's social and political lives. If you work with youth, you know that Internet technology is central to their daily routines. Read this book to understand how these new tools are empowering creativity, social connection, and activism.

Anyone Interested in Big New Ideas   This book offers insight into how people are using the technologies that are driving radical changes in our society, politics, and economy. Over the last 150 years, we've moved slowly from a society that values industrial goods to one that primarily values information. And within just the last ten years, technological innovations have begun to shift the means of production to average people. Sitting in our living rooms, we can reach, inform, and educate millions of our peers. Look to the conclusion of each chapter for a summary of the key changes, and to the Big Picture essays and interviews from leading technology visionaries for a view of what's to come.

How to Read This Book

This book is intended to serve as a handbook. It introduces you to the various technologies popular among youth and shows how they're used in practice by nonprofits, political campaigns, and the occasional for-profit.

I'm assuming that you have a set of organizational objectives and are looking for tactics to achieve those objectives. In this case, you may be asking such questions as, "I've heard about social networks. I wonder if there's a way we could use one to achieve our goals?" The structure of the book works well to answer these types of questions. (Please note, however, that although the division of chapters by technology is helpful for the purposes of the book, few organizations would seek to use a technology in isolation.) The chapters discuss the following topics:

Blogs are simple Web publishing systems that enable nontechnical people to create Web sites in the format of a personal diary. In Chapter One, we'll look at how blogs are becoming the primary tool that young people use to frame and share observations about politics, relationships, and the world in general. Over the last several years, blogs have grown into a major alternative source of information, vying with the commercial mass media in terms of their ability to frame current events. In order to become effective in the political space, politicians must understand the role of blogs and engage the blogging community. Nonprofits have discovered that maintaining a blog has numerous benefits, such as involving young supporters, strengthening community ties, and advancing key issues.

Social networking sites allow people to create personal profiles, mingle with friends, and define an identity online. In Chapter Two, we'll look at how these Web sites have become "third places" similar to coffee shops, bowling alleys, and roller rinks; they are places where young people "hang out." In the process, they define their identities, form connections with peers and organizations, and learn about and undertake civic action. To understand young lives, you need to understand social networks. Organizations have been conducting campaigns on these networks, with varying success, to recruit young activists, promote issues, and raise money.

Video- and photo-sharing sites, which we'll explore in Chapter Three, are Web sites that enable people to publish and share videos and photos easily. The widespread ability to view, create, and share these forms of media has established a vivid new avenue for online conversation. Videos and photos offer a sense of realism and authenticity that was not available in the text-focused World Wide Web of yesteryear. Online video's unassailable and widely accessible replaying of events has toppled several political careers. At the same time, video and photo sharing has enabled organizations and politicians to engage more deeply with supporters.

Mobile phones have become woven into the social fabric of youth life. In Chapter Four, we'll discuss text messaging—the short messages that are like e-mail for mobile phones. Text messaging has become a primary method of communication among young people. It offers immediacy unrivaled by any other technology—you can send and receive a text message from any place, at any time. Using text messaging, political campaigns and organizations have been able to cost-effectively mobilize and recruit supporters. This chapter also discusses several other features available on most mobile phones.

Wikis are Web sites built through ad hoc collaboration. In Chapter Five, we'll discuss the ways in which wikis can be used to aggregate knowledge and coordinate efforts. Wikis also exemplify how a decentralized group of people, connected to one another by the Internet, can jointly produce a work as great as, or greater than, one produced by a traditionally structured hierarchical organization. There is more to be gained by putting trust in supporters than by exerting tight managerial control.

Online maps offer much more than driving directions. In Chapter Six, we'll explore the wide range of possibilities that online mapping offers to politicians and nonprofits. Maps reveal powerful patterns and relationships previously hidden in a sea of data. New online mapping tools are easy to use, inexpensive, and a great way to support advocacy campaigns.

Virtual worlds are three-dimensional representations of reality . . . and fantasy. Although they may seem like games, they are places in which real social lives unfold. People purchase property, build homes, meet one another, conduct business, and generally live their lives in these places. In Chapter Seven, we'll look at several entrepreneurial organizations that have conducted successful advocacy and fundraising campaigns in virtual worlds. Be forewarned, however, that virtual world successes are few and far between. Challenges are numerous.

The Conclusion synthesizes the topics, strategies, and trends discussed throughout the book. It wraps up with a view toward the future.

The Big Picture is a series of essays and interviews that run between each chapter. Leading thinkers in the fields of nonprofit organizations, technology, and politics take a step back to look at the big ideas shaping the online world today and tomorrow.

The Conversation Continues Online

This book's Web site (www.mobilizingyouth.org) offers an extensive collection of resources and links to other sites referenced in the book, including up-to-date information that couldn't fit in the confines of a printed book. My contact information is also on the Web site if you would like to get in touch. This is a collaborative venture—a product of the hundreds of organizations and people who shared their strategies, thoughts, and results. I welcome you to join the conversation, and look forward to seeing you online.

Endnotes

1. Today you would not normally set up a text-messaging campaign to send to a standard phone number, as in this example. You would use a shortcode instead (see Chapter Four on mobile phones). At the time in 2004, however, shortcodes were relatively new, and using a standard phone number was a much easier route.

2. www.sacredheart.edu/pages/3917_poll_results.cfm

3. Population facts and estimates are derived from the U.S. Census Bureau Population Projections 2000 to 2050, available at www.census.gov/ipc/www/usinterimproj/usproj2000-2050.xls.

4. UCLA's Higher Education Research Institute, "National Norms for Fall 2005," *The American Freshman*, p. 1.

5. www.ksg.harvard.edu/ksgnews/Features/opeds/050107_shaheen _volpe.html

6. www.idealware.org/articles/social_networking_genocide.php

7. www.forbes.com/technology/2007/09/24/facebook-microsoft -investment-tech-cx_pco_0924paidcontent.html

   www.web-strategist.com/blog/2007/08/17/the-numbers-from -facebook-themselves

8. Although you might make a good case that mobile phones fall some- what outside this rubric, they are nevertheless a key technology in use by young people and are integral to the technical landscape of their lives. As such, they're quite appropriate for the context of this book.

9. The following Web site offers a great review of Web 2.0 trends: www.squidoo.com/introtoweb20. Thanks also to www.adaptive path.com/ideas/essays/archives/000547.php and Oreilly Radar's Web 2.0 report for focusing this particular list.

CHAPTER 1

Blogging

When Strom Thurmond ran for president, we voted for him. We're proud of it. And if the rest of the country had followed our lead, we wouldn't have had all these problems over the years, either.

—Senator Trent Lott, December 5, 2002

This statement from a Mississippi senator at the one hundredth birthday of former South Carolina senator Strom Thurmond may sound like benign birthday flattery—if it weren't for the fact that Thurmond's 1948 presidential campaign promoted racial segregation. A young ABC News reporter assigned to cover the event concluded that Lott's comment might imply that he also supported segregation. The reporter thought he had a major news story. But ABC's senior staff disagreed, deciding to run the story briefly on television at four-thirty in the morning and to publish a short piece about it on its Web site.[1] By the next day, the story was effectively dead in the mainstream press.

But it did not go unnoticed in the "blogosphere," that massive decentralized group of people who publish online personal journals. Several politically oriented bloggers read the story and began to investigate. They found that Lott had voted against the renewal of the Voting Rights Act and the Civil Rights Act; opposed the Martin Luther King holiday;[2]

affiliated himself with the Council of Conservative Citizens, classified as a hate group by the Anti-Defamation League; and wrote articles for publications espousing white separatism.[3]

Bloggers filled in details that were missing from the original report, and the story spread rapidly across the Internet.[4] Within a week, thousands of bloggers had republished it, and many called for Lott's resignation. Sensing a grassroots groundswell, the mainstream press ran the story again, only this time reporters added the historical details that bloggers had uncovered. The press turned the issue into a full-blown scandal. Lott quickly lost the support of the White House and his Senate colleagues; he resigned as Senate Republican leader on December 20, 2002.[5]

Bloggers had arrived: their intense focus on an obscure story forced it to national attention. Mainstream media were no longer the sole conduit through which current events became News.

For many people, particularly youth, blogging is more than a source of political news; it is a mechanism for self-expression, identity formation, and entertainment. According to a recent Pew Internet and American Life survey, about twelve million Americans keep a blog, and fifty-seven million Americans read them. Over half are under the age of thirty, and most view blogging as a creative way to share their experiences with others.[6] The impact of blogging in the political and social spheres has been so sudden and wide reaching that social scientists, marketers, politicians, and many others are struggling to understand how it affects their domain.

Although blogging's role in modern life is complex, its premise is simple. *Blogging software makes Web publishing easy.* Once the province of highly technical webmasters, Web publishing is now about as difficult as sending an e-mail. Within ten minutes, anyone with access to a computer can create a blog, publish an article, and call themselves a blogger. One key innovation of these publishing systems is that they allow the reader to *talk back.* After every article, a "comments" area invites written response. Popular blog articles have become long conversations between readers and the original author.

Over the past several years, blogging has evolved into a distinct literary and media form. Although there is no official body that determines what qualifies as blogging, bloggers generally value personal and authentic language, are willing to listen to and allow criticism in comments, write frequently, and participate in the community of bloggers by writing comments on related blogs. The first blogs took the form of personal diaries. Today, however, businesses, politicians, and nonprofit organizations use blogs for a variety of purposes. Growth has been explosive: fewer than fifty blogs existed in 1999, but now over seventy million populate the Internet.[7]

This chapter explores the ways organizations have used blogs to achieve mission-related objectives and build relationships with bloggers. Bloggers can profoundly affect public perception of a candidate, issue, or organization. It's vital to establish credibility and connection with the blogging community in order to have a voice in this increasingly important forum.

How Organizations Are Using Blogs

Starting an organizational blog is one of the fastest routes for telling the story of your candidate or cause, demonstrating expertise in your field, and engaging supporters in conversation. They are easy to set up and inexpensive to maintain. For many organizations, blogging may be the ideal gateway to participation in the Web 2.0 movement.

As a point of introduction to blogosphere vernacular, *posts* is the term used to refer to blog writings. The word is used interchangeably as a noun and verb—for example, "Don't bother me, I'm working on a blog post" or "I'll be ready to eat dinner after I post to my blog." I'll employ these linguistic conventions throughout this chapter.

Providing Limited Participation in a Story

Mitt Romney's "Five Brothers" blog lies at the heart of his presidential campaign's Internet strategy. In shades of the *Brady Bunch*, Romney's five sons write about their dad, the issues they face, and life on the

campaign trail. Tagg, the eldest at age thirty-seven, loves the Red Sox
and has three kids. Craig, the youngest at twenty-six years old, would
like to meet Conan O'Brien someday. On the day I visited the blog,
Josh, thirty-one, had just posted a photo of himself and his two children visiting a state fair in Iowa. A funnel cake stand was illuminated
in the distance. You could almost hear the American flag flapping gen-
tly in the wind and the sounds of the carnival rides. Without sounding
scripted or "spun," the blog reinforced Romney's key campaign message:
family values.

From a communications standpoint, the Romney campaign has scored
a big hit. The blog medium helped the campaign deliver a message
that sounds (and probably is) authentic. At the same time, it's also a
message that has been carefully crafted to contrast Romney against his
twice-divorced competitor, Rudolph Giuliani, who no longer speaks
with his adult children.

The mainstream media have picked up on this angle in dozens of articles and television spots. They echo the family values sentiment in such
statements as this from the *Times* Online: "The brothers are so handsome and wholesome that they bring to mind the Osmonds,"[8] and
this from the *Washington Post:* "Wholesome does not really begin to
describe the five adult children of Republican presidential candidate
Mitt Romney, who for the past few weeks have been sharing such details on Five Brothers."[9] If nothing else, the blog serves as a continuous
feed of the family values message to the press. But it's also a hit with
supporters. According to rankings from Alexa.com, the blog is the most
popular part of Romney's Web site outside the home page.[10]

From a technical perspective, the Romneys are using blog software to
publish content to the Web. It provides the brothers with a simple tool
for posting new material every day. The campaign hired a designer to
make the blog look good, and the software does the rest.

However, the blog provides the campaign with more than a Web publishing system: it offers a framework for telling a story. Blogs add a date
and time stamp to each article and insert the most recent article at the

top of the page. This reverse chronological structure creates a serial-like quality which suggests that a new installment is coming soon. The Romneys don't need to invent new ways to keep supporters interested; the blog automatically provides a known storytelling device.

Before reading a word, experienced blog readers expect the Romneys' blog to offer an honest, personal, and straightforward account. Organizations that rehash promotional writings better suited for marketing brochures find that blog readers are extremely critical. Readers will berate these as "fake blogs" or "flogs." Generally, the Romneys' blog does meet readers' expectations, although it runs some risk of being perceived as a flog, for unlike most blogs, it limits interactions between authors and readers. Comments are accepted, but controversial ones are left unanswered. The Romneys have responded to a question about campaigning on Sundays as Mormons, but ignored a question asking about the brothers' willingness to volunteer for the Iraq War.[11] However, they don't delete these questions. The campaign successfully walks the line between marketing and authenticity by leaving challenging comments on the site.

The blog gives the campaign an approachable and personable face while telling a great ongoing story. It keeps supporters engaged while avoiding "off-message" conversations. It may be possible to increase youth engagement by making this interaction richer, but the Romneys manage to make effective use of their blog while staying within the limits of their comfort zone and campaign strategy.

Offering Deep Participation and Social Connection

Amnesty International aims to engage and connect human rights activists around the world. It has 2.2 million members in more than 150 countries. Traditionally, the organization used newsletters and e-mail alerts to communicate with members. Although these media worked, Amnesty felt uncomfortable being the "sole authoritative voice" and wanted to create a more balanced relationship between staff and activists. In contrast to Romney, the organization thrives on community-driven conversation and debate. Starting a blog was a natural fit.

The Amnesty blog features five topic areas and engages readers in a lively discussion via comments. Blog posts convey timely news, upcoming Amnesty events, and ways to take action. Although Amnesty continues to offer authoritative analysis, it also invites supporters to create dialogue around that analysis. Amnesty starts the story, and supporters then make it their own.

Amnesty's blog gives activists a source of inspiration and a space to connect with one another. By playing host, Amnesty is able to take the pulse of activist thought and action. It monitors and participates in these discussions in order to inform future action. Compared with a newsletter or e-mail alert, the blog offers a much richer forum for dialogue, community building, and learning.

One of Amnesty's key objectives is to encourage *offline* action, which the blog achieves. On the day I visited, a recent post in the "Student Activism" area called for students to spend some of their summer vacation sending postcards. Another article reported the successes of the previous summer's postcard-writing campaign, which resulted in the release of five prisoners of conscience from Belarus and Israel.[12] Amnesty's blog both asks for participation and shows results from past involvement, a method of engagement often called "closing the feedback loop." The loop begins when a supporter takes action and closes when the organization shows the results of that action.

Organizations often fail to close the loop due to limited time or financial resources. However, it's one of the most effective methods for retaining and engaging supporters.[13] Young supporters want to know that their efforts have not gone to waste, and the blog offers an inexpensive and quick way to close the loop.

Whereas the Romney campaign considers conversation around difficult issues a potential risk, Amnesty thrives on this type of discussion. Dan McQuillan, Amnesty's interim Internet director, says that the organization is still in the process of exploring social media, but that thus far, use of such technology as blogging has led to richer conversation around human rights issues, generated action, and resulted in access to new audiences.[14]

Ways to Use Blogs

Blogs can be used to

- **Announce**
  - Events
  - New products, services, and initiatives
- **React immediately** to public criticism or praise
- **Convey** organizational messaging and identity
- **Involve** constituents by asking questions and listening to responses
- **Close the feedback loop**
  - Give results of fundraising efforts
  - Tell volunteers what they've achieved
  - Report back from conferences and events

Reporting Alternative News

At age seventeen, Gwen Araujo was brutally murdered after several men discovered that she was biologically male. As the trial of the accused murderers began, the Community United Against Violence (CUAV), a nonprofit dedicated to preventing violence against the lesbian, gay, bisexual, and transgender community, started a blog to document the proceedings. CUAV's bloggers were intimately familiar with the issues and provided an alternative analysis of the trial while the mainstream media delivered sensational sound bites. The blog provided a forum for the community to vent their anger, share frustrations, and watch the trial unfold from the perspective of like-minded individuals.[15]

The mainstream media don't always report a story in depth, due to a number of restraints. Some stories don't appeal to a wide enough audience, certain advertisers will find some content objectionable, and television time and print space are limited resources. As a blogger, you are free of these limitations. You can use a blog to tell the story from the perspective of your constituency and to provide depth where the mainstream media have glossed over the issues.

Improving Internal Communications

The qualities of blogs that resonate so well with supporters can also improve an organization's internal communications, creating opportunities for collaboration, discussion, and ad hoc documentation.

Matias Fernandez Dutto, a PR strategist and management consultant specializing in social technologies, presents this excellent list of the benefits of using a blog internally:[16]

- It improves participatory spirit, collaboration, and the capabilities of team learning. It is ideal for running projects and working with heterogeneous teams. It is also useful to promote dialogue and find lateral ideas outside the team.

- It allows integrating conversations with a shared vision. It is an excellent means for the leaders to communicate.

- It is the space where interpretations and different points of view come up so that any member of the organization can discuss and debate them.

- It is an excellent means for the employees to achieve an integrated vision of the company by joining in conversations.

- It implies an open communication platform that allows new ways of relating and coordinating actions among the organizational members and between the latter and the network of external relationships.

- It becomes the written memory of the organization. Furthermore, writing conveys emotional stability, which eventually promotes the process of organizational development.

- It speeds up the transference and transformation of knowledge to make ideas flow easily and take learning into action.

Moreover, blogs can help create a workplace in which young people thrive. Although an extended discussion of internal organizational practices is beyond the scope of this book, keep this capability in mind if you're thinking about starting a blog.

You can also use a blog to keep the story in the news. The mainstream media coverage of the Gwen Araujo case died after the first trial, but CUAV provided ongoing blog reporting and analysis of the second trial. Eventually, the blog drew the attention of the mainstream media and kept the story in the public eye. For grieving members of Araujo's community, the blog offered some reconciliation. It created a space for reacting to, supplementing, and influencing the mainstream news. At the same time, it served as a forum for discussion and support.

Harnessing Super-Supporters

Teens are often much more enthusiastic authors and readers of blogs than their adult counterparts, according to the Pew Internet and American Life Project.[17] Pew classifies 8 percent of the population as Internet "omnivores," that is, users who consume the Internet with fervor. These users see the Internet as a "platform for participation and self-expression," and they tend to be young. More than half of heavy Internet users are under the age of thirty (versus one in five in the general population), and 42 percent are students with access to high-speed and wireless networks at school.[18]

Some organizations are blessed with a contingent of these active young supporters, but may find it difficult to harness their collective energy. One solution is to create a *community blogging platform,* an umbrella site where super-supporters can operate their own blogs. This approach can strengthen community, centralize activity, and maintain the vital interest of young supporters.

The Obama 2008 campaign launched one of the first community blogging platforms in the political sphere. In a few minutes, supporters can create their own blog and start posting about Obama, or whatever else they see fit. On the day I visited the community blog, one young supporter posted images of himself and a few friends canvassing in the Iowa rain. Another reported highlights from Obama's speech at the Yearly Kos convention. The headline from another read, "Senator Obama wake up! You are losing and it's time for change!"

As you can see, the community blog offers a space for both support and criticism, and the campaign benefits from both. These blogs have allowed supporters to create their own grassroots marketing propaganda, while also increasing the campaign's ability to quickly understand the zeitgeist of its support. Blogs are an early-warning sign: if candidates are indeed losing the race, they'll hear about it first on the blog.

Unlike the Romney campaign, which follows a top-down communication strategy that offers limited space for supporting and reacting to the campaign, Obama's blogging strategy allows his super-supporters to engage with the candidate on many different messages—and to give feedback to the campaign. If a message doesn't work, the campaign will hear about it and can quickly adjust. The blog functions as a massive and inexpensive focus group.

At the same time, it harnesses the energies of super-supporters to cocreate campaign messages and spread these messages throughout their network of friends. Romney's sons may be charismatic personalities and frequent writers, but there are only five of them. They can't hope to match the reach of Obama's thousands.

Adopting a community blogging strategy is not without risk. After you have made an investment in software and time, there is a real possibility that no one will make the effort to create a blog under your umbrella. Potential bloggers have so many possible avenues for creating online content that you will have to convince supporters that your umbrella is better. A community blog with a lot of activity will attract new supporters. Conversely, a sparsely populated one will convey a lack of interest and a sense of irrelevance.

To counteract this risk, your organization will need to make an up-front investment in blog marketing and an ongoing commitment to blogger outreach. You'll need someone to guide your community blogging initiative to ensure that your bloggers remain active and engaged, while providing incentives to do so. Clearly, this level of commitment would strain the resources of many organizations. For those that can manage it, however, a community blog provides a compelling method for engaging supporters and learning from them.

Blog Fundraising

According to market research company comScore Media Metrix, blog readers are 11 percent more likely than the average Internet user to have incomes of or greater than $75,000. They tend to make more purchases online and also spend 6 percent more than the average Internet user.[19]

Clearly, these statistics don't refer to the majority of young people. But it's worth mentioning that many organizations use their blogs to raise funds from readers.[20] An engaging story puts people in the right frame of mind to donate. When addressing young audiences, however, it may make more sense to ask for another form of participation. Many young people seek authentic engagement and the opportunity to participate beyond writing a check.[21] However, see the chapter on social networking for one fundraising method that seems to be working among youth.

Creating a Sounding Board

In the discussion of Obama's blog, I touched briefly on the idea of using a blog to conduct market research. Some people use their blogs *primarily* in this way, posting new ideas, possible strategic directions, and preliminary campaign materials to the blog and inviting feedback prior to making a commitment. Martin Kearns, executive director of Green Media Toolshed, describes this approach:

> I am the type of yahoo who gets lots of thoughts and thinks better "externally." . . . Unfortunately, it means that I say lots of dumb things . . . but I get to throw them out and get snagged by fellow bloggers. It catches the mistakes or reinforces good ideas and helps me edit more of my thoughts. . . . I know the language, writing, and thoughts are often way more convoluted than I would ever kick out in a meeting or for work products. I also mess up typing and spelling all over the place. However, I am pretty comfortable with the idea that I am not stupid and that cranking stuff out on the blog helps me refine my thoughts. I am verbose. I am comfortable that I make mistakes and I am not perfect. . . . Seeing my thoughts online may actually serve to make me more comfortable with the idea that some mistakes are OK.[22]

Some organizations would be wise to use their blogs as Kearns does. In February 2007, the Buffalo chapter of the American Red Cross put up billboards with the following headline: "Terrorist Strike Leaves City in Chaos. November 9, 2009." In small print, the advertisement described a biochemical attack.

The billboard incensed many people in the community, who decried it as an act of fear mongering. One frequent Red Cross donor described her reaction: "I find it absolutely despicable that this organization has chosen to further the unwarranted state of fear that many citizens of this country currently live in by advertising in this manner. . . . The money spent on this absurdity should have gone to those in need. I will not yet withdraw my monetary support; but I am greatly disheartened by this distasteful waste."[23]

On February 21, citing negative reactions from the community, the Red Cross removed the billboards.[24] If the Buffalo chapter had taken Kearns's approach and vetted the advertisement on its blog, it would have saved thousands of dollars and the ire of many supporters. Allowing blog readers to participate in the design and direction of the organization's initiatives would have also generated loyalty. Young people, in particular, want to know that their opinion matters. Using a blog as a sounding board demonstrates your commitment to hearing other opinions.[25]

You don't have to set up your own blog to do market research, however. On a daily basis, over seventy million bloggers are creating a mounting treasure trove of data. You can harvest this data for key insights about your supporters and organization. When young people talk about your issues, you can learn what they're saying. When they speak about your organization, you'll hear about it. Setting up systems to track blogosphere conversation serves as an inexpensive form of market research, using one of the biggest focus groups on the planet. It can also function as an early warning system for breaking news that affects your organization.

To learn more about easy ways to track
issues in the blogosphere, head to

mobilizingyouth.org/resources/blogs_research_tool

Building a Training Tool

"AFL/CIO Endorses Homer Simpson"

"Video Shows That Maggie Is a Revolutionary New Kind of Leader"

"Looking and Sounding Presidential, Krusty Klown"

These headlines were featured on the home page of the New Organizing Institute's blog in summer 2007. Trainees enrolled in NOI's week-long boot camp for young progressive activists ran a mock race for president in which they selected characters from *The Simpsons* as their candidates and waged political warfare against each other. NOI's directors turned the blog into a simulated media channel, giving trainees permission to post at will. As the week progressed, the trainees reveled in their ability to create and distribute faux campaign propaganda. They posted interview transcripts, campaign videos, and breaking news stories. They explored the concepts of Web metrics, earned media, and microtargeting. The blog provided an outlet for creativity while teaching the trainees how to run an Internet campaign.

The blog offered an engaging learning environment that won rave reviews from trainees. It wasn't the focus of the institute's efforts or even an ongoing project. Instead, the organization made creative use of a blog to support a primarily offline project. Blogs enable multiple authors with little technical expertise to publish photos, video, and written text to the Web. Most people use them to publish articles in diary format, but by being creative, you can apply the benefits of blogging to other purposes. You may find that the blog offers a compelling alternative to traditional tools, such as PowerPoint presentations.

Managing Blogger Relations

After the Trent Lott episode, politicians, corporations, and nonprofits realized that they needed a blogosphere strategy. One year later, Republican senator Rick Santorum was quoted equating homosexuality with bestiality. The progressive blogosphere ignited. The same bloggers who lacerated Lott condemned Santorum. But this time the GOP was prepared to take control of the message first. President Bush intervened early to express support for Santorum and frame the story before the bloggers could take control of it. Bush promoted a softer interpretation of the bestiality comments, and the mainstream media reflected this muted stance. Public outrage was contained, and Santorum kept his job.[26]

Without a doubt, Bush's preemptive strike tactic was effective, but it required major political muscle and would be a difficult strategy to maintain over the long term. Instead, many organizations have begun to build relationships with bloggers that enable them to have a degree of influence in terms of promoting stories, framing issues, and responding to breaking news.

Like their audiences, bloggers expect personal conversations. They respond to sincere efforts to engage in their community, and to people who build relationships prior to a pressing need. Identify bloggers who are naturally aligned with your organization's positions and get to know them. Supply them with original content for their posts. Human Rights Watch provides ongoing story leads and issue analysis to help bloggers write new stories. This effort builds credibility and puts the organization in a strong position to ask favors at a later date.

A handful of elite political bloggers now wield tremendous influence, but like celebrity reporters, they're in constant demand and are therefore more difficult to contact. However, they rely on so-called B-list bloggers for story sourcing. By looking at comments and links on an elite blogger's site, you can begin to understand the structure of his or her network.[27] You can reach out to the less popular bloggers and become a trusted source to them. In turn, they will feed your perspective and ideas to the elite bloggers.

By developing trusted relationships and treating bloggers as a core part of your outreach efforts, you can take a proactive role in shaping news that affects your organization. You'll also be prepared to respond rapidly to negative news and to promote your achievements.

Microblogging

One of the fastest-growing phenomena on the Internet is known as *microblogging*. Microbloggers write just a sentence or fragment at a time, and their postings are less formal and more frequent. If a blog tells the story of someone's day-to-day life, microblogging describes it moment to moment. Young people use microblogging sites like Twitter and Jaiku to write one- or two-sentence updates about what they're doing at that precise moment.

So far, microblogs are being used primarily to communicate among friends, but they offer fertile ground for engaging young people in civic and political life. LiveEarth uses microblogging to advocate for environmental conservation; San Francisco mayor Gavin Newsom keeps constituents apprised of events at City Hall; NASA builds community support through a live connection to the happenings at its Moffett Field facility; and conferences such as South by Southwest enable attendees to share the event with friends who weren't able to make it. At press time, Wired Online was considering using microblogging to gather real-time intelligence from a broad swath of amateur journalists.

term

The promise of microblogging is just beginning to unfold. Learn more at
mobilizingyouth.org/microblogging

How Blogs Work

In this section, we'll look both at the basics of blogging software and at more recent innovations that have added a wide array of options.

Blogging Basics

All blogging software shares three core components:

1. A simple mechanism for publishing text and images to the Web[28]

2. An automated system that displays posts in reverse-chronological order

3. A mechanism for readers to submit public comments about a post

To understand these components in context, let's look at two screenshots from the popular blog software Blogger, created by Evan Williams (who also has contributed a Big Picture essay to this book). Figure 1.1 shows the user interface for publishing text and images to the Web.

Figure 1.1. Screen for Writing a New Blog Post

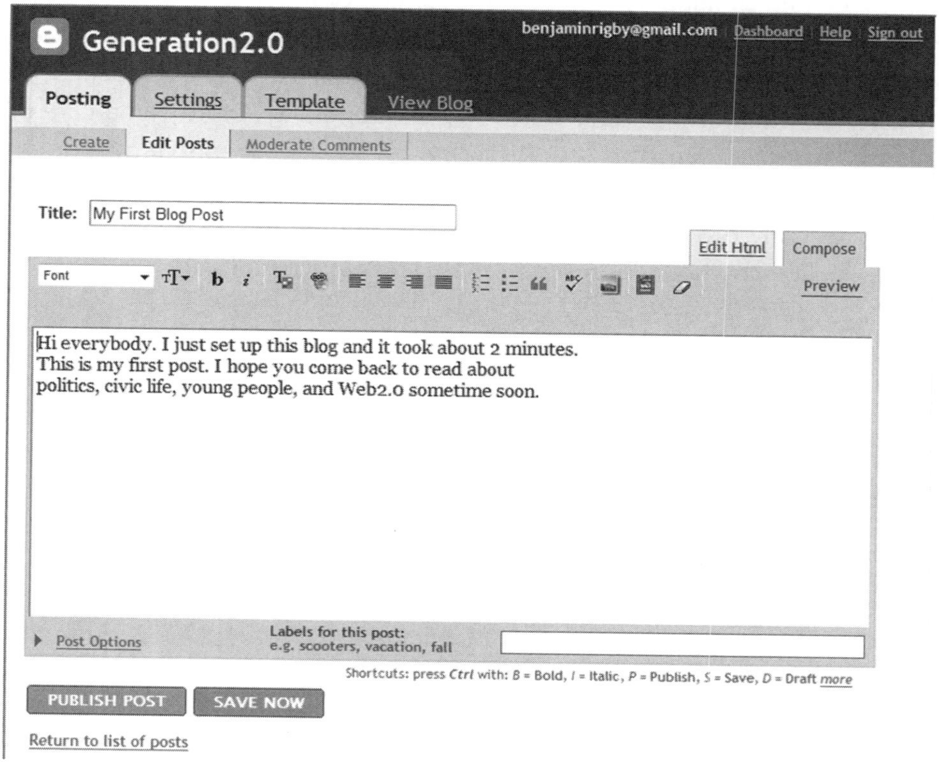

As you can see, the simple interface looks similar to such document-editing software as Microsoft Word. Type in the white box, and click "Publish Post." Blogger's automated system then generates a Web page that displays the new post at the top of the page. It also builds in a link that allows readers to comment on the post. Figure 1.2 shows two sample articles I've posted to my new blog.

Figure 1.2. Two Posts on My New Blog

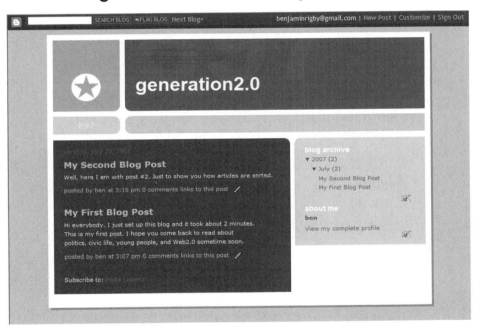

The most recent post is listed at the top. Note the comments link beneath each post. Most blogging software allows the blog owner to choose whether he or she wants to allow public comments, allow approved comments, or not allow any comments. During the two-minute setup process, I chose this design template from among many possibilities. Most blogging software offers a range of predesigned templates from which to choose. If you have a bit more technical knowledge, you can customize the blog design to match your organization's brand identity.

Other Key Blogging Features

Blogging software in its early form comprised only the aforementioned three core components, which facilitate easy Web publishing in diary format. The meteoric rise in the popularity of blogging, however, was brought about by the somewhat later addition of several components, which encouraged people to share and distribute their blog postings. The following are brief descriptions of these newer features.

Permalinks   Over time, numerous posts accumulate on a blog home page. On the earliest blogs, it became difficult to find an individual post. To give directions, a blogger would have to say something like "Go to myblog.com and scroll three-fourths of the way down the page and look for the post called 'blogs are easy.'" Permalinking systems solve this problem by making a copy of each post at a distinct Web address (URL). With permalinks, a blogger can give much simpler directions, such as, "Go to myblog.com/blogs-are-easy."

Trackbacks   Book authors cite references with footnotes or endnotes. Bloggers cite references using trackbacks. These are not ordinary references, however. Trackbacks weave the blogosphere together, inserting the citation on both the referenced and the referring blog.

> Learn more about trackbacks and related
> technologies, such as pingbacks, at
> **mobilizingyouth.org/trackbacks**

Blogroll   A blogroll is a list of links to favorite blogs; its name derives from "honor roll." Bloggers use their blogrolls to express affinity and respect for other bloggers. The convention has helped create a sense of community among bloggers and facilitated the flow of readers among blogs. A listing on a popular blogroll can raise a blog from obscurity to prominence. In the words of one researcher, "links and pageviews are the currency of the blogosphere . . . [and] the most reliable way to gain traffic [readership] is through a link on another [blog]."[29]

o   o   o

Combined with blogging's core components, these newer features tie the network of bloggers together, creating a symbiotic blog universe. They encourage readers to jump from blog to blog following personalities and stories. Bloggers stand to benefit by becoming active participants in a blogging community: frequent commenting, reviewing, and posting generate increased readership.

You'll also find the following three features in use on blogs. However, they're not exclusive to blogs. In fact, they underpin most Web 2.0 technologies. We'll discuss them throughout the remainder of this book.

Feeds   Using what is known as a *feed reader*, you can read stories from many blogs all in one place. Most blogs display a link that indicates an available feed. See bottom left of Figure 1.2. You'll see a link that says "Subscribe to: Posts (Atom)." Clicking this link will launch your Web browser's mechanism for adding a feed to your feed reader of choice. Sometimes this link reads "Subscribe to Feed" or simply "RSS," which is the name of one popular feed technology (there are several). Unfortunately, the words and graphics used to indicate an available feed are not consistent across blogs.

Learn more about feeds at

mobilizingyouth.org/feeds

I've told my feed reader (Google Reader) to get the feeds from about a hundred blogs. Google Reader lists the headlines in a centralized location. If an article piques my interest, I click the headline to read the entire story. Feed readers save minutes of clicking, scanning, and waiting for pages to load.

Feeds are one of the most important innovations driving the Web 2.0 movement. They've enabled people to quickly scan a large number of blogs and other types of Web content, such as bookmarks, news, photos, and videos. Moreover, feeds have enabled *computers* to quickly scan, import, and use large quantities of data (such as blog posts) by formatting the data according to known standards.

Tagging   A tag is a short phrase or keyword that identifies a piece of content. For example, if this chapter were a blog post, I might tag it with the following phrases: "blogging," "microblogging," "young people," "Rock the Vote," "Generation 2.0 book," "nonprofit," and "politics." These are my self-selected descriptors for the contents of this chapter.

Like feeds, tagging is one of Web 2.0's primary enabling technologies. By entering this simple list of phrases, I've accomplished the following:

- **Helped search engines find my work.** I've given search engines a starting point for categorizing my blog post. If someone searches for any of these phrases, the engine will have to do less work to identify a relevant result.

- **Created my own flexible organizing system.** Over time, I will be able to view all my content according to tags. For example, I might want to see all my blog posts that match the tags "microblogging" and "Generation 2.0 book." By using this combination of tags, I can quickly find relevant content.

- **Contributed to a Web-wide organizing system.** By tagging my own work, I've joined the worldwide community of taggers. If I were to do a Google search for "young people" and "blogging," I'd get results from people that self-categorized their work using the same tags. This organizing system has come to be known as a *folksonomy*, or a taxonomy of the folks.

Like feeds, tagging is relevant to all types of Web content, including photos, videos, blog posts, and bookmarks. Most modern software systems are turning to tagging as a model for organizing content and turning away from the more rigid "foldering" system.

Learn more about tags at
mobilizingyouth.org/tags

Widgets   Widgets go by many names, including gadgets, badges, or modules. They are mini Web pages that can be placed within other Web pages. Your organization can create a widget and ask supporters to place it on their blogs, Web sites, and social networking pages. Supporters become key partners in promoting your campaign: blog visitors can interact with your organization without ever visiting your Web site.

For example, to conduct a fundraising campaign, create a compelling widget about your cause and ask supporters to put it on their blogs. (Figure 1.3 shows an example.) The donation processing occurs directly in the widget. Your supporters have become the field team that spreads your call to action.

Figure 1.3. A ChipIn Widget for Barbara Davis Center for Childhood Diabetes Embedded in a Supporter's Web Site

Widgets are fairly new and still evolving. They may dramatically reshape the Web by reducing the importance of an organization's Web site. In a "widgetized" future, all interaction with supporters and potential supporters occurs within the widget. An organization's main marketing task becomes persuading supporters to place a widget on their blogs and social networking profiles. Maintaining a robust central Web site becomes a secondary priority.

Learn more about widgets at
mobilizingyouth.org/widgets

How to Get Started

If you're not already familiar with blogging, the logical first step is to start reading and commenting on blogs. Use a blog search engine, such as technorati.com, to find blogs in your field. Read them on an ongoing basis. If you're interested in nonprofit technology, start your search with the tag "nptech." Many nonprofit technology bloggers use this tag to identify their posts. As you read, pay attention to the writing style and the use of comments, blogrolls, tags, and other features specific to the blog software in use. Bookmark favorite blogs or, even better, add them to your feed reader. Get to know the bloggers in your field, and post comments when you can add value to a discussion.

Choosing Blog Software

When you're ready to get started with your own blog, you'll need to choose blog software. First decide if you'd like to operate a standard blog, a community blogging platform, or a feed-only blog. These blog types are described in more detail in the next sections.

Get help choosing blog software at
mobilizingyouth.org/blog_software

Standard Blog

The great majority of organizations operate what I will refer to here as standard blogs, which allow one or multiple authors, comments, and a range of miscellaneous features specific to the blog software. Some people distinguish among standard blogs according to the number of people who have posting privileges. A blog that allows a single person to post is called a single-user blog, as compared to a multiuser blog or group blog, which allows multiple people to post. Today, most blogs allow either single or multiple authors.

Community Blogging Platform

The Obama example discussed earlier showcases use of a community blogging platform. This software allows your organization to host numerous supporter blogs.

Feed-Only Blog

In this type of blog, you dispense with a Web site and offer information only to feed readers. Practitioners of this approach treat their blog more as a news service than as a space for interaction. The primary advantage of this configuration is that you don't have to spend time designing a blog, responding to comments, or sorting through comment spam. However, you don't gain the advantages of interaction with supporters, search engine optimization, permalinks, or ad revenue. In addition, there is no popular blogging software that supports a feed-only blog. For these reasons, the feed-only blog is not widely used.

Comment Spam

Unless you turn on your blog's comment-approval system, anyone will be able to post a comment. Spammers can then post irrelevant comments with links to their (usually pornographic) Web sites. Turn on your approval system to prevent comment spam, but be sure to approve valid comments quickly enough to keep the conversation flowing.

Other Types of Blogs

You might also hear about video blogs (vlogs) or photo blogs (plogs). As their names suggest, these blogs primarily feature video or photos. Another popular type of blog is a mobile blog or moblog, which is created from mobile phones or devices. Some blogging software is configured to automatically post text messages and videos or photos sent from mobile phones. These blogging forms are an effort to carve out a niche as bloggers seek ways to distinguish their work. However, they're all variations on the theme of a standard blog, and many standard blogs also feature video, photo, and content from mobile phones.

Finding a Vendor

After determining which blog type is the best fit for your content and community, you'll next need to select a software vendor. Because most blogging software is free (or has a trial period), you can experiment with a few options before making a decision. Take advantage of online blog software reviews, such as those available at Idealware.org. The site lists the following key considerations when selecting blog software:[30]

- Consider whether you need more than a simple blogging tool.

- Decide whether you need to tailor the blog's appearance.

- Determine if someone with technical skills will be available to set up the blog.

- Weigh control and integration versus ease of getting started.

- Consider the technical expertise of the people who will be posting.

Idealware helps you think through each of these considerations and goes on to recommend specific software on the basis of your organization's situation. One of the primary considerations is whether to install the blog software on your own server (installed) or to hire a vendor to host it for you (hosted). Installing your own software will give you more control, but will require technical expertise. For most organizations, hosted blog software will adequately serve needs while limiting expenses.

Optimizing for Search Engines

One of the great secrets about blogging is that it dramatically improves search engine rankings. Search engines take two primary factors into account when ranking results: keyword density and inbound links.[31] Keyword density refers to the number of times a short phrase or word appears in the text of a Web page. An inbound link is a link to your blog from another Web site or blog. If your organization operates a blog, you'll address both factors without making any special effort. If you post with some frequency, you'll naturally write relevant keyword phrases. If you write interesting articles, people will link to your blog.

By taking a few extra steps, you can *optimize* your blog for search engine "discoverability." Put strategic thought into the keywords that are most relevant to your organization. By developing a list of about fifty keywords and using them frequently in blog posts, you can focus search engine rankings around the topics that attract your supporters. Go one step further by tagging your posts. Be sure to find and use this feature of your blogging software. Grow your inbound links by actively pursuing relationships with other bloggers. Every time you post a comment on another blog, it generates a link back to your blog. In short, your search engine rankings will get better as you become a more active blogger.

Reaching Out to Bloggers

Bloggers are not traditional media, so the last thing a PR person should do is create another column on a spreadsheet that includes bloggers in future e-mail blasts.

—Church of the Customer Blog[32]

Bloggers consider themselves unlike professional mainstream journalists. In general, they prefer outreach efforts that demonstrate a personal interest in their writings. To get started, find bloggers with whom you'd like to connect and

- Mention their names on your blog. Most bloggers track mentions of their names.

- Link to their blogs from your Web site or blog.

- Leave comments on their blogs.

- Pitch your story, but

    o Demonstrate that you have read their blogs and that you can offer something of value to their readers.

- Keep messages short and conversational.

- Include a note that indicates that the message is not a form letter.

- Offer a phone number, e-mail address, and Web site URL.

• Understand that e-mail pitches don't work well for reaching top bloggers. Try calling them.[33]

• Give them some bit of exclusive information or inside access.

• Avoid marketing-speak.

• Cultivate a long-term relationship.[34]

• Do all of these things before you have a pressing need. If you're launching a new campaign and want a blogger to write about it, it will help to have this preexisting relationship.

Forum vs. Blog

term

Forum, discussion group, and *message board* are synonymous terms describing software that lists a series of discussion topics. Whereas a blog usually features one or a small group of primary authors, a forum is open to the public. Visitors can submit new topics or respond to existing ones. All topics are treated with equal weight, as opposed to in a blog, where comments are less noticeable than the original post. Forums tend to be more text-heavy, and feature long lists of topics with few images or video.

For a more detailed discussion of the differences between forums and blogs, see

www.commoncraft.com/archives/000768.html

Strategic Considerations

Blogging might seem to offer a quick path to joining the Web 2.0 movement, but operating a *successful* blog requires strategic planning. The following sections discuss questions and issues that can help you focus your efforts.

Be Authentic

Blogs have come a long way from personal diaries, but, as I've mentioned, readers still expect them to be written in authentic and personal tones. Copy that sounds as if it came from a marketing brochure will not be well received. To connect with young readers, take advantage of the fact that a blog is an *alternative* to marketing materials. It creates a forum for unscripted, dynamic, and personal conversation. Creating personal connections with your supporters is the primary benefit of operating a blog.

Devote Time to Blogging

Setting up a blog takes ten minutes. However, creating a blog that draws readers requires posting frequently, managing comment spam, and making efforts to join the community of like-minded bloggers. Blogging is an ongoing daily project. Maintaining positive blogger relations and regular blog reading, writing, and posting must be scheduled priorities.

Clarify Objectives

What are you trying to accomplish with your blog? The question seems rather obvious, but many organizations start a blog without thinking it through. Explicitly answering this question will help you focus the content and writing style of your posts and the way that you interact with supporters. Here are some possibilities:

- Telling a story that advocates for a candidate or issue

- Connecting supporters with one another

- Creating a space for supporters to express ideas and creative thought

- Conducting market research

- Attracting new supporters

- Reporting news

- Raising your organization's search engine ranking

- Establishing your organization as an expert in the field

- Preparing to respond to timely events

- Supporting a broader campaign

- Showing the impact of your organization

- Fundraising

- Improving internal communication

If the purpose of your blog is to tell a story, for example, your blog is going to look radically different than if you're seeking to improve internal communication. Write a list of objectives and then outline the ways in which the blog will meet those goals.

Tag Smartly

Tags tie a community of bloggers together. You can join the community simply by using tags common to bloggers in your field. Before you begin a blogging project, research tags by looking at the tags in use on related blogs. Develop a list of tags that you'll use frequently. In the Web 2.0 world, tags help define your brand, except that you share and codevelop this brand with fellow taggers.

Integrate Broadly

Consider the ways in which a blog can complement the range of your organization's activities. For example, you can use a blog to enhance communication surrounding a traditional direct-mail piece. Print an exciting lead-in on the mailer and then steer people to a blog post to discuss the topic. Blogs don't have to operate as independent entities— use them creatively to encourage communication.

Release Control

For many organizations, one of the biggest hurdles in starting a blog has nothing to do with software. The obstacle is fear of losing control. Blogging requires a willingness to relinquish some control over branding and messaging. It encourages greater openness and a flattening of organizational hierarchies. It invites constituents to have a conversation not only with your organization but also with *you*, the real people who work behind the scenes. Blogs also ask constituents to converse with each other. They will not always say nice things.

Blogging purists will say that operating a successful blog *necessitates* shifting the very structure of your organization—making it more open, transparent, and responsive to constituents. Certainly, some organizations have used blogging to facilitate these types of changes. Others, such as the Romney campaign, use their blog to tell personal stories around a tightly controlled message. However, even the Romneys embrace a degree of openness. By not deleting controversial comments, they demonstrate a commitment to the spirit of blogging.

The benefits of blogging diminish as you add more controls. When you strip opportunities for social interaction, the blog becomes more like a marketing brochure or advertisement. Before starting a blog, review your objectives. If your organization wants to broadcast a message, create a Web site or run an advertising campaign instead.

See the Big Picture essay by Beth Kanter for more thoughts about this topic.

Participate in the Blogging Community

As I've mentioned elsewhere, when you start to blog, you become part of a community of like-minded bloggers. Your organization undoubtedly has developed expertise in a given field. Think about how you can contribute that expertise to the community. Read other blogs and post comments, and start discussions. When someone posts a comment on your blog, respond quickly to encourage lively conversation. Keep tabs on discussion in your field by running frequent blog searches on relevant keywords.

Challenges and Opportunities

If you're like most nonprofits and smaller political campaigns, you're underfunded, short on time, and still trying to figure out how to make the best use of Web 1.0 technologies, such as e-mail lists and online donations. Blogging seems like a lot of work. It is. Operating a successful blog will require many hours of strategic planning, reading, writing, and interacting with supporters.

However, blogging does not add a categorically new task to your organization's busy schedule. It extends the reach and efficacy of the work that you're *already* doing. Chances are that your organization does some degree of advertising, community outreach, and market analysis. Blogging enhances your ability to accomplish these tasks, particularly for organizations that work with young people.

But blogs also fundamentally shift the nature of these tasks. Consider advertising, for example. The objective of advertising is to promote your organization, candidate, or cause. Currently, you're probably using a traditional advertising model: printing ads in newspapers or magazines, sending direct mail, buying online banners, or maintaining a brochure-like Web site. This form of advertising requires that you craft and broadcast a message that will appeal to your target audience.

Like an ad campaign, blogging promotes your organization, candidate, or cause. You achieve the same end result, but through radically different means. Supporters read your blog, learn about your point of view, and discuss your issues, because the experience is valuable to them. Instead of *targeting* supporters, you *engage* them. Instead of spending time writing taglines and brochures, you spend time in conversation. "Brand building" is not a result of maximizing viewer impressions; it occurs as a result of doing substantive work. You post a well-reasoned and persuasive article, and it generates discussion, which attracts interested people. You learn about the "market" through conversation and comments. You build connections between people who care about your issues. With few financial and technical hurdles, blogging allows you to jump directly to the important work of your organization.

In the upcoming chapters we'll talk about mobile phones, social networks, video and photos, mapping, and virtual worlds. Almost every campaign that uses these technologies also uses a blog. For example, social networks have built-in blogging tools. Virtual world residents actively discuss the evolution of their worlds on blogs. Online video creators post their latest work to their blogs. You'll also see that the technologies supporting blogs, such as tagging, feeds, and widgets, also support many of the other Web 2.0 campaigns. Blogging is the foundation and the glue for many Web 2.0 initiatives.

Blogs also demonstrate many of the concepts that underpin the Web 2.0 movement:

Emergent Behaviors   When a software application is open ended, people invent uses for it that suit their needs. In the examples discussed in this chapter, we saw uses ranging from the delivery of a crafted message, in the case of the Romney campaign, to the formation of a creative space for young trainees, in the case of NOI's organizing efforts. These organizations used similar blogging software, but because it provides a minimum of structure, each organization adapted it to support very different activities. This lesson applies to more than just software. In many of the most successful campaigns in the following chapters, you'll find an organization creating a loose framework that empowers supporters to develop their own meaning and direction. As cocreators, supporters are more engaged, interested, and effective.

The Rewards of Sharing Information   The more you post, comment, and link, the more popular your blog will become. Sustainable advantage in Web 2.0 is not about maintaining control; it's about delivering value to a community over time. The elite bloggers are those who share quality thoughts, information, and analysis most often. Information hoarders and proprietary systems don't do well in the Web 2.0 world.

The Web as a Conversational Medium   Blogging encourages organizations to have conversations with supporters, and supporters to talk with one another. In order to have this dialogue, organizations must be willing to reveal an unpolished and personal side. Marketing messages and advertising campaigns have their place, but blogs are not it. This unspun quality resonates with young supporters in particular. They appreciate the candor, transparency, and openness that blogs encourage. For organizations, the ability to have these conversations creates new opportunities for making deep connections with supporters.

o   o   o

Blogging is not without its critics. The most significant criticism is that blogging is created for and by a privileged class. Blogs are written and read by people with Internet access. In theory, anyone can set up a blog in minutes, but in reality, this capability is available only to those privileged with a computer and a network connection. Lack of access excludes millions of people worldwide.

Blogs don't solve the problem of access among the underrepresented. Most of the technologies discussed in this book, in fact, should be understood in this socioeconomic context. However, blogs put the tools of information production in the hands of millions of people who didn't have these tools just a decade ago. Young people can distribute their creative endeavors as widely as Madison Avenue can. Organizations can cost-effectively communicate with Internet-enabled supporters about their ideas, issues, and perspectives.

Blogging is not a cure-all, or even a replacement for traditional tactics, such as advertising. However, it's an alternative that works. The influence of blogging will continue to grow. Many young people blog on a daily basis, and they're becoming more active citizens as they observe life and inject a thought or criticism into the public dialogue. Organizations that learn to navigate the evolving blogosphere stand to benefit from the involvement of this vital cohort.

Endnotes

1. http://journalism.nyu.edu/pubzone/weblogs/pressthink/2004/03/15/lott_case.html

2. www.sfgate.com/cgi-bin/article.cgi?file=/chronicle/archive/2002/12/14/MN189376.DTL

3. www.thenation.com/blogs/thebeat?pid=208

4. *The Economist* describes the relationship between the mainstream press and blogging after the Lott episode as follows: "The mainstream media was initially blind to his [Lott's] remarks perhaps because it is used to such comments. But the 'blogosphere'—websites of opinion and news, first known as weblogs—denounced the remarks vigorously, and would not let up, finally forcing others to take notice." "Mississippi Burning," *The Economist*, Dec. 21, 2002, p. 39.

5. http://en.wikipedia.org/wiki/Trent_Lott

6. www.pewinternet.org/pdfs/PIP%20Bloggers%20Report%20July%2019%202006.pdf

7. http://technorati.com/weblog/2007/04/328.html. Technorati tracks over seventy million blogs and counts more than 120,000 being created each day.

8. www.timesonline.co.uk/tol/news/world/us_and_americas/article2116172.ece

9. www.washingtonpost.com/wp-dyn/content/article/2007/06/08/AR2007060802781.html

10. http://alexa.com/data/details/traffic_details?url=mittromney.com

11. Thanks to this story for some information about the Romneys' blog: www.washingtonpost.com/wp-dyn/content/article/2007/06/08/AR2007060802781.html.

12. For a summary of the postcard writing campaigns, see www.amnestyusa.org/action/summer/Summer2007.pdf.

13. www.ingentaconnect.com/content/klu/team/2003/00000009/00000002/05120922

14. Unfortunately, Amnesty doesn't release any other metrics that would confirm the efficacy of this blog, such as conversation rates or visitation figures per blog section. This quotation is from a recording from a panel session on human rights blogs, featuring Amnesty: http://archive-c02.libsyn.com/podcasts/880d27015813032ed2eca010f2339ae8/46b41495/netsquared/2Human_Rights_New_Communication_Technologies_BreakoutSession2.mp3.

15. www.netsquared.org/blog/britt-bravo/10-ways-nonprofits-can-use
    -blogs

    www.gwenaraujo.blogspot.com; www.cuav.org/about.php

16. www.globalprblogweek.com/2005/09/19/dutto-internal-blogs

17. www.pewinternet.org/PPF/r/166/report_display.asp

18. www.pewinternet.org/pdfs/PIP_ICT_Typology.pdf

19. *Behaviors of the Blogosphere: Understanding the Scale, Composition and Activities of Weblog Audiences,* Aug. 2005. www.comscore.com/blogreport/comScoreBlogReport.pdf.

20. For more information on blog fundraising, see www.on philanthropy.com/site/News2?page=NewsArticle&id=5216.

21. www.pacefunders.org/pdf/05.06.05%20Final%20Version%201.0.pdf

22. www.network-centricadvocacy.net/2004/03/nonprofit_advoc.html

23. www.thinkmoderate.com/2007/02/fear-mongering-red-cross-bill boards-to.html

24. www.thinkmoderate.com/2007/02/fear-mongering-red-cross-bill boards-to.html

25. Thanks to Beth Kanter to turning me on to this example. It's featured in her slide show at www.slideshare.net/kanter/bridge-confer ence-fundraising-20-session.

26. www.utsc.utoronto.ca/%7Efarrell/blogpaperfinal.pdf

27. www.emergence-media.com/wiki/index.php/Blog_Outreach:_How_ to_Pitch_Bloggers

28. You may be familiar with content management systems (CMSs), which also aim to facilitate Web publishing. Blog software is a type of CMS. Most CMSs allow a more freeform organization of content, whereas blogging software enforces the reverse-chronological list of articles.

29. www.utsc.utoronto.ca/%7Efarrell/blogpaperfinal.pdf

30. www.idealware.org/blogging_software/2006/06/how-to-choose.php

31. Search engine providers protect their search algorithms with an Area 54–like secrecy. Except for a few insiders, no one is exactly sure how to obtain one of the top listings. Dozens of speculative books have been written on the subject, and an industry of search engine optimization consultants attempts to help organizations navigate their way to a top listing. Each specialist offers a combination of science and black art, but most agree that the two factors I've mentioned are critical.

32. www.churchofthecustomer.com/blog/2007/04/the_myth_of_cul.html

33. These tips are from Robert Scoble, one of the world's top bloggers: http://radio.weblogs.com/0001011/2005/02/16.html#a9452.

34. Several of the tips here are from www.emergence-media.com/wiki/index.php/Blog_Outreach:_How_to_Pitch_Bloggers, and from http://beltwayblogroll.nationaljournal.com/archives/2007/04/tips_for_blog_o_1.php.

THE BIG PICTURE

Overcoming the Barriers to Blogging

Essay by Beth Kanter

Beth Kanter is a trainer, social-media coach, consultant, and author of Beth's Blog (http://beth.typepad.com), where she writes about how nonprofits are using social media for social change. Her blog is a veritable treasure trove of information—and was indispensible in writing this book.

Many nonprofit professionals in the United States are thinking about how to integrate blogs and other Web 2.0 tools into their organization's outreach, marketing, and fundraising plans. Some have gone so far as to do a bit of research and experimentation, but they still need to convince skeptical coworkers, board members, or bosses before going any further.

Unfortunately, however, nonprofit leaders frequently run head-first into a number of significant barriers to adoption when undertaking a blogging strategy. These fears can typically be grouped into a few common themes.

Loss of Control Over Messaging and Branding

"What if a blog reader complains about our organization so that everyone can read it? What if their complaint is not based on facts or the truth?"

These objections are by far the most common concerns that keep many organizations from starting a blog. Similarly, they might drive other organizations to turn off the commenting feature on their blog, thinking that this is the best way to control the conversation but ending up only defeating the purpose of blogging.

Truth be told, people are going to complain, and complaints aren't always based on the facts. But isn't it better that you hear from your constituents so that you can (1) address their perceptions directly and (2) use their comments as an opportunity for free market research? Many nonprofit professionals I've talked to feel that the feedback they get from comments on their blog is well worth the possibility of being criticized. Some organizations even measure the return on investment of their blogs by evaluating how many useful business insights the comments generate.

Loss of Editorial Control

Many organizations are used to publishing pieces that go through many layers of editing until the content is perfect. In some cases it may take many months before the piece finally sees the light of day. Compare this to a blog, where the writing is more like a conversation, it's not necessarily perfect, and posts are published rapidly.

Blogging has been dubbed "conversational media." Just as spoken conversations often dispense with perfect grammar and usage, sometimes blogs have typos, awkward phrasings, and errors. But this informal language is authentic, immediate—more *human.* Doesn't your organization want to engage in a richer conversation with constituents?

If certain stakeholders are concerned about making public typos, some blogging platforms offer a draft feature. Organizations can use a tag-team approach in which at least one staff person reviews a post in draft form before it is published.

Too Time-Consuming and Distracting

Blogging takes time to do well. Depending on the scope of the blog, it can take anywhere from four to eight hours or more per week to write, review, and maintain the blog. One way to minimize the time commitment is to share blogging responsibilities among several staff members. This not only spreads out the workload but also helps organizations work across silos. Another approach is to focus instead on "comment blogging"—that is, leaving comments on the blogs of other organizations and writers in your topic area.

If an organization's staff members are writing about their program areas, the discipline of reflecting on a topic every day can help deepen these individuals' subject expertise. Their blogging work can be viewed as an essential program responsibility, and can in turn provide some important paybacks to the organization, such as enhanced organizational reputation. Some nonprofits look at the blogging process as inexpensive professional development for staff members.

The Ideas Are Too Imperfect

As many seasoned professional bloggers know, they may often "think out loud" or publish a post that is not crystal clear. Someone might read it and leave a comment to that effect, while also providing some clarification. Nonprofits that have adopted blogging take this feedback as a gift that helps them clarify a message and solicit thoughts on an idea before investing more time and resources on implementation. Over and over again, I hear from nonprofit professionals who are blogging that this is one of the key benefits.

o   o   o

Although all these concerns can be quite real for many nonprofits and, in some cases, prevent them from starting an organizational blog, I've found that the benefits can far outweigh the drawbacks. Blogging can deepen your staff members' expertise in a subject, help you test ideas before they become set in stone (or before you've invested time and resources), and enable a more authentic conversation with constituents.

Web 2.0 and social media tools offer many possibilities for nonprofits to raise awareness of their work, connect with younger donors, raise money, find volunteers, and achieve other tangible benefits. There are challenges, of course, but these can be mitigated with low-risk forms of experimentation and learning in order to reap powerful rewards.

THE BIG PICTURE

The Story of Blogging

Interview with Evan Williams

Evan Williams seems to know where the Internet is going before the rest of us do. He created one of the first massively popular blogging software applications, Blogger, which was eventually purchased by Google. He went on to found Obvious Corp, which created Twitter—one of the most talked-about Internet sensations. I interviewed Evan in summer 2007. An edited portion of the transcript is presented here.

In the beginning, a lot of content publishing on the Web basically meant, "We have something in print, and we're going to put it on the Web." So newspapers and magazines translated to the Web, and it made a lot of sense because of the advantages in terms of distribution and cost.

But when it came to personal publishing, it wasn't so much an evolutionary matter, because personal publishing wasn't really something that was widely done. Before the Web, there were 'zines and newsletters and different attempts by a very small minority of people to do something in publishing. But the idea of a person actually publishing on a regular basis wasn't established in print, because the medium didn't allow people to do so in a way that made sense for an individual: it was too costly and too time-intensive. When the Web came along and eliminated the cost, however, it still didn't provide the context or the framework in which to do such publishing.

GeoCities was one of the early personal publishing Web efforts. It made it very easy to create a Web page to share your ideas and thoughts, but there wasn't the mechanism for personal publishing. To use the technical term, there wasn't content management.

Personal publishing and content management came together in the form of the blog. It was one of the first Web-native formats, because you could write something online and publish it instantly. And you could publish multiple times a day if you wanted to, because there's no economic cost. The post could be as short as a sentence or infinitely long, especially once comments came into it.

Traditional print media also don't take advantage of the hyperlink, the core element of the Web. Blogs very much take advantage of the hyperlink, which allows you to write something as short as a sentence or even a word, but link it to something out there in the world and provide context for your view.

Blogging really lets information flow and a billion voices bloom, so to speak. People can tune in to whatever they want. That's powerful.

The Power of Microblogging

Twitter is another tool along the same lines as blogging. I don't know if it will be as profound, but I think there will be situations and uses in which it does something that nothing else can do, based on its real-time and mobile aspects.

Twitter is designed around the now. At any event, be it a concert, protest, or political convention, it gives you the ability to send a message to a lot of people at once, in real time, when they're out and about. You can get your message out to people very quickly and can potentially move people, move crowds, move all kinds of things.

Essentially, Twitter is a way to let people know what you're doing or thinking at any given time, in the moment, and to find out what those you care about are doing. The concept is very simple. You say, "I'm eating at this restaurant." And you send that message via text or via the Web, and those who are interested tune in and know that.

The heart of it is sharing thoughts and feelings in real time, and there's something that's really fun about both sending and receiving. If you're using Twitter, especially if you're using it on your mobile phone, you get these messages from people, and they aren't the type of messages that require a conversation or a reply. They're just an image or an idea sent from someone you may know or from someone you may not know but from whom you're at least interested in getting updates.

A lot of people use Twitter as a sort of a journal to capture moments in their lives for their own use. One neat side effect is that people build a log of all the significant (and lots of insignificant) things that have happened to them over the last year, at exactly the times they happened. Using Twitter builds a personal-life time line.

What I've observed over the last eight years of working on these types of technologies is that people want to share. It's that idea of sharing what's going on in the moment, and receiving messages about what's going on in the moment, that's fun. It plays off our desire to be social and to connect with one another.

As people live more and more of their lives on the Web, it simply can't be a one-way medium. It's just not interesting enough to people. That's why MySpace is the number one trafficked site on the Web. People want to interact. The Web is essentially a social medium. Whereas in the past the Web may have been more about e-commerce, advertising, or the consumption of content, now it's about "socialness." It's hard to think of a Web 2.0 application or anything useful or interesting online that doesn't have a social component.

CHAPTER 2

Social Networking

[Young] people are doing things on [social networks]. They're hanging out. They're dancing in front of digital mirrors. They're patting their friends on their digital backs. They're increasing the strength of their relationships through sharing. They're consuming and producing cultural artifacts that position them within society. They're laughing, exploring, and being entertained.

—danah boyd[1]

Social networks have become *places* where young people spend a considerable part of their lives. In these places, they explore and form their identities, socialize, and, as boyd says, "write themselves into being."[2] Social networks are today's bowling alleys, roller rinks, and drive-ins. They welcome jocks and nerds, the politically engaged and the apathetic, the outcasts and the in-crowd. If you're between thirteen and thirty years of age, there's a very good chance that you "hang out" on a Web site that defines itself as a social network.

A recent study by the Pew Internet and American Life Project found that 55 percent of teens used social networks. Almost half visited one daily, and nearly a quarter of teens visited several times per day.[3] College students are the heaviest users. Approximately 80 percent of U.S. college students maintain a profile at the popular social network Facebook.[4]

Usage is also surging for the postcollege set. The fastest-growing group on Facebook is people over twenty-five.[5] These figures are not limited to Facebook or to the United States. The same trends are playing out across the world on hundreds of social networking Web sites.

The following features define social networks and distinguish them from other types of Web sites:[6]

- *The profile page:* a page that allows you to describe yourself through text, video, and music

- A *network of friends:* a public or semipublic list of friends, usually displayed as small photographic icons

- A *public commenting system:* allows friends and strangers to write a short note or statement that will be displayed publicly on your profile page

- A *private messaging system:* enables friends to send private messages to you via your profile page

Contrary to public perception, most of the groups that form on social networking sites are *not made up of strangers.* Although people may browse profiles of others who are unknown to them, most use social networking sites to support preexisting real-life social groups.[7] Friends use them to meet up and hang out, just as they would in cafés or bars.

Social networks are also as diverse as public spaces in any vibrant big city. MySpace is the most popular and highly trafficked. Facebook attracts a majority of college students in the United States and is growing exponentially. Young teenagers love Bebo. Older teenagers prefer Xanga. Newshounds like Digg. African Americans spend time on BlackPlanet. Filipinos visit Friendster, Brazilians hang out on Orkut, Chinese on QQ, Japanese on Mixi, and Koreans on Cyworld. Muslims connect on MuslimSpace and Christians on Christianer. There is a social network for every niche and geographical region.

How Organizations Are Using Social Networks

Social networks may appear to offer nonprofits and political campaigns a prime opportunity for spreading a message and promoting civic action among legions of young people. But as suggested by the list of social networks in the preceding section, these communities are fractured and nuanced. Hundreds of social networks exist, and within each network, people have self-organized into thousands of subgroups and cliques. Opportunities exist for recruiting new supporters, advocating for causes, and fundraising, but success requires a concerted and well-considered effort.

Recognizing these difficulties, several entrepreneurial nonprofits have formed social networks made up almost entirely of activists dedicated to social causes. These communities offer fertile ground for promoting your candidate's or nonprofit's issues.

By contrast, some organizations have decided to build their own social networks from scratch. By taking complete control over the branding, features, and structure of the social network, they attempt to focus social activity around a specific set of issues. This approach requires an extremely active and committed group of supporters.

In this section, we'll explore campaigns that use a number of the aforementioned social networks, as well as those that specifically target cause-oriented networks or build custom networks.

Recruiting and Advocacy with a Persona

Every year, the Humane Society of the United States runs a campaign to fight the Canadian seal hunt. In 2007, it used the most popular social network, MySpace, to advocate for change, recruit new supporters, and drive civic action. The Society created a persona named Sunny the Seal to serve as the campaign's focal point. This fictional harp seal came to life on a MySpace profile page. Here he introduces himself:

> "Hello everyone! My name is Sunny, and I was just born in the Gulf of St. Lawrence. I'm here to write about all my new experiences here on the ice. I'm a little scared, 'cause my mom and dad told me about a seal hunt where people come and kill seals. How could anyone do such a cruel thing?"[8]

Sunny's story unfolds over the course of the three-week hunt. A team of four dedicated Society staff members carefully planned and executed the narrative. Prior to the hunt, the team selected key moments in a young seal's life and integrated them with the horrors that would transpire during the hunt. They also researched how young people use MySpace to communicate with friends and planned to use these same methods to chronicle Sunny's life.

In addition, the team looked at ways to generate excitement for the campaign outside of MySpace. They prepared to use traditional online tactics, such as e-mail lists and link agreements with sympathetic partner organizations. Because MySpace offers a limited toolkit for building Web pages, the Society also developed a freestanding Web site (www.protectseals.org) to offer more robust functions, such as mailing-list sign-ups and fundraising and petitioning forms.

The campaign got under way in mid-March, when the harp seals birth their pups. The Society jumpstarted the campaign with an e-mail to its mailing list that instructed people to visit Sunny's MySpace page, become his friend, and spread the word. Campaigners reached out to celebrities and other seal groups asking for their support and participation. Much of their efforts went into relating Sunny's saga via the MySpace profile and interacting with people who started to follow the story. The narrative builds when the hunters arrive in early April and concludes with Sunny's untimely death on April 17.

In the process, the group made use of almost every MySpace capability:

Personal Details   The team developed a back story and personality using MySpace's built-in profile-building tools to define Sunny's tastes in music, favorite television shows, and list of heroes. These details appear in preformatted areas that are common to all MySpace profiles.

Blog   MySpace lets users publish a blog in which the latest entries appear on the user's profile page. Humane Society team member Rebecca Aldworth spent the duration of the hunt blogging from the ice in the voice of Sunny, vividly describing the horrors of the hunt and the joys of being a young seal. The blog developed a strong following, as people returned to learn if Sunny survived the day's hunt. Fans encouraged Sunny to stay strong, and posted comments of support and promises of action.

Bulletins   MySpace bulletins allow you to send a message to your entire friend list. It's the equivalent of an e-mail distribution list, with the added benefit that the message is publicly displayed on the profile page of each friend. A bulletin has a viral effect: it's seen not only by your friends but also by *their* friends. The Society sent frequent bulletins using a chatty and informal writing style.

Top Friends   One of the core elements of a social network is the friends list. MySpace allows users to select and order their "Top Friends" (see box on friending), to be displayed prominently on the user's profile page. Sunny listed the Humane Society in the topmost position.[9] The remaining spots were used to highlight celebrity supporters and other environmental organizations, such as Bryan Adams, Pamela Anderson, Sarah McLachlan, Al Gore, and Greenpeace, as shown in Figure 2.1.

Figure 2.1. Part of Sunny the Seal's MySpace Profile Page

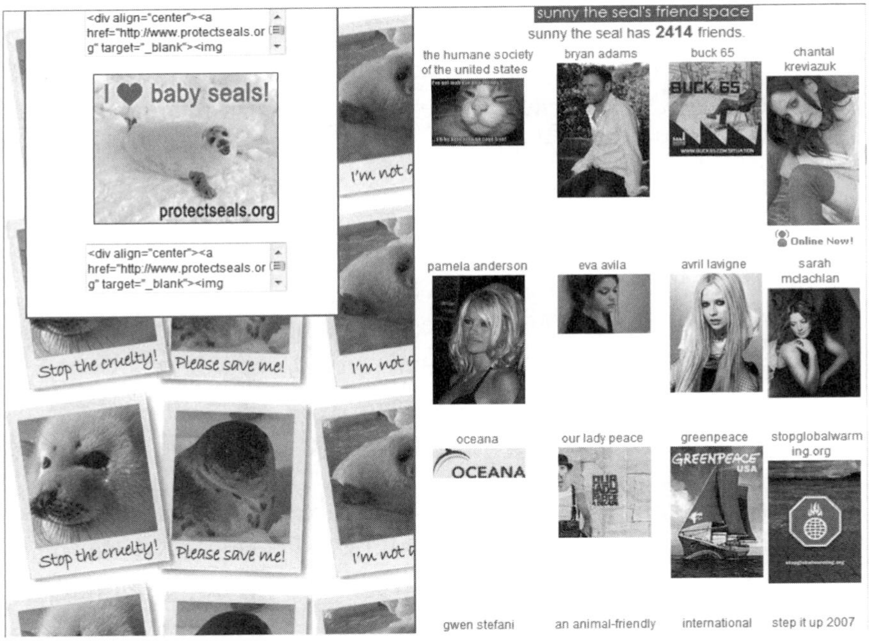

Note the widget at left. To place this widget on your own profile page, you would copy and paste the code shown immediately below the graphic. At right, Sunny's top friends.

Embedded Media   Like most social networks, MySpace allows users to embed media from other sources into their profile pages. Sunny embedded four types of media:

- *Music.* MySpace revolves around music. Sunny's profile featured a meditative track by Sarah McLachlan, which sets the mood for experiencing Sunny's story.

- *Video.* Sunny posted graphic videos of the seal hunt and cute movies about seals. They added a vivid quality to Sunny's experience.

- *Photo.* Sunny's photo slide shows depict "stop the hunt" rallies and cheering supporters. They convey a sense of community and togetherness.

- *Map.* Sunny's profile features a map showing the locations of his supporters, which helps demonstrate connectedness.

Widgets   Widgets are small chunks of Web content, such as graphics, video clips, or animations, that friends can place on their profiles, blogs, and sites to show affinity or support. As mentioned in Chapter One, widgets allow supporters to help you advertise your cause or Web site. The Society created a series of widgets featuring photos of seals and calls to action, such as "Stop the seal hunt!" and "I [heart] baby seals!" (as shown in Figure 2.1). Each widget linked directly to ProtectSeals.org.

For more information on widgets, see

mobilizingyouth.org/widgets

By the campaign's end, the MySpace profile attracted two thousand friends and fourteen thousand unique visitors. Traffic to the ProtectSeals .org Web site increased by 50 percent; five hundred new people signed up for the mailing list; and hundreds of supporters self-reported taking action. Although the Society made donation tools available on its Web site, it reports that it raised only "a small amount." Overall, the Society's team feels that the campaign delivered a positive return on its investment by giving supporters a "sense of connection to our organization."[10]

Clearly, using MySpace as a core campaign tool is still experimental. You can't expect dramatic results. Although the Society was pleased with the results of its campaign, by my measure, it spent a lot of time and effort for a limited return on investment. However, the Society did develop experience and expertise in social networking that will put it in a stronger position to achieve better results with its next Web 2.0 effort.

Friending

Social networking enthusiasts use the word "friend" as a verb, as in "Will you friend me?" The noun for the act of making friends on a social network is "friending." MySpace and Friendster users started a phenomenon known as hyper-friending, friend collecting, or friend whoring.[11] A friend collector accumulates as many friends as possible without regard to personal connections. Organizations have adopted this tactic because most social networks allow you to broadcast a message to all friends — it's like e-mail marketing for social networks.

The friend collecting trend has motivated anthropologists to examine the changing definition of friendship as it applies online. Young people typically use social networks to interact with a small group of known friends. The majority of people on a large friend list, however, may not be part of this group. Many are complete strangers; some are organizational entities. Although there are not yet words to distinguish a known-friend from a stranger-friend or an entity-friend, these differences exist and are intuitively comprehended by young people. Despite their understanding of the nuances of online friendship, however, many young people struggle to navigate these new social complexities.[12]

Recruiting "Door-to-Door"

To elect Peter Franchot to the office of Maryland comptroller, twenty-three-year-old organizer Jacob Colker turned to social networks. But instead of building a profile in order to drive supporters to it, as the Humane Society did, Colker visited profiles of likely volunteers and asked them to volunteer for Franchot's campaign. He undertook the online equivalent of knocking door-to-door.[13]

First Colker identified MySpace and Facebook as the social networks most likely to host a large number of potential Franchot supporters. Young voters already favored the candidate, and these social networks are populated with mostly eighteen- to twenty-five-year-olds. He then narrowed his list to college students living in Maryland, majoring in political science, and self-identified as holding liberal political views.[14] He then began the grueling work of sending messages to potential volunteers one by one. "It's tedious work for one lucky campaign staffer," he said. "You need a computer-savvy person to sit there on the Web sites and try to talk to as many people as possible."[15]

In four weeks, Colker outmaneuvered Franchot's two-term incumbent competitor, recruiting an army of about two hundred people, or 80 percent of the campaign's volunteer staff. They dropped fifty thousand fliers, made fifteen thousand phone calls, and pushed their candidate to victory. Colker acknowledges that winning a campaign takes more than a volunteer workforce; it requires fundraising, field organizing, press tactics, and advertising. But Colker estimates that the volunteers brought in 7 percent of the votes for the candidate, which had a significant impact on this second-tier race.[16]

Young people hang out online, but that doesn't mean that your campaign needs to limit itself to online action. Colker's methods provide an excellent example of using social networks to drive offline action. They also show that, just as in real life, the time spent making individual and personal connections produces results. In a sense, sending messages and posting comments on profiles is akin to shaking hands in the digital era, as danah boyd discusses in her Big Picture essay on this topic.

Conducting Advocacy on a Niche Network

So far, we've discussed the category leaders, MySpace and Facebook, two massive networks that host millions of people with diverse interests. But many networks target narrower audiences.

Digg appeals to people who love news—and competition. Its one million members submit, rank, categorize, and comment on breaking news. When Diggers like a story, they "digg" it by submitting it to

Digg's Web site. Stories that are "dugg" the most appear prominently on the site's home page. Using this method, most-liked stories rise from obscurity to the attention of Digg's considerable readership. (Figure 2.2 shows an example of Digg's "Top in Political News.") On any given day, Digg is approximately the one hundredth most popular Web site in the world.[17]

Figure 2.2. The Top Ten Political News Stories on Digg.com, December 13, 2007

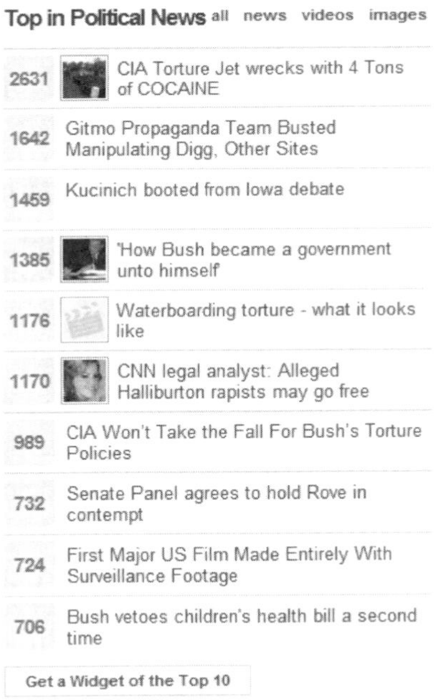

Top in Political News all news videos images

2631	CIA Torture Jet wrecks with 4 Tons of COCAINE
1642	Gitmo Propaganda Team Busted Manipulating Digg, Other Sites
1459	Kucinich booted from Iowa debate
1385	'How Bush became a government unto himself'
1176	Waterboarding torture - what it looks like
1170	CNN legal analyst: Alleged Halliburton rapists may go free
989	CIA Won't Take the Fall For Bush's Torture Policies
732	Senate Panel agrees to hold Rove in contempt
724	First Major US Film Made Entirely With Surveillance Footage
706	Bush vetoes children's health bill a second time

Get a Widget of the Top 10

The number of "diggs" per article is listed to the left of each article headline.

Diggers who "break" a story first earn recognition from the community. Members vie to be the first Digger to uncover the day's most popular news. Discovering good stories first is the currency of this social network.

Digg's largest user group is made up of people ages eighteen to twenty-four; 88 percent are eighteen to thirty-nine; 94 percent are male; and a majority resides in the United States.[18] Clearly, Digg's members represent a sliver of the world's population.[19] For organizations seeking to promote issues among this demographic, Digg provides an ideal environment. Jonathon D. Colman of the Nature Conservancy (www.nature.org) uses Digg and similar "social news" sites to promote a wide array of events, announcements, and discoveries relevant to his organization. In April 2007, Colman promoted the successful results of one of the Conservancy's major campaigns, a $120 million effort to finance conservation of British Columbia's twenty-one-million-acre Great Bear Rainforest.[20] Such a feat involved two years of work, the formation of a coalition of four large nongovernmental organizations, and extensive government negotiation. Promoting the story raised awareness for the need to preserve forests, attracted new supporters, and confirmed that existing supporters' efforts were effective.

By the time Colman sought to promote the Conservancy's campaign results, he had already become a regular Digg contributor. He typically spent about five minutes daily browsing news in his topical specialty, and his submissions had become known for their quality and credibility. Within one hour of submitting the Great Bear Rainforest story, nature.org received 2,127 visitors from Digg and 3,747 over the course of four days. At the end of that time, 836 people "dugg" the story, and 56 people commented on it.[21] They provided congratulatory commentary, panegyrics about the forest, and also criticism of the Conservancy's campaign. In short, the Digg campaign engaged the community.

"Nonprofits have been stymied by online communities, what they're for, how to build them, and how to engage them," Colman says. "[The Conservancy's] guiding philosophy is to engage people where they're already being active." Requiring only a small daily investment of time, Colman's efforts resulted in a boost in visibility within a community of likely supporters.

This example illustrates the wide variety of social networks. Digg and other social news sites offer a much different experience than MySpace. Digg's members derive social value from participating in the community, but all interactions revolve around news. For nonprofits and political campaigns, this high degree of focus offers an opportunity. Unlike social networks with tightly knit cliques where uninvited strangers are unwelcome, Digg offers a simple route to community acceptance: *post interesting stories.* By adding value to the social news community via an authentic and ongoing effort, you will open a reliable avenue for advocacy.

Note that Digg is one among many content-oriented social networks, each with a focus:

- StumbleUpon: Review new Web sites

- Del.icio.us: Share bookmarks

- Yelp: Write reviews of local establishments

- DeviantArt: Share art

- YouTube: Share videos

- Freecycle: Give and receive gifts

- Flickr: Share photos

Each of these social networks is oriented around a specific type of media or content. Like Digg, these networks value active and engaged community members. The first step in making an impact in these networks is to become a credible participant.

Raising Money

In early 2007, several young entrepreneurs realized that social networks could enable low-cost, friend-to-friend fundraising campaigns. Using these networks, they could integrate social issue awareness directly into the flow of everyday life. The entrepreneurs hoped that this social networking–based advocacy and fundraising approach would open the floodgates to fundraising among nontraditional donors, such as young people.[22] Let's examine two recent examples, one more promising than the other.

Change.org

Launched in February 2007, www.change.org is a social networking site dedicated to causes. Like most social networks, it enables participants to create profiles, send messages to friends, and keep a personal blog. As a member of the social network, the user joins like-minded individuals in groups oriented around specific social issues, nonprofit organizations, or political candidates. For example, members can join the Stop Global Warming group, the Doctors Without Borders USA group, or the Fred Thompson group. Hundreds of groups exist in each category, and each contains a set of tools for members to support their cause of choice, either through a pledge to take action or by fundraising.

At the time this book went to press, the top nonprofit listed at Change.org, Friends of New Orleans, had raised only $375 and had 760 supporters. Change.org suffers from a predicament common to new social networks: it needs to convince young people either to switch from their current social network or to use two social networks. This task, though not insurmountable, is monumental, to say the least. Less than a year old, Change.org doesn't provide a viable solution at the moment, but its founders may yet have the energy and enthusiasm to overcome the obstacles. For the purposes of this book, the site demonstrates the enormous difficulty in developing a social network from scratch.

Causes

Twenty-four-year-old entrepreneur Joe Green used a different tactic to launch the fundraising tool he called Causes. Instead of building a brand-new social network, he developed a Facebook application that is integrated directly into this popular social network. Using the tool, Facebook users and organizations can start a "cause," choose a 501(c)(3) organization to become the beneficiary, and then use Facebook's built-in communication tools to promote the cause among friends.

In concept, Causes is similar to Change.org. In practice, however, it has been much more effective, for the simple reason that it makes use of existing social connections rather than building new ones. Causes currently boasts 2.5 million users and adds thirty thousand on an average day. It has raised about $300,000 in the few months since its launch. The largest group, Support Breast Cancer Research, has 1.5 million supporters and has raised $31,649. Almost all of the money will go to Boston-based Brigham and Women's Hospital.[23]

In response to recent news about a professional football player involved in a dog fighting ring, University of Arizona graduate Bradley Kraay started a group called Stop Dog Fighting Now. He chose Pit Bull Rescue Central as the group's beneficiary. Within a month, the cause gained 287,756 members and brought in over $10,000. In an interesting twist, Pit Bull Rescue was completely unknown to Kraay. He chose it from Causes' list of 501(c)(3) organizations. The funds from Kraay's campaign are a windfall for the all-volunteer organization, which has annual gross revenues of just $82,000.[24]

For some nonprofits, Causes has been a fundraising marvel. For the majority, it's an experiment that hasn't yet delivered results. Most Causes groups have attracted only a few members and less than $10. However, the Support Breast Cancer and Pit Bull Rescue examples show that with a popular cause, good timing, and an enthusiastic organizer, the system works.

o   o   o

Change.org's struggles and Causes' early successes illustrate a foundational Web 2.0 concept: a product or service becomes more valuable as the number of people using it increases. Causes and its users are able to raise funds and awareness much more effectively because it was built on top of a dynamic existing social network. The strength of the network matters more than anything else. To engage young people in online activism, you'll find it much easier to go where they are, rather than to build a new place where you want them to come. Having understood that it was fighting an uphill battle, Change.org recently launched an application on Facebook to compete with Causes.

Engaging an Existing Community

Today, Care2 is a dynamic social network consisting of more than seven million activists. It bills itself as the "largest online community of people passionate about making a difference." The site offers an array of online services to facilitate civic activism and connections between activists and nonprofits.

In 2001, Care2 was a much smaller organization that communicated with its member nonprofits and activists via e-mail. It sent e-mail on behalf of its nonprofits to the members most likely to support a particular nonprofit's cause. It matched members with nonprofits on the basis of demographic information supplied by the member.

In this year, Care2 conducted a scientific experiment. The group wondered what would happen to the level of activism if it allowed members to communicate with each other, rather than through the nonprofit-to-supporter e-mail channel. The activism level was measured using a number of criteria, such as signing petitions, donating money, and sending e-cards. To empower member-to-member communication, Care2 developed several social networking tools that enabled members to speak among themselves online.

Care2 found that the level of activism among the treatment group *doubled* in six months. Members encouraged and engaged each other. Each new post to a discussion group resulted in a 2 percent increase in the likelihood of someone's taking action. Overall, people who posted were 78 percent more likely to take action than those who did not.

Comparing the social networking experiments of Care2 and Change.org is illuminating. Both attempted to empower activists by connecting them with each other and with nonprofit organizations. Care2 added social networking features to an already vibrant and active online community. Change.org built a place for activist-based social activity and then sought participants. These organizations learned a profound truth: social networks reinforce existing communities. Don't build a new social network without one.

How Social Networks Work

In the introduction to this chapter, I briefly touched on the core features that define social networks. Let's examine these features in more detail.

Profile Page

The profile page comprises the heart of someone's social networking identity. Most networks allow an individual to customize his or her page in a variety of ways, such as by adding music, video clips, and photos. A profile often contains demographic information, such as gender, age, and location, in addition to conveying the user's personality and affinity through music, a list of interests, and photos. As danah boyd says, "Profiles let you write yourself into being via collage."[25] Figure 2.3 shows a typical MySpace profile page.

Figure 2.3. A MySpace Profile Page

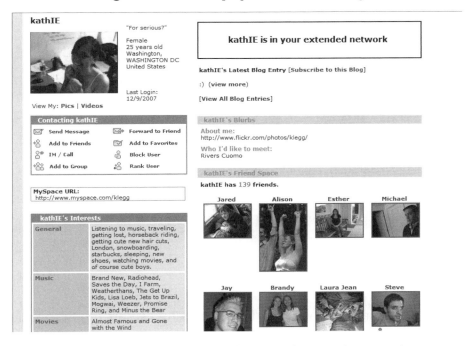

The components of the page, such as the area showing demographic information and the box describing interests, are common to many profiles.

Public or Semipublic Network of Friends

After you have created a profile page, most networks encourage you to connect with friends. Social networks provide an array of tools to help you find friends who are using the same network. Upon finding a friend, typically you send an invitation to that person. If he or she accepts, a small photo is added to your profile. In a short time, you develop a visualization of your friend network. Figure 2.4 is a screenshot showing part of my Facebook friend list.

Figure 2.4. Example of a Facebook Friend List

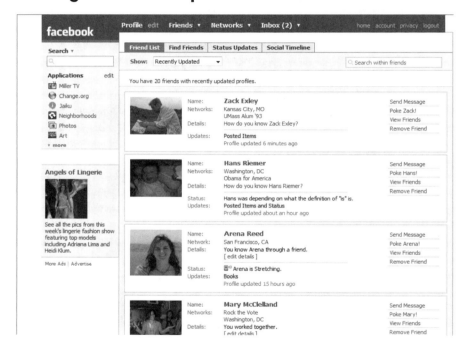

On many social networks, these friend lists are public, or public among people who have confirmed friendship to one another. Because you can see your friends' friends, and their friends, and so on, the network becomes traversable. You can navigate quickly from the profile page of a good friend to the page of someone whom you've never met. Although this person is a stranger, the social network creates a link (albeit remote).

Public Commenting System

To the uninitiated, one of the most peculiar aspects of social networking is the public commenting system. Most social networks enable one friend to write a publicly viewable message to another. On the first social networks, these spaces were designed to feature testimonials, such as "Harry is the greatest friend in the world." However, many people use this space to deliver personal messages. Here's a typical example from a MySpace page:

> "Hey Square what you up to anything good. lol. Clearly ive got nothing better to do with my time. How was CSI Sorry silly question. Dont forget about tea next monday if you do i will get very very cross. No more mash for you then. Xxx"[26]

Despite the personal nature of these messages, they are available for any MySpace visitor to peruse. (This one was on the first MySpace profile that I clicked from the MySpace home page.) This type of public exposition of personal details has led to privacy and personal security concerns—especially on the part of parents.

Private Messaging Systems

Recognizing that many people do not want to expose their personal conversations to the general public, many social networks developed private messaging systems. These work like Web-based e-mail systems, but are confined to a given social network, as messages can be sent privately between individuals on the network. Recently, some social networks have added the ability to send messages to e-mail addresses.

o   o   o

All social networks share these four features, but they're not always clearly described or delineated as such. Each network applies its own set of distinctive names, as well as additional technologies that intertwine with these core components. MySpace offers *bulletins,* Facebook provides *the wall.* Bebo touts its *white board,* and Xanga promotes its *journals.* These elements differ primarily in name.

However, there are also some profound differences. For example, Facebook allows software developers to write applications that have privileged access to data about its members. These are called Facebook applications. Causes (mentioned above) is one such application. By allowing third-party software developers to launch applications within its walled garden, Facebook has become much more than a social network; it has become a *social networking platform.* Since launching this capability, Facebook has experienced dramatic growth. Competing social networks are now trying to mimic its success by offering similar platform-like features.

The overarching lesson is that, in some significant ways, social networks work similarly. They're places where people come to interact on a frequent basis. From a technical perspective, however, there exist wide differences that significantly affect the environment for launching and managing a social networking campaign.

Getting Started

Despite the wide differences among social networks, learning the lingo and technical idiosyncrasies is not terribly difficult—it just takes time. Sign up for an account on your social network of choice and spend a week or two using it. But don't do it alone. It's imperative that you interact with close friends on the network. It will be difficult to understand the social significance of the tools without experiencing the ways in which they enhance (or alter) your existing relationships.

If you don't know which social networks your supporters use, spend time browsing networks and profiles. Use built-in search tools to find people who list interests aligned with your organization. If you have a way to contact existing supporters, ask them to take an online survey about their use of social networks. Web sites like SurveyMonkey.com make it easy to administer this type of poll.

When you're browsing social networks, pay close attention to widgets. Their name makes them sound like small trivialities, but they're one of the most powerful ways to disseminate your message across the Internet. What types of widgets do you see most often on the profile pages of your supporters? What can your organization offer that adds value to your social networking community? Some widgets do more than advertise: they accept donations, send text messages, and play music. Be sure to understand the range of widget possibilities before crafting your campaign strategy.

For more information on using widgets strategically, see
mobilizingyouth.org/widgets

You probably began this chapter with a passing familiarity with MySpace and Facebook. We've discussed these and several other social networking sites. The next paragraphs briefly describe some other networks so as to give you a sense of their wide range and diversity.

For a more comprehensive list of social networks, see
mobilizingyouth.org/social_networks

Hi5 Launched in late 2003, Hi5 is one of the leading social networks. The site targets teens and twentysomethings and has over sixty million members. Most of Hi5's traffic comes from outside the United States. It's the number one ranked site online in Portugal, Ecuador, Costa Rica, El Salvador, and Guatemala, and it ranks at number two in Jamaica, Honduras, and the Dominican Republic.

Gather Gather is a social networking site with a heavy focus on content. It allows you to publish blogs (called "articles"), which others can tag and rate according to usefulness. Articles and images with the highest rankings appear on the home page and generally gain more visibility on the site. Gather also allows users to create and join groups, where they can share images and articles with people who have similar interests.

StumbleUpon   This site allows you to surf the best-reviewed sites on the Web while blogging about your favorite content and connecting with others who have similar interests. StumbleUpon is one of the fastest-growing social networks.

LinkedIn   LinkedIn focuses on creating and maintaining professional contacts. You can use the site to touch base with former coworkers and classmates, find people employed in the nonprofit sector, and obtain professional references. The site, currently boasting over ten million members, supports the creation of groups and has a dedicated category for nonprofits.

Strategic Considerations

The examples in this chapter demonstrate the fragmented universe of social networks. These networks are every bit as varied and unique as the world's most dynamic cities (see Fred Stutzman's Big Picture essay that compares social networks to cities). Although they have become an integral part of young lives, social networks are not a cure-all for organizations looking to recruit, engage, or activate young supporters. Appealing to young people on these networks requires research, subtlety, authenticity, technical know-how, and commitment. No single strategy will work for all networks. Before you launch a campaign, carefully consider the qualities that make your target social network and supporters unique. The following sections discuss questions and issues that will help you focus your efforts.

Calculate Opportunity Costs

If you're working with young people, chances are that they already spend time on a social network or networks. Your supporters' choice of network(s) will determine the range of practical and technical possibilities. If potential supporters are spread across many networks or even within a single network, the task of reaching them becomes more difficult and expensive. After some experimentation and measurement,

Care2 determined that its per-friend acquisition cost on MySpace was $12.27 Does this level of investment make sense for your organization? Once you find your supporters' networks of choice, roughly calculate the cost of conducting a campaign in these spaces. In many cases, there may be a more cost-effective way to interact with supporters.

> Care2 created a social networking ROI calculator. Find it at
> **http://www.frogloop.com/social-network-calculator**

Understand Social Dynamics

How do people interact with one another on their social network of choice? What actions and behaviors are valued? Who are the leaders and followers?

In *The Tipping Point,* Malcolm Gladwell popularized the notion of "connectors" and "mavens." He theorizes that you can lead crowds by influencing the *influencers.* Some network theorists disagree. They believe that group dynamics drive social movements, and recommend influencing the *easily influenced.*[28] Anthropologists will tell you that both theories have merit. Groups behave differently at different times. Identify group and individual motivations and then craft your campaign to guide both leaders and followers without condescension or marketing spin. Most young people appreciate an honest and forthright approach.

You can build credibility by enhancing the community. Some social networks offer easy entry to the "inner circle." In the case of content-focused social networks (such as Digg), community members respect those who add value to their community. People who submit interesting news on Digg are respected. This concrete definition of community value can offer a clear path for your campaign strategy. As an organization, you'll undoubtedly have more resources at your disposal than many individuals. Apply these resources to adding value to a social network.

Figure Out Friending

If you read the news about social networks, you might determine that social networking is about making the most friends. These "friend collecting" stories draw the majority of media attention. However, the value of a friend differs by social network. On MySpace, more is better. On Facebook, authentic connections between individuals are valued more than the quantity of friendships. Neither is worse or better, but they are distinctly dissimilar. If you understand the nature of friendship on your network of choice, you can develop a more focused campaign strategy.

Fit Social Networking into Your "Ecosystem"

Josh Levy from the Personal Democracy Forum calls social networking "part of a participatory ecosystem."[29] How does social networking fit within the broader context of your campaign? Do you have other ways for people to participate? Social networks are just one area in which people can interact with one another. Think about complementary ways in which people can take action and communicate. Most important, create mechanisms to motivate *offline* action. In-person meetups have been shown to make people more likely to become an activist.[30]

Build Your Own Social Network?

Businesses are great candidates for custom-built social networks. Their hierarchical structure makes it easy for the boss to say, "Use this social network." But most nonprofits and political campaigns will find this path difficult. Be warned that many organizations have tried this route and failed. Persuading people to switch or add social networks will require a lot of effort. Consider this option only if you have an ultra-energized group of supporters or a compelling need that's not being served by other social networks. Such organizations as Care2 succeeded with this approach because they built social tools around a network of people who were already online and engaged with their organization.

Instead of building your own network, think about adding social features to your existing Web site. You can add a blog, a commenting area, or a discussion group. Offer widgets. There are ways to gain many of the benefits of a social network without building one from scratch. Services like KickApps aim to provide skilled software developers with tools to incorporate socialization features into existing Web sites.

If you're set on building your own network, some new services eliminate many of the technical costs. Unlike Care2, you don't have to build it from scratch. For example, Ning.com allows you to create a customized social network in a matter of minutes.

> For a list of build-your-own social network tools, see
> **mobilizingyouth.org/resources/social_network_build**

Tell a Story

The Humane Society's Sunny the Seal campaign demonstrated the art of good narrative. The Society could have created an organizational profile that contained a litany of seal hunting offenses, videos, and photos. However, it would have neither captured people's imaginations nor tugged at their heartstrings. Sunny personalized the seal hunt while also giving the campaign a sense of momentum. The story line engaged supporters and encouraged them to return daily. It gave context to the textual information, photos, videos, and music that would have been lifeless otherwise.

Dramas play out across social networks every day. Study these dramas and learn how to tell your story in a way that will be familiar and compelling to your audience.

Encourage Participation and Let Go

Web 2.0 is predicated on the idea that users define the things they use. Your role as a campaign organizer is to provide structure and guidance and to encourage communication among supporters. The first part of this task is to define multiple ways in which supporters can take action and meet each other. Fortunately, social networks were designed with participation in mind. Use your network's built-in tools to encourage involvement.

But you must also be willing to let supporters take your story and run with it. They will post comments, use your graphics on their profiles, and dream up ways of participating that you could not have imagined. If you encourage this kind of open-ended participation, supporters will internalize your cause and make it their own. Consider how you'll respond when supporters start to modify your story. Design it from the start to become more compelling as they personalize it.

Get comfortable with negative comments. They spark discussion, and, when constructive, they can help you learn more about your supporters, make smarter decisions, and demonstrate a willingness to listen. Even nonconstructive comments have value. They often create an inverse reaction among people who support your organization and cause. It gives them a rallying cry and binds them together.

Letting go of control can significantly enhance your organization's relationships with supporters and the resulting strength of your campaign. But what if participation goes too far? How do you draw the line between harsh criticism and hateful language? Discuss the issue among your staff and share your thoughts with supporters. With some advance planning and consideration, you'll be ready to address harmful participation if it should occur.

Spend Time on Your Social Network

If there's a key lesson contained in the examples in this chapter, it's that social networking needs people's active attention. You can't simply create a profile and expect results. A social network is a place where people hang out, talk, and pass the time. To be effective, you can't stand silent among them. People will friend you, request friendship, post comments, and send messages. Make staff time for becoming an actively participating member of this community, or enlist a volunteer who is already engaged in the network.

If you don't have the time to work like this on a network, consider an advertising strategy instead. You can buy ads on social networks with none of the commitment of becoming a community member. This approach may be a more effective way of reaching social network inhabitants for organizations with limited time.

Be an Organizer

There's a good reason that social networking campaigns need nurturing from people. Social networks are groups of . . . people. There's a tendency to call people "users" or "target audiences." (I'm as guilty of using these terms as anyone.) But such language obscures the fact that computer users are human beings. In social networks, online groups behave a lot like offline groups. Intrusions by unknown individuals or organizations are repelled, marketing spin is disdained, and authenticity is valued.

To be effective in this environment, you have to behave more like an organizer and less like a marketer. Instead of broadcasting messages, identify and develop leadership and encourage supporters to reach out to each other because they believe in your shared values. Bring people together and give them the tools to act on behalf of these shared values. Build a network of relationships that is deep enough to provide a foundation for community action—and offer social rewards for individual action. Show supporters why they should advocate for an issue and then encourage them to do it.

Ask for Help

Are there other organizations in your field interested in your campaign? Do they already have an established presence on a social network? Ask them to send a message to their friends about your campaign. Form a mutually beneficial social networking coalition. The most effective nonprofits reach out for help and collaborate frequently.[31]

Make a List of Actions

How will new supporters interact with your campaign? What are you asking them to do? Many campaigns do a great job of storytelling but neglect to capitalize on the enthusiasm and empathy that their story generates. Develop a list of actions that you'd like supporters to take.

Create easy pathways for supporters to perform these actions. For example, if you want someone to sign a petition but your social network does not have a petition function, direct the person to petition forms on your Web site via strategically placed links.

Tackling large social issues can seem daunting. Make doing so more manageable by keeping your list of actions small. The Genocide Intervention Network created a list called "Ten Ways You Can Take Action Right Now."[32] Each action was followed by a link to a Web page that enabled a supporter to take that action.

Measure Results

How will you know if your social networking campaign is successful? Was it worth all the effort? Was there something else you could have done with better results? If you set up a plan for measuring results, you'll have the answer to these questions at the end of your campaign. One easy way to measure results is to develop metrics based on your list of actions.

For example, for a three-month-long MySpace campaign staffed by one part-time person, you might develop the following list of action-oriented goals and associated data for comparison:

We want to

- Make ten thousand friends.
- Sign 10 percent of those friends to sign our mailing list.
- Get 1 percent to volunteer for our annual event.

In the past, we have

- Spent $3 per new member to sign our mailing list
- Spent $25 to recruit one new volunteer through our traditional e-mail campaigns
- Tasked one employee with managing the campaign to recruit new members and volunteers, which required ten hours per week over a three-month period

Keep track of staff time and dollars spent on your social networking campaign, and you'll know how it compares to your historical experience and to other options.

Challenges and Opportunities

Social networks are difficult environments in which to run campaigns. They're fragmented in terms of technical capabilities, demographics, and even terminology. Their popularity is also ephemeral. Last year, MySpace dominated the field of social networks. This year, Facebook has become the darling of the press and technophiles alike. Like most technologies and social phenomena discussed in this book, social networking is in an embryonic phase. Organizations are exploring new tactics and strategies every week. None of them has yet discovered a magic social networking formula.

The popularity of these networks will shift, feature sets will expand, and campaigns will continue to deliver positive and negative results. Regardless of all the changes, social networking is here to stay. It has already become a staple of young social lives. To understand young people and the Internet of tomorrow, it's essential to comprehend social networking. This claim is bold, I know. But the concepts that underpin social networking are becoming the trends shaping the Internet, commerce, and social life *online and offline*.

Our society is becoming one in which conversations have a perpetual shelf life and an unseen audience of millions. We're gaining new notions for friendship that defy our words to describe them. Online connections are strengthening offline relationships. In some circles, a lack of Internet access can become a cause for social exclusion. In short, social networks have become places in which life happens—but it's the life of people networked to every other computer user on the planet.

The implications are complex and sometimes bewildering. Many campaigns have achieved only mediocre results. However, each effort brings the organization—and the people who work for it—one step closer to understanding the shape of things to come. I posit that people with these experiences are better positioned not only to conduct social networking campaigns in the future but also to understand many of the technologies and campaigns described in this book.

The short history of social networking has shown that people move from huge networks to smaller and more intimate ones. In the future, social networks will specialize further as contingents break off and migrate. Networks will also merge as businesses aggregate their holdings. At press time, Microsoft has made an investment in Facebook that values the company at $15 billion. However, shortly thereafter, a cabal of companies led by Google launched a new standard called Open Social, which intends to rein in Facebook's rapidly growing advantage. It creates a common social networking platform.

Some people speculate that the social networking applications of tomorrow will be "social aggregators." Aggregators consolidate social networking interactions, allowing you to easily maintain accounts on multiple networks. This approach makes it practical to keep up relationships and profiles across networks, but also, more important, across social groups. In real life, we change how we express our personalities ever so slightly when we move between various social circles. We speak to our parents using different words and cultural references than we use with our friends. We are more formal at work, more casual at home, and more stylish for a night out on the town. At the moment, social networks do not allow for this type of differentiation. Social aggregators may fill the void, enabling us to manage multiple identities effectively.

Social networks will also become visually more dynamic. In fact, they may merge with virtual worlds as the faster computers required to render three-dimensional graphics become available to more people. Social networks will also move to mobile devices and use global positioning systems to identify your proximity to friends. Strolling down Main Street may become a mixed-reality experience in which your online social network intermingles with your offline experience. Learning about these networks today will serve as a foundation for understanding social life in the next few decades.

Endnotes

1. danah boyd is a PhD candidate at the School of Information (iSchool) at the University of California-Berkeley and a fellow at the Berkman Center for Internet and Society at the Harvard Law School. boyd prefers her name to be written with lowercase letters. This quotation is from "Friendster lost steam. Is MySpace just a fad?" Apophenia Blog, Mar. 21, 2006. www.danah.org/papers/FriendsterMySpace Essay.html.

2. www.ft.com/cms/s/0/59ab33da-64c4-11db-90fd-0000779e2340 .html

3. www.pewinternet.org/PPF/r/198/report_display.asp

4. http://blog.softtechvc.com/2005/10/the_facebook_un.html

5. www.mediabuyerplanner.com/2007/07/30/facebook-issues-site-stats

6. Thanks yet again to boyd for elucidating these common components: boyd, danah, "Why Youth [Heart] Social Network Sites: The Role of Networked Publics in Teenage Social Life"; in David Buckingham (ed.), MacArthur Foundation Series on Digital Learning, *Identity* volume, forthcoming.

7. boyd, danah, "Social Network Sites: Public, Private, or What?" Knowledge Tree 13. http://kt.flexiblelearning.net.au/tkt2007/ ?page_id=28, May 2007

   www.powerhousemuseum.com/dmsblog/index.php/2006/12/20/ shirky-and-boyd-on-problems-of-reality-in-second-life

8. http://profile.myspace.com/index.cfm?fuseaction=user.viewprofile &friendID=167879261. You can find case study write-ups at www .frogloop.com/care2blog/2007/5/7/sunny-the-seal-melts-hearts-on -myspace.html and at http://beth.typepad.com/beths_blog/2007/06/ using-social-ne.html.

9. Interestingly, the Humane Society of the United States (HSUS) is not listed in an official capacity anywhere on the profile. Sunny frequently refers to HSUS and provides links to HSUS Web sites, but does not acknowledge that HSUS is his creator. The fiction is not broken.

10. www.frogloop.com/care2blog/2007/5/7/sunny-the-seal-melts
    -hearts-on-myspace.html

11. Friendster was one of the first social networks.

12. For an excellent discussion of this topic, see danah boyd's paper
    "Friends, Friendsters, and MySpace Top 8: Writing Community into
    Being on Social Network Sites," available at First Monday, Dec.
    11–12, 2006: www.firstmonday.org/issues/issue11_12/boyd/
    index.html.

13. http://weblogs.chicagotribune.com/news/politics/blog/2006/10/
    the_virtual_campaign.html

    www.nancyschwartz.com/social_networking_and_nonprofits.html

    http://hotlineblog.nationaljournal.com/archives/2006/12/
    on_the_download_20.html

14. Most social networks ask your political orientation as a standard
    profile question.

15. http://hotlineblog.nationaljournal.com/archives/2006/12/
    on_the_download_20.html

16. www.nancyschwartz.com/social_networking_and_nonprofits.html

17. Alexa is a Web site ranking service. Digg hovers around Alexa's one
    hundredth top Web site mark. www.alexa.com/data/details/
    traffic_details?q=&url=digg.com

18. http://snook.ca/archives/other/digg_us_centric

    www.federatedmedia.net/authors/digg

19. Digg's CEO states that Digg's membership and readership are
    becoming increasingly diverse. See http://blogs.zdnet.com/
    micro-markets/?p=446.

20. www.nature.org/wherewework/northamerica/canada/work/
    art14771.html

21. www.nten.org/sites/nten/files/nten_ntc07.pdf

    http://digg.com/environment/5_MILLION_ACRES_of_the_Great
    _Bear_Rainforest_saved_from_logging

    www.treehugger.com/files/2007/07/ecogeek_of_the_4.php

22. www.techpresident.com/node/385

23. www.nonprofittechblog.org/project-agapes-causes-facebook
    -app-now-at-25-million-users

    www.personaldemocracy.com/node/1458

24. The last year for which records are available;
    www.guidestar.org/NpoDocuments/47/0068/91-2/16000-4191.pdf

25. boyd, danah, "Friendster lost steam. Is MySpace just a fad?"
    Apophenia Blog, Mar. 21, 2006. www.danah.org/papers/
    FriendsterMySpaceEssay.html

26. http://profile.myspace.com/index.cfm?fuseaction=user
    .viewprofile&friendid=202589226

27. www.christine.net/2007/04/7_tips_for_succ.html

28. http://socialmarketing.blogs.com/r_craiig_lefebvres_social/2007/
    03/fallacies_of_bu.html

29. www.personaldemocracy.com/node/1116

30. www.sierrasummit2005.org/sierrasummit/coverage/r076.asp

31. Crutchfield, Leslie, and Heather McLeod Grant, *Forces for Good*, San
    Francisco: Jossey-Bass, 2007. See also www.forcesforgood.net.

32. www.genocideintervention.net/advocate/action/thingstodo

THE BIG PICTURE

Digital Handshakes in Networked Publics:
Why Politicians Must Interact, Not Broadcast

Essay by danah boyd

danah boyd is a PhD candidate at the School of Information at the University of California-Berkeley and a fellow at Harvard Law School's Berkman Center for Internet and Society. Her research focuses on the role of social media in public life. If you're interested in how young people are using the Internet, chances are that danah has written something about it. As I researched for this book, I discovered that if you click around enough, you'll eventually arrive at danah's work and will be thankful you did—her insights and research elucidate the complex interplay of technology and youth.

Much to my dismay, American politicians primarily treat the digital world as yet another broadcast medium. They seem to think that they will be worshipped online if only they port their TV-styled material to the Internet. With this framework in mind, they pay consultants to build structured, formalized content for citizens to passively consume. When these endeavors fail to capture massive attention, politicians blame the medium.

Even in 2004, when politicians everywhere were discussing the potential of the Internet thanks to Howard Dean, most political campaigns recognized digital citizens only to the extent that they typed in their credit card numbers to support campaign finance. They never seemed to understand that there were people behind those wallets. Of course, I cannot fully blame the campaigns—they were trying to do what the e-commerce entrepreneurs tried a few years earlier. Yet, as venture capitalists learned the hard way with the burst of the tech bubble, there's a lot more to the Internet than online shopping.

By and large, two practices dominate everyday people's use of the Internet: information access and communication. Both are about interaction and engagement—with content and with other people. The result of everyday participation is the collective formation of networks—networks of people, networks of information, and networks of people juxtaposed with information. As such, the Internet is not simply a broadcast medium, but a "networked public." Just as with the offline equivalent—parks, malls, town squares, and so on—people come together for a variety of different purposes, including socialization, status negotiation, consumption, and civic engagement.

The manifestation of networked publics is most visible with the current wave of online communities—social networking sites like MySpace and Facebook, media-sharing sites like YouTube and Flickr, and blogs. These sites are not simply spaces for information dissemination; they are networked publics where people gather en masse to do the things that they would normally do in public places. In doing so, they help construct a new public sphere.

To their credit, political candidates understand that the services that help construct networked publics are important. They are rushing to social network sites to mark their turf and using YouTube to spread their message, but, all too often, their awkwardness shows. They know that the sites are important, but they don't seem to know why or what to do with them. Although it is certainly possible to grandstand in networked publics, the social norms demand authenticity, a quality that is typically hammered out of most candidates at a young age.

Consider the "friending" phenomenon, in which social networking sites allow participants to list others as "Friends." The concept of Friends can be confusing because most people don't use this feature to list their closest and dearest; they list all the people whom they envision as part of their imagined audience. If they imagine that their profile will be viewed by just a few, they're likely to list only close friends; those seeking mass attention are far more likely to nurture thousands of connections. Not surprisingly, politicians are seeking fairly broad audiences, so they (or at least their interns) run around trying to collect as many Friends as possible. The problem is that their enthusiasm more closely resembles that of a dorky fourteen-year-old boy trying to appear popular than that of a celebrity supporting and nurturing fans. Their profiles have no life to them—and no one wants to have a Death Eater as a Friend.

It is critical to understand the reasons why people collect strangers and celebrities (of which politicians are typically one or the other) on social networking sites. The primary reason has to do with signaling identity information. A connection to Barack Obama or John McCain or even Stephen Colbert signals political affiliation, political engagement (or lack thereof), and philosophical bent. The second reason is to create an open channel for communicating with the public figure through comments. In other words, citizens use politicians for their own purposes, not to validate a snazzy new media campaign.

Having millions of Friends means nothing if politicians don't create a platform where they will listen to and validate people's woes. The primary place for said interactions is through comments. On MySpace and Facebook, Friends can leave comments or wall messages—pithy remarks that are publicly displayed on an individual's profile. Getting comments makes a person look cool, but comments are also embedded in a social contract of reciprocity. Comments are not left on politicians' profiles simply to be consumed by the aide who controls the profile; they are crafted to provoke a response by the politician or by anyone visiting the politician's page.

Furthermore, comments are a form of social currency. Receiving comments from cool people makes the recipient look cool. Imagine what would happen if politicians sincerely reached out to some of their Friends and began commenting. Whenever bands do this, teens go wild and tell all their friends. For some of the most politically engaged young people, this would be a huge energizer. All of a sudden, the candidate would go from being one of nine thousand Friends that a person has to someone who leaves a message and is visible by all of that person's Friends, many of whom are probably not connected to the candidate. The key is that these need to be genuine messages rather than mass-produced spam. Sadly, we see no such effort by politicians on social networking sites. They think of their profile as a way to advertise themselves, rather than as a jumping-off point to engage in a networked public.

Politicians stand little chance of activating Friend connections if they fail to nurture those relationships or understand the social norms that exist in networked publics. A Friend online does not automatically mean a vote offline. Simply having a digital presence doesn't convert people. Having a MySpace profile that looks like an ad campaign doesn't convince anyone to vote for you.

Whenever I encourage campaigns to reach out and connect to the citizens of the networked publics, I'm told that politicians don't have time for this, or that it's easier to broadcast. There's no doubt that broadcast is easier, but it's not nearly as effective as meaningful encounters. Politicians know that even in an era of TV, they have to travel state-to-state to talk to people on their own terms in their own world. They also spend countless hours on the phone nurturing potential donors. For many young adults today, public life is primarily experienced online. By not taking the time to engage in networked publics, politicians are failing to engage those who spend much of their day there. It's time to start acknowledging networked publics and begin digitally shaking hands.

THE BIG PICTURE

The Vibrancy of Online Social Spaces

Essay by Fred Stutzman

Fred Stutzman is a PhD student and teaching fellow at the University of North Carolina's School of Information and Library Science. He is also cofounder of ClaimID, a service that allows people to manage online identity from a single location (instead of creating separate logins for every site). He writes frequently about information, social networks, identity, and technology.

Over the last few years, millions of us have come to know sites like MySpace and Facebook as social spaces, where the virtual and the real collapse and where a sense of community and interaction is integral to the experience.

In her 1961 book *The Death and Life of Great American Cities*, writer Jane Jacobs described the "sidewalk ballet" of a vital real-world urban environment. Jacobs argued that a vibrant and diverse city should possess four characteristic design elements. These elements can be applied to our virtual social spaces as well.

First, Jacobs argues that a city should be of mixed use, its multifunction form creating necessary activity throughout the day. We can see an analogy in the Facebook Newsfeed. When participants log into Facebook, they receive a list of recent activity in their social network. A message may inform you that a friend has written on another friend's wall, or that a friend has posted an event.

Second, Jacobs writes that a city should have "short blocks," allowing pedestrians to explore novel paths that create interest in their environment. In a social network, we declare our identity as we describe our interests, tag each other, and post on walls and message boards. These "digital traces" are often hyperlinked, permitting endless point-and-click exploration of the social space. As it happens, humans are very interesting to each other, and social networks provide endless opportunities to explore those we know and care about.

Third, a city's buildings should have a variety of architecture and styles, enabling residents of different social strata to meet in a shared place. Love it or hate it, the unending ability to customize MySpace profiles provides a significant level of variety. It drives learning and adoption of the service, as individuals collaborate to make their space better represent their identity.

Finally, Jacobs argues for density, so that different populations are interspersed. Indeed, online social networks are concentrated, but in this sense they are unlike any neighborhood. Social networks allow for the centralization of a person's network in a single place. Geographical boundaries are rendered insignificant as we connect across place and time. The social network allows work friends to intermingle with grade-school friends in an odd, often awkward dance.

We know that online social networks represent meaningful digital spaces to millions of people. We flirt, we interact, we do business, and we seek out information and gratification, finding a complex social world at our fingertips. It would be wise for all of us to pay attention to Jacobs's ideas. We will find both the meaning and the letter of her laws instructive.

CHAPTER 3

Video and Photo Sharing

At a press conference for his 2006 Senate reelection campaign, Republican George Allen pointed at twenty-year-old S. R. Sidarth and made this remark:

> "This fellow here, over here with the yellow shirt, macaca, or whatever his name is. He's with my opponent. He's following us around everywhere. . . . Let's give a welcome to macaca, here. Welcome to America and the real world of Virginia."[1]

Sidarth, a native Virginian of Indian descent and a senior at University of Virginia, captured the statement using an inexpensive video camera (see Figure 3.1). He had been videotaping Allen throughout the campaign in the employ of Allen's challenger, James Webb. When Webb's campaign staff saw Sidarth's video, they weren't exactly sure what *macaca* meant, but it sounded derogatory, and they ran with that interpretation.

Webb's campaign worked furiously to ensure that the public saw the video in this light, uploading it to YouTube, a Web site used to publish and share video; reaching out to the mainstream press; and calling in favors with bloggers. The online video became a focal point for the story as over four hundred thousand people watched the grainy image

**Figure 3.1. Allen Points at Sidarth
in the Infamous "Macaca" Video**

George Allen introduces "Macaca"

▶ ❙◀ ━━●━━━━━━ 00:13 / 01:02 ━━❗◀)) ⬚ ⬚

✉ Share   💟 Favorite   📑 Add to Playlists   🏳 Flag

Rate: ★ ★ ★ ★ ☆   Views: **282,592**
421 ratings

Comments: 614   Favorited: 415 times   Honors: 0   Links: 5

of Allen bullying the young Sidarth. Eventually, it was shown on television to an audience of millions.

Prior to the "macaca incident," Allen was leading by 16 percentage points. Allen's campaign didn't even consider Webb to be a viable challenger.[2] After the incident, Allen's support plummeted, particularly among youth. He swung from plus-23 points to minus-17 points among voters ages eighteen to twenty-nine.[3] On election day, Allen lost by 9,329 votes. Political analysts regard Webb's victory as one of the key races that led to the 2006 Democratic takeover of the U.S. Senate.[4]

Many factors contributed to Allen's loss, including smart moves by Webb's campaign, television broadcasts, and YouTube's system for uploading and sharing videos. Without amplification by the mainstream press, the story may not have gained statewide and national exposure. Without YouTube, however, the Webb campaign would have been entirely reliant on the mainstream press to promote the story. Instead, it used YouTube and a network of supporters as its personal broadcast network.

The video became a rallying cry for the campaign, giving volunteers a concrete method for offering their support. Every time the video was viewed—which YouTube publicly tabulates and displays automatically—Webb's campaign created one more negative impression about its opponent. Of course, no one knows how this incident would have unfolded before the era of online video sharing, but it's reasonable to assume that the video was an influential factor in Webb's victory.

Photo- and video-sharing sites, which I'll refer to as media-sharing sites, provide nontechnical people with simple and free tools to publish photos and videos to the Web. They also offer a group of features that facilitate sharing these media files. The Web sites share several defining characteristics:

- *Easy publishing tools.* Before media-sharing sites came into being, formatting, uploading, and coding a Web page to display photos and videos required technical expertise. Media-sharing sites removed almost all of the technical complexity.

- *Social features.* Media-sharing sites offer a variety of methods for sharing and discussing media files, such as comment areas and tools for sending photos and videos to friends.

- *Publishing to personal sites.* One of the key media-sharing innovations was a simple method for publishing media files directly to social networking profiles, blogs, and Web sites. It's often been said that MySpace was a primary factor in YouTube's growth, as millions of MySpace visitors used the service to put videos on their profile pages.

- *Low cost.* Most media-sharing sites do not charge for their services or have a tiered pricing plan that includes a free option.

Thanks to the low cost, relative absence of technical hurdles, and easy methods for sharing, people have been creating, distributing, and consuming visual media in huge numbers. According to a recent report by the Pew Internet and American Life Project, over 75 percent of young people watch online video, and about 50 percent upload photos. Perhaps most interesting, a majority of young people watch video *with friends*—the activity has become a real-life social event.[5]

The significant effect of this media explosion is that average people and organizations are telling video- and photo-based stories to ever wider audiences. Using media-sharing sites' social features, audiences are also talking back. In many instances, a compelling video or photo becomes a spark for conversation and a focus for online community action. Organizations are taking advantage of these opportunities to promote their causes and more fully engage supporters.

How Organizations Are Using Media-Sharing Sites

Inspired by spectacular stories like Webb's come-from-behind victory, many organizations have attempted to create similarly "viral" video sensations. However, there's no concrete formula for creating a video campaign that spreads exponentially online, and therefore the results often disappoint. Prudent organizations are experimenting with the aspects of video and photo that have a higher chance of success. The following examples describe these experiments, both to elucidate the range of opportunities and to set expectations for results.

Watching Opponents

In the political realm, following your opponent with a video camera has become a standard campaign tactic. Politicians now must assume that every moment of their public life is minutes away from becoming Internet news—and stands the chance of becoming a mainstream press story. The possibility brings a new level of responsibility and pressure to public office.

Nonprofits and activists have used similar tactics in their work. They train the watchful eye of a camera on their adversaries' every move to force increased public accountability. For example, an organization called Cop Watch patrols the streets of Brooklyn, New York, with cameras in hand. They keep an eye out for unnecessary interrogations, which they view as a form of harassment. Monifa Bandale of Cop Watch says, "Typically, once we start taping, the police leave."[6] This tactic is also common among protesters who record police movements in order to document and prevent abuses.

Responding to News

On the flip side, organizations use video-sharing sites to respond immediately to events that affect their domain. For example, John Edwards, the Democratic candidate for president, published a two-minute video response to President Bush's 9/11 memorial speech that has been watched by over 127,000 people on YouTube. Prior to the age of video sharing, Edwards would have been limited to a sound bite on the mainstream news—and only if his campaign worked hard enough to secure an interview. Now when relevant news breaks, politicians and nonprofits no longer have to depend exclusively on the mainstream press to broadcast their positions.

Reporting Alternative News

In the vast majority of cases, nonprofit organizations use media-sharing sites to report on their own planned activities, rather than stalking adversaries or responding to news. They create mini media channels to energize and inform existing supporters, attract new supporters, and document their organization's work.

In June 2007, for example, Oxfam International reported news from its campaign to protest the G8 Summit, the annual meeting of the leaders of the eight biggest and most powerful economies. Oxfam's yearly event aims to praise leaders who support its agenda and berate those who do not. The highlight of its efforts was a publicity stunt involving papier-mâché effigies of the G8 leaders' heads. Team members donned these costumes and romped through town to comical effect. Each day, they uploaded videos about their antics to YouTube and photos to a popular photo-sharing Web site called Flickr. Like YouTube, Flickr offers a low-cost method for publishing and sharing images.

Throughout the summit, Oxfam's team supplied supporters with frequent updates and in-depth reporting via Flickr and YouTube, in addition to daily reporting on its blog. These media channels intertwined to create rich and thorough coverage of Oxfam's activities. Clearly, no other media outlet would have been interested in providing this level of focus. In the pre-media-sharing world, Oxfam might have reported the event via e-mail newsletters. But with media-sharing tools at its disposal, Oxfam was able to offer comprehensive reporting. (Figure 3.2 shows Oxfam's YouTube channel.)

Was it worth the effort? It's hard to say. The campaign's most-viewed video was watched 1,413 times. The average number of views for the top nine videos was 441. Most photos were seen about 80 times. Oxfam earned a lot of media attention because of this "Big Heads" stunt, but it's unclear if the YouTube and Flickr efforts delivered any concrete results. Certainly, the videos did not generate as much excitement as those from the Webb campaign, and the G8 leaders did not alter their behavior as a result of the campaign.

I present this example because it clearly demonstrates *how* to create a mini news channel for supporters on both Flickr and YouTube. It also points to the challenges inherent in using media-sharing sites to offer alternative news. Oxfam experimented, and we can learn from its experience. Instead of simply broadcasting news, it could have made better use of the medium by relying more on the *sharing* aspect of media-sharing sites. As some of the next examples demonstrate, when you ask for participation, enthusiastic supporters can become a wellspring of creativity.

Energizing and Focusing Supporters

Ned Lamont's 2006 campaign to become the Democratic nominee for the U.S. Senate made better use of YouTube's tools to encourage supporter involvement. The campaign asked supporters to create, upload, and share videos promoting its candidate. Supporters responded enthusiastically, creating about 350 videos that ranged from serious issue analysis to utter parody.

Figure 3.2. Oxfam's YouTube Channel
(c. December 2007)

Three of the more humorous videos poked fun at Lamont's competitor, Joe Lieberman, for embracing George Bush on the Senate floor. The videos replayed this moment dozens of times to a cheesy love-song soundtrack, reinforcing Lamont's central campaign message that his competitor was more Republican than Democratic. People watched these videos seventy-five thousand times. Other supporter-created videos were also watched tens of thousands of times.

The videos became a focal point for the campaign, giving supporters a rewarding outlet for their energies. At the same time, the campaign worked behind the scenes to ensure that this "grassroots video" story became the focus of mainstream press articles, helping Lamont stay in the news and relevant to a wider audience. The combination of populist support, authenticity, and humor appealed strongly to Connecticut Democrats. Although he was initially considered unlikely to win, Lamont beat Lieberman, the incumbent Senator and former vice presidential candidate, to win the Democratic nomination.[7]

This example shows how media-sharing sites like YouTube provide a low-cost and easy-to-use platform for harnessing supporters' creative energies. Lamont's staff offered loose guidelines ("make videos in support of our candidate") and a clear objective within a defined time frame ("win the Democratic nomination on Election Day"). Then, with no technology investment, they engaged supporters over a long election cycle while also weaving a good story for the mainstream press. Many factors contributed to Lamont's victory, but the YouTube component played a critical role in keeping his opponent on the defensive and providing a constructive avenue for super-supporter involvement.

Engaging Supporters in Conversation

Web 2.0 technologies promise closer ties between politicians and their constituencies. In particular, online video provides a practical method for politicians to pose questions, view responses, and respond in turn. In contrast with large, staged "town hall" events, it gives politicians a low-cost forum for ongoing and intimate dialogue.

Clinton's Failed Attempt

Senator Hillary Clinton was one of the first to experiment with using online video to have a conversation. Soon after she launched her presidential campaign, she released a video on her Web site titled "Let the Conversation Begin." In it, she answered written questions from supporters and pledged to post a video each week in the same format. The video was shot in a presidential-looking room with professional lighting. Clinton, impeccably coiffed, talked for thirty minutes, speaking as if she were reading a script. Her campaign released the video, *not* on a video-sharing site, but on her Web site, which provided no mechanism for viewers to post comments or to respond in any way. This broadcast approach was decidedly nonconversational, and although she did answer supporters' questions, she did so in a canned, traditional format. One young supporter critiqued her performance in a YouTube video: "You should post more videos to a place like YouTube [and] not only on your personal Web site, because it shows that you are more open, more willing to listen, and more willing to engage in real dialogue."[8]

After three weeks of so-called conversations, the Clinton campaign cut the program. Although it eventually put these videos on YouTube, the campaign did not use any of YouTube's tools to respond to questions or comments. Perhaps campaign advisers decided that a more open-ended strategy was too risky or time-consuming.

Clinton, Take Two

Learning from its misguided first foray, the Clinton campaign made a second effort to use online video. This time, it made much better use of the participatory nature of the tools. In a video posted to YouTube, Clinton asked supporters to vote for her official campaign song or to submit their own song ideas in video format. After each week of the contest, Clinton made a video in which she reviewed the submissions. She laughed at the absurd, poked fun at the angry, praised the kind, and encouraged additional submissions. By the end of the campaign, she received over two hundred thousand votes, three thousand comments, and one million views.

These videos are, by far, the most-viewed videos on Clinton's YouTube channel. The Clinton team crafted an effective media-sharing campaign that drew mainstream media attention, hundreds of thousands of viewers, and a multitude of engaged young people. Simultaneously, the campaign helped counteract the stereotype of Clinton as cold and humorless. Of course, this effort wasn't nearly as substantive as her first initiative, but it shows a smart use of YouTube to generate buzz, encourage supporter participation, and reinforce campaign messaging.

Miller's Authentic Dialogues

In a much less high-profile effort, George Miller, a Democratic congressman from California, embraced the opportunity to have a straightforward video-based conversation with constituents. In a two-minute YouTube video, he launched a campaign called "Ask George." In this handheld video, Miller sat casually in his office chair and asked supporters to engage with him in a dialogue about the Iraq war. He invited participation via numerous avenues:

- Shoot a video of your question and upload it to YouTube, SplashCast, Blip.tv, or Google video. Tag the video with the phrase "askgeorge."

- Post a question on your blog and tag it "askgeorge."

- Join the "Ask George" group on Facebook and post your question there.

- E-mail a question to george.miller@mail.house.gov with the subject "Ask George."

Miller also sent video cameras to Capitol Hill to ask questions of passersby.

He faced tough questions. Constituents thanked him for his willingness to listen, but wanted to know why they should trust him. They didn't believe that he was making good on his promises to end the Iraq war. Miller acknowledged these questions, gave summarized two-minute responses, and then offered longer in-depth answers. Constituents asked follow-up questions, which he also addressed.

Tag Clouds and Folksonomies

term

Tagging is a critical component of the video- and photo-sharing ecosystem. A tag is a word or short phrase used to identify and categorize a piece of content (see Chapter One for an introduction to tagging).

Flickr popularized what is now called the *tag cloud* (see Figure 3.3). The cloud shows popular tags all on one page; larger font sizes are used to indicate greater popularity. By looking at a tag cloud, you can very quickly visualize a person's interests or interests shared among a group of people.

The tag cloud becomes an organizing system. It enables the community to define its own categorization, which has come to be known as a *folksonomy,* or a taxonomy of the folks. A folksonomy encourages user participation while freeing the media-sharing entity from the task of categorization. It has enabled media-sharing sites to grow quickly while maintaining logical navigation systems, and it simultaneously encourages chance encounters between like-minded individuals. Two people might come across each other's work simply by using the same tags.

Figure 3.3. A Nature Lover's Top 150 Tags in Tag Cloud Format on Flickr

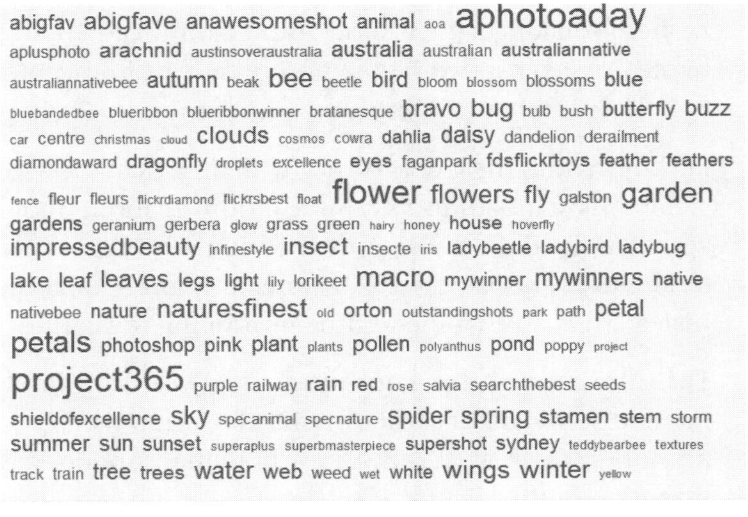

abigfav abigfave anawesomeshot animal aoa aphotoaday aplusphoto arachnid austinsoveraustralia australia australian australiannative australiannativebee autumn beak bee beetle bird bloom blossom blossoms blue bluebandedbee blueribbon blueribbonwinner bratanesque bravo bug bulb bush butterfly buzz car centre christmas cloud clouds cosmos cowra dahlia daisy dandelion derailment diamondaward dragonfly droplets excellence eyes faganpark fdsflickrtoys feather feathers fence fleur fleurs flickrdiamond flickrsbest float flower flowers fly galston garden gardens geranium gerbera glow grass green hairy honey house hoverfly impressedbeauty infinestyle insect insecte iris ladybeetle ladybird ladybug lake leaf leaves legs light lily lorikeet macro mywinner mywinners native nativebee nature naturesfinest old orton outstandingshots park path petal petals photoshop pink plant plants pollen polyanthus pond poppy project project365 purple railway rain red rose salvia searchthebest seeds shieldofexcellence sky specanimal specnature spider spring stamen stem storm summer sun sunset superaplus superbmasterpiece supershot sydney teddybearbee textures track train tree trees water web weed wet white wings winter yellow

Miller's effort won widespread kudos on blogs and YouTube and has so far attracted about sixty-six questions and ten thousand viewers. Although these viewer numbers certainly don't compare with Clinton's high-profile effort or a television broadcast audience, Miller has created an environment for *substantive* political dialogue. He provides a model for using the Internet to overcome some of the structural barriers that divide politicians and the common person.

Engaging Supporters with Contests

The Nature Conservancy launched an annual photo contest in 2006 in which it invited entrants to submit "stunning nature images . . . representing the diversity of life on Earth." It created two categories: Best Nature Photo and Best Photo from a Place We Protect. To collect submissions and facilitate interactions among supporters, the organization formed a Flickr group. About three thousand people submitted photos to the group in 2006. The numbers surged to over thirty thousand in 2007.

Many of the photos have generated active discussion and have been viewed many times. Anecdotally, I clicked a serene photo of a tree in a springtime meadow. Viewers had posted 141 comments, and it had been viewed 14,747 times.[9] Most of the comments praised the photographer for taking a great shot. Some reminisced about a memory or wrote poems inspired by the photo. At least fourteen comments invited the photographer to submit the photo to other Flickr groups.

Flickr provides the Conservancy with an instant, low-cost technical system. Its standard tools handle group creation, photo uploading and aggregation, and view count tabulation. The Conservancy doesn't need to identify vendors, create software, or manage ongoing operations. Instead, it is able to spend time promoting the contest on its Web site.

The Conservancy also gains incidental Flickr Web traffic. People interested in scenic nature will discover the group while browsing related photos. In this way, it draws new potential supporters simply by participating in the Flickr community.

Finally, the contest aligns closely with the Conservancy's mission. People who submit and view photos are those most likely to support the protection of natural lands. And by submitting to the Best Photo from a Place We Protect category, people must necessarily research the Conservancy's worldwide initiatives.

Many nonprofits have recognized these benefits and started similar photo contests. If your campaign addresses an issue with any sort of visual element, Flickr offers a low-risk method for implementing a user-generated contest. Some other examples:

- March of Dimes' "So You Wanna Be a Coin Star?" photo contest: best photo of the place where you keep your spare change

- Creative Commons' "Swag Photo" contest: best photo of a product that uses the Creative Commons license

- Jumpstart Ford's "Freedom from Oil" contest: best photo that delivers the "Freedom from Oil" message to the American auto industry

Making Petitions More Vibrant

Petitions are a tried-and-true method for involving supporters in an advocacy campaign. Typically, petitions entail adding your signature to a long list. The cause may be energizing, but the process is usually dull. Media-sharing sites enliven the act of asking for signatures and signing a petition.

For example, Oxfam conducted a campaign to convince Starbucks to sign a licensing agreement that would result in higher prices being paid to Ethiopian coffee farmers. The story of this campaign begins with a protest. Via e-mail, Oxfam invited supporters and members of the Ethiopian community to protest at several Starbucks locations throughout the world. It filmed these protests and put the footage on YouTube.

Organizers then contacted Ethiopian bloggers and asked them to put the video on their blogs. Oxfam sent another e-mail to its supporters asking them to watch the videos. The videos were viewed about fifteen thousand to twenty thousand times. Starbucks posted a response video on YouTube, which generated buzz in the blogosphere. Within a week, views of the Oxfam video doubled to fifty thousand. Oxfam fueled the fire by filming and uploading interviews with Ethiopian farmers telling their side of the story.

To supplement the video activity, Oxfam started a Flickr petition asking supporters to take a photo of themselves with a sign that said "I support Ethiopian coffee farmers," which generated submission of 577 photos. Although it didn't attract a comparatively large number of people, the Flickr petition took only minutes to set up, and it identified over five hundred super-supporters. Oxfam knew that these people would be great candidates for taking further action.

With a critical mass of people paying attention to the issue and participating through multiple channels, Oxfam asked supporters to send Starbucks e-mails, faxes, and postcards, and to make phone calls and store visits. Oxfam estimates that ninety-six thousand supporters took action. Within a few weeks, Starbucks and Ethiopian farmers signed an agreement to end their dispute. Oxfam considers the campaign a great success.[10] Both YouTube and Flickr played an influential role, bringing the petition to life and helping identify strong supporters.

Building a Community

Social entrepreneur Gregory J. Smith started the Children at Risk Foundation (CARF) to send Brazilian street children into foster care. Since 1993, the organization has worked on the outskirts of São Paulo, offering education, emotional support, and resources tailored to individual children. In 2006, Smith began a Flickr group.

An accomplished photographer, Smith frequently posts photos about Brazilian street life. He invites others to submit photos that convey positive images of the environment and youth issues. To date 1,045 people have joined this group. Most photos depict children facing and overcoming difficult living situations.

It's clear from reading posted comments that this community does not consist of young people. As a group, they're concerned about youth issues, but the photographers are older folks with the means to travel and who own camera equipment. However, the example shows how a photo-sharing group can serve as a foundation on which community grows. The community is small, just over a thousand members, but they are committed and joined together by a passionate common interest. Submitting photos to the group gives them a reason to connect with each other on a frequent basis.

Hosting Media Content

Media-sharing sites sit at the crossroads of Web hosting and social networking. Thus far, I've limited discussion to social networking uses, which are less obvious to those unfamiliar with the space. However, it's important to note the much simpler but equally important role that media-sharing sites play as inexpensive Web hosts.

A Web host leases space on a server to hold an organization's content (Web site, videos, images) and "serves" it to Web visitors. Typically, hosts charge according to the bandwidth that Web traffic consumes. Videos and high-resolution photos require a lot of bandwidth. In addition, once uploaded, these digital assets are often exceedingly difficult to organize. Many nonprofits struggle with hundreds of assets in one unmanageable directory.

Historically, these issues dissuaded most organizations from making extensive use of videos and, to a lesser extent, photos.[11] Media-sharing sites solved both the cost and organizational issues. They lowered the cost to near-zero and offered tools such as tagging to help people sift through large media collections.

Organizations have turned to such media-sharing sites as Photobucket, Flickr, and YouTube to serve as a simple repository for their digital media assets. They then use these assets on their Web sites and social networking profiles. Many MySpace profiles, for example, feature videos from YouTube. Photobucket is the top choice for MySpace users to store their photos. Such campaigns as the Humane Society's Sunny the Seal, discussed in Chapter Two, make extensive use of media-sharing sites to support the effort. They use few of YouTube's social tools, relying on YouTube instead as a free and easy-to-use Web host.

Photo and Video Widgets

Media-sharing sites (as well as a host of specialized companies) offer widgets that display a selection of content. For example, you can create a Flickr widget that shows a slide show of photos matching a particular tag. If I wanted to show a series of randomly selected photos from the winners of the Nature Conservancy contest, I would make a widget that pulled photos with the tag "BestNature-TNC07." I could then place this widget on my social networking profile to show my affinity for this organization (not to mention a series of stunning photos).

How Media-Sharing Sites Work

Like other social networks, media-sharing sites have their own unique mix of features. I described many of the common characteristics in earlier sections of this chapter, but the best way to familiarize yourself with these sites is to open an account and start viewing and publishing media. Let's look at a few screenshots to give you a better idea of how these common features are implemented on leading sites. Figure 3.4 shows the YouTube upload form.

Publishing a video on YouTube requires only that you complete the form; several of the options it offers (as shown in Figure 3.4) are worth exploring:

- *Tags.* They're one of the most powerful methods for organizing data across and within Web sites, as mentioned frequently throughout this chapter.

- *Date and map options.* If you expand this box, you're able to enter the location, date, and time at which you filmed your video. Adding this information is called geotagging: attributing latitude and longitude coordinates to a media file. Geotagging allows the aggregation of media by *place.* You can travel a map of the world seeing photos from

Figure 3.4. YouTube Upload Form

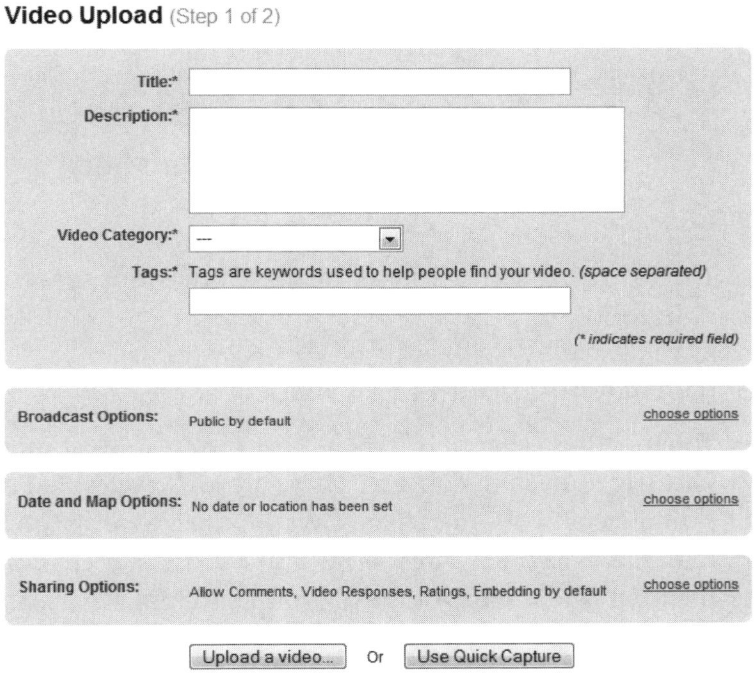

Video Upload (Step 1 of 2)

Title:*

Description:*

Video Category:* ---

Tags:* Tags are keywords used to help people find your video. *(space separated)*

(* indicates required field)

Broadcast Options: Public by default   choose options

Date and Map Options: No date or location has been set   choose options

Sharing Options: Allow Comments, Video Responses, Ratings, Embedding by default   choose options

Upload a video...   Or   Use Quick Capture

anyone who has provided this information. See the mapping chapter for more information.

Sharing options. If you expand this box, you're able to turn various sharing options on or off, such as comments, video responses, ratings, and "embedding." In this context, embedding refers to giving someone permission to put your video on his or her Web page, blog, or social networking profile.

How to Get Started

As I mentioned earlier, the best way to get started is to sign up for an account and to begin exploring. I've discussed Flickr and YouTube because a wide majority of political and nonprofit campaigns make use of them. However, there are a handful of others, and one of these might have a particular feature that fits your needs.

For a list of popular video- and photo-sharing sites, go to
mobilizingyouth.org/vid_photo_sites

The following sections describe some quick tips for setting off on the right foot.

Create Your Own Channel or Group

YouTube has "channels"; Flickr has "groups." Most media-sharing sites have an equivalent concept. These are Web pages that enable you to centralize all your media, give you options to write introductory text material, and often offer social tools, such as discussion groups or commenting fields. Start your own group and join others. You'll quickly get a sense of how they work.

Use Tags

I can't overemphasize the importance of tagging to so many Web 2.0 technologies, and particularly to photo and video. Tagging systems are integral to organizing your media assets effectively so that you can find them later and so that others can discover them. Tags allow you to organize assets into groups and bind you to the group of *people* who use the same tags. By using one tag across media-sharing sites and blogs, you can effectively create (and give your supporters a way to create) a collection of media across the Internet. Before beginning a campaign, familiarize yourself with tag "vocabulary" by looking at tag clouds, and think about the tags that you will use and the ways in which you will encourage their usage among supporters.

For example, to ensure that your campaign's media can be found easily, choose a rarely used tag. The Nature Conservancy asked contest entrants to tag their photos intended for the Best Nature Photo contest category with "BestNature-TNC07." The Conservancy could be fairly confident that this tag would be unused on the Web. A poor choice would have been "Nature Photos," because millions of unrelated photos are likely to be tagged with this phrase.

Evaluate Equipment Needs

Most campaigns will be fine using point-and-shoot cameras. But if your audience is expecting very high quality resolution or if you'll need to print posters or reproductions later, do a few tests with your equipment to ensure that the results are satisfactory.

Edit Your Photos and Videos

If you want to edit your photos or videos prior to sharing them, there are now a multitude of online services available. For example, at JumpCut.com, upload your video and an audio file, and you can merge the two in a few minutes. JumpCut also has an array of sharing tools similar to YouTube. For advanced editing needs, you can also purchase desktop software, such as Apple's Final Cut Pro. For a great online photo editing service, head to Picnik.com.

For a list of photo and video editing resources, head to

mobilizingyouth.org/vid_photo_edit

Choose a Quality Level

If you're familiar with producing professional videos or photos, be aware that producing for the Web is different. Frame rates, aspect ratios, and dots per inch are not consistent with other media. Before you shoot new material, browse media-sharing sites to get a feeling for the dimensions and quality of other work. High-quality production values are difficult to achieve. If you're *not* seeking professional results, you don't have anything to worry about. Media-sharing sites were designed for the consumer with an inexpensive video or still camera. Use the default settings and you'll be fine.

If you need to display high-quality video, a media-sharing site may not be the right place for your organization. Video quality is often subpar. Consider, instead, an account with a host that specializes in video. You will pay a lot more, but if you need quality, it's the best option.

Research Legalities

Using a media-sharing site to host your videos and photos makes a lot of sense. These sites offer inexpensive pricing options and smart organizing tools, and they're improving these tools all the time. But be sure to explore the terms of use on your media-sharing site of choice. By uploading your assets to these sites, you are giving away some rights. For example, YouTube retains the right to distribute and modify any material for any purpose.

Strategic Considerations

Before developing a campaign that relies on media-sharing sites, you may want to consider the following questions and issues.

Have Conversations

Explore the ways in which your organization can use video and photos to generate lively discussion. You can build an ecosystem of communication: ask for participation, respond, and repeat. Encourage supporters to interact with one another—video and photos can make these interactions more vivid.

Media-sharing sites have dramatically reduced barriers to communication—distance, cost, and time. Talking *at* your constituency using the broadcast model is no longer the only option.

Consider Production Values

In certain instances, production values don't matter. Don't worry about editing the most perfect video. Think about media sharing as a video conference call. You might comb your hair in advance, but when you're on the call, you're engaged with people, listening and talking. In order to be present, you can't take the time to worry about imperfections. Video conversations are not formal productions.

Some media campaigns are not in fact conversations. Some media are intended to get a conversation started through a careful presentation. For example, CARF's photo group is dedicated to high-quality photos of at-risk youth. A poor-quality submission would be inappropriate in this context. Determine the strategic worth of production values to your campaign. Some highly persuasive videos require deep thinking, planning, and a focus on production values.

Practice Brevity

Internet video is not television, and young people are loath to sit through a thirty-minute video. Look to Congressman George Miller's example. He prepared two-minute responses to questions asked by supporters *in addition to* in-depth answers for those interested in a more complete discussion. He acknowledged both the attention span of Internet users and the fact that complex issues cannot be fully addressed within the confines of this span.

Be Funny

News content is the most popular category across age ranges, except for those viewers ages eighteen to twenty-nine. Young people like comedy: more than half of young people say that they use the Internet to watch funny videos.[12] Hillary Clinton's experiences with online video testify to this reality of young tastes. Obviously, comedy is not appropriate for all topics. However, when you can maintain the mission of your organization and incorporate humor, make an effort to do so.

Find Your Niche and Use the Right Tools

Network television produces high-quality entertainment that appeals to a broad range of people. Your organization will have difficulty competing with television on the same terms. Ask yourself what you can provide that is not available in mainstream media or elsewhere.

And when you find your niche, take advantage of a media-sharing site's tools to make your message more compelling. Oxfam created a mini-channel that delivered Oxfam-specific G8 Summit news that supporters couldn't find anywhere else. However, it didn't use the participatory tools that might have strengthened supporter engagement and delivered better results.

Encourage Subscriptions

Most media-sharing sites offer some sort of membership function. By joining a photo or video group, a supporter will receive regular updates about your campaign. If you succeed in persuading people to join your group, you can engage them over the long term. Ensure that you learn about and take advantage of your media-sharing site's subscription options.

Integrate with a Broader Campaign

Media-sharing sites enable you to run an entire campaign using only their sites. However, the tools are limited. Remember that one of the most important elements to any campaign is the story. Ask yourself if you can effectively convey your story on the media-sharing site alone. If the answer is no, develop a strategy for incorporating the media-sharing site into your broader campaign. Many organizations craft a campaign that operates across Web 2.0 technologies, such as social networks, media-sharing sites, and blogs.

Use a Flexible Content License

The ability to copy and remix media is one of the major factors in the growth of Web 2.0 technologies. Supporters take their favorite videos and photos and "mash them up" into new creations. The process of being able to remix endears people to your organization, because you supply them with the raw materials they need to express themselves creatively. Enable your supporters to mashup your content legally by using one of the Creative Commons' licenses that retain some rights while giving away important remixing rights.

Mashup

term

A mashup is a compounding of two or more media or data sources. For example, Ned Lamont supporters mashed up a video of George Bush embracing Joe Lieberman with love song music. In an example of a data mashup, an enterprising software developer mashed up Google Maps with housing listings from craigslist. The result was a new creation that showed the housing listings placed appropriately on a Google Map (housingmaps.com). For a comprehensive listing of data mashups, point your browser at www.programmableweb.com/mashups.

For more information about licensing, see

mobilizingyouth.org/creative_commons

Challenges and Opportunities

We're in the midst of a dramatic shift in the creation and consumption of media. Growing up in the 1980s and 1990s, young people could reasonably expect that a majority of their visual knowledge would come from three sources: their own eyes, television, and mainstream printed media. Within the past ten years, the sources that provide our images of life on earth have multiplied a thousandfold. We're seeing new visual perspectives that aren't tied to our own experiences or to an organization that intends to earn revenue from its imagery.

As more people participate in the creation of media, our relationship with media shifts. That the television is no longer our primary visual media device is only part of the story.[13] Our perception of images as professionally produced products is giving way to thinking of images in terms of conversation. Online media-sharing sites are becoming the outlet for this form of dialogue.

In the future, mobile phones will play an increasing role in pushing this transformation. Well over half the world's population has the ability to photographically document any scene at any time. Although the cameras are usually low quality and incidental to a consumer's mobile phone purchasing decision, the simple fact of their ubiquity has profound implications. Without making an explicit decision to become a photographer or videographer, millions of people own and carry photographic devices. With barriers so low, millions of new people will join the ranks of those already participating in visually documenting our world.

Media-sharing sites are aggregating this visual documentation. They are becoming the Wikipedias of imagery. Envision a place—any place. It's likely that numerous people have documented it with photos and videos from various angles, at different times of day, and over a span of many years. Collectively, we have developed a historical visual record of nearly every place on earth. This record is currently distributed on dozens of types of media and among millions of people. It exists on photographs in shoeboxes and VHS cassette tapes in an attic. However, as more people use media-sharing sites—and as they tag and geotag their visual imagery—the record will start to come together in a centralized fashion.

Microsoft is developing a fascinating software product called Photosynth to bring meaning to such massive collections of visual information. Given a large number of *ordinary photos* of a specific place, the software can assemble a coherent and navigable three-dimensional space. It has the potential to turn the database of Flickr photos into a photographic model of earth. Unlike a mapping application, such as Google Earth, which uses mechanically produced satellite imagery to generate its models, this model is constructed from the handmade photographs of its thousands of contributors. It becomes a reflection of collective memory.

o o o

It's no wonder that nonprofits and politicians haven't figured out exactly how to use photo- and video-sharing sites. We're only just beginning to understand the complex social, economic, and technical movements that these sites are catalyzing. However, if the history of the shift from radio to television teaches us anything, it's that we'll need to adapt in a short time. In September 1960, Richard Nixon learned this lesson in debates with his television-savvy opponent, John F. Kennedy. Kennedy performed better on television and won the nation's top elected position. The world learned a broader lesson: that a technology like television could reshape politics, debate, and democracy.[14]

We're at a similar point in history, only this time, the power to influence the national dialogue is shifting to the average person. As agents for social change, nonprofits and politicians are in an exciting position to encourage and shape this evolution.

Endnotes

1. www.washingtonpost.com/wp-dyn/content/article/2006/08/14/AR2006081400589.html

2. www.rediff.com/news/2006/nov/10uspoll.htm

3. www.wusa9.com/news/news_article.aspx?storyid=51530

4. Incidentally, one of the other key races was the Tester-Burns contest in Montana, in which camera-toting Tester supporters filmed Burns disparaging firemen. They uploaded the video to YouTube, and it may have also influenced this election.

5. According to the Pew Internet and American Life Project, 57 percent of Internet users have watched online video, and most of them share their video discoveries with friends. Among eighteen- to twenty-nine-year-olds, the figure goes up to 76 percent. Forty-seven percent of teens say that they upload photos to the Web, and 28 percent report tagging media. www.pewinternet.org/pdfs/PIP_Teens_Privacy_SNS_Report_Final.pdf

6. www.techsoup.org/learningcenter/internet/page5287.cfm

7. Lieberman then registered as an Independent and ran against Lamont in the general election. Lieberman's popularity among Republicans tipped the scales in his favor, lending a final twist to this political

drama. Thanks to the following article for much of the information used to write this example: www.slate.com/id/2147255.

8. www.youtube.com/watch?v=IBK_J-ueyVU&watch_response

9. www.flickr.com/photos/matilde/122113258/in/pool-thenature conservancy

10. www.oxfamamerica.org/whatwedo/campaigns/coffee/starbucks

   www.netsquared.org/blog/britt-bravo/notes-ntc-age-you tube-using-video-online-reach-masses

   www.netsquared.org/blog/britt-bravo/oxfam-uses-flickr-to -advocate-for-ethiopian-coffee-farmers

11. Due to their simpler file format, photos have always been easier to manage than videos.

12. www.pewinternet.org/pdfs/PIP_Online_Video_2007.pdf

13. For information on Internet usage encroaching on television watching, see www-03.ibm.com/press/us/en/pressrelease/22206.wss.

14. For a good discussion on the topic of television in the Nixon-Kennedy presidential debates, see www.museum.tv/archives/etv/K/htmlK/kennedy-nixon/kennedy-nixon.htm.

THE BIG PICTURE

Political Life on YouTube

Interview with Steve Grove

Steve Grove is the head of news and politics at YouTube. He directs programming including You Choose '08 (YouTube's political coverage for the 2008 election), Citizentube (YouTube's political video blog), and citizen journalism on the site. In his frequent video reports, he exudes a smart, hip style that reflects attributes that are driving the use of online video as a conversational medium. I interviewed Steve in summer 2007. An edited portion of the transcript is presented here.

What differentiates video from other tools is that it's a tangible and compelling medium. Video has the power not just to tell stories but also to *show* stories and allow candidates and voters to demonstrate their positions, interests, and perspectives on an issue.

In the nonprofit world, groups like Stop Genocide Now on YouTube have broadcast video straight from Darfur. Instead of just hearing about why Darfur is a problem, you can see pictures of children without parents in a refugee camp, and feel the effects of the conflict that's taking place there. The group also asked a question of the presidential candidates in our YouTube political debate with CNN, showing orphaned refugee children alongside the question asker to demonstrate the impact of what's happening in Darfur.

We have hundreds of thousands of videos uploaded to the site each day, and hundreds of millions of videos seen on the site per day. There's never before been such a collection of eyeballs on video or still content.

But the challenge is to find ways to get your voice to rise above the cacophony of other voices. Another challenge is in remembering that the medium isn't just a shrunken TV screen for distribution of your content. The medium is more like a window into the world of Web interaction.

If you're not viewing your video or your content as a communication tool that cuts two ways, then you're going to have a harder time achieving takeoff on your content. Online videos are a two-way conversation. If you don't have a way for other people to contribute to what you're doing, to comment on it, to share it, or to post their own videos in reply to it, you're not fully taking advantage of the community.

The democratizing part about this is that it doesn't matter who you are. It's a real meritocracy out there. Compelling content is what sells. You can be a kid in your bedroom, a mother in your kitchen, an executive in your office, a television executive in your studio, a sports star on the pitch, a movie star on the screen—if you have a piece of compelling content, that's what people are going to watch.

YouTube Politics

We are first and foremost a platform for political discussion. Because of the power of video and the way that people have begun to use the platform for politics, we've become the world's largest town hall for political discussion. When we think about politics on YouTube, we keep three words in mind: access, education, and empowerment.

We're giving voters and candidates access to each other. Add to that issue groups, voter registration organizations, and anyone with a stake in the election and a political opinion to share. They have access to each other that they wouldn't have had before, and there's no filter. There's no media man in the middle to say yea or nay on content. It's purely a decision of the masses, and what they want to do.

Once that access is put in place and connections are made, people have opportunities to be educated—to learn about the issues and where the candidates stand and to reach out to other people who might not otherwise have become educated. Campaigns and issue groups also have a chance to inform voters about how they think our country should be run.

And finally we think about empowerment. We are empowering people who might not have been a part of the political dialogue in the past to speak up and be heard on the same level as politicians.

We create initiatives and programs that address these three things, but at the end of the day it's really our users who define our programming, and our users who use these tools to ultimately improve the political process.

THE BIG PICTURE

Telling Stories That Make an Emotional Connection

Essay by Jonah Sachs

Jonah Sachs is principal and creative director of Free Range Studios in Washington DC. This article originally appeared in *The NonProfit Times* and is reproduced with permission. I find his thoughts on storytelling particularly compelling for any organization working with youth and technology: he asks us to take a step back from the technology and to think about the people behind the computer screens.

As nonprofits become increasingly sophisticated about communication tools and audience outreach, the frequency of contact between organizations and their constituents also increases. You've got your e-mail newsletter neatly scheduled, your Web site shined, perhaps even a Web 2.0 tool ready to go. The conversation has clearly started.

But for many, the conversation people have been so eager to initiate feels a little flat. There's often a sense of discontinuity between one communiqué and the next. The conversation tends to circulate within a distinct and often small "choir," or set of die-hards. And the emotional drive that brought you to work for something other than the promise of riches, and brought your members into the fold, has taken a back seat to something that feels, well, more mechanical.

How do you get out of this high-volume, low-value communications rut? You don't need the latest Web 3.0 blog package. You need the oldest communication method known to human beings. You need stories.

Why People Need Storytelling

People tend to support nonprofits and the causes they champion because of an emotional connection. When you're not trading in cold hard cash, you're trading in hope, compassion, and, yeah, maybe sometimes guilt or fear. Emotion drives people to try to tackle the world's problems. But emotions are a human-scale response, and the world's problems are anything but human scale. How do you bridge this gap? How do you keep the emotional inspiration alive when your issue drowns you in a sea of statistics, policy proposals, and case studies?

Stories were invented specifically to bridge this gap, to translate the complex, gray-area experience of the faceless many into the simple, graspable experience of the single individual (or small group).

Here's what happens when you create an effective story around your organization or issue:

- The inherent justice of your efforts becomes apparent in a way that appeals to people's sense of right and wrong. Emotional connection increases.

- Serial communications become welcomed as the story continues to unfold. A key quality of stories is that they engage the listener (or viewer) to seek its end or next episode.

- The story begins to self-replicate as it's passed from one listener (or viewer) to the next. Self-replication is a basic attribute of stories, and the Internet has supercharged that function. The message expands beyond the choir.

How to Begin

So how do you create a story around your organization or issue? The good news is that there are established, can't-miss formulas out there. In fact, the fantastic work of Karl Jung and Joseph Campbell suggests that the ability to understand and absorb certain specific story elements is shared by every human being on the planet, as has been throughout history. Just watch a movie like *Star Wars* (written under the tutelage of Campbell) to see how even the most out-there subjects like fantasy sci-fi can reach mythical proportions if they use the right storytelling forms.

To begin the process of telling effective stories, imagine a simplified world that your issue or organization inhabits. In this world, identify the following:

- **The Heroes:** Who are they? What are they trying to achieve? What person, historical figure, even animal or mythical creature might represent these heroes? Think beyond your organization's employees when searching. The hero need not be you! Oftentimes it is our constituents or those we are trying to help who emerge as the most compelling heroes in our stories.

- **The Villains:** Every story needs a bad guy. People just won't accept a struggle without a villain, and with no struggle there is no story. Who stands in our hero's way? Are they identifiable individuals or a set of problems that can be personified in a character or person? Villains should feel evil in your story, but that doesn't mean you have to vilify your opposition. We don't have to personally attack other people to show the problem as evil (although at times, such attacks have undeniably worked).

- **The Catalyst:** Stories begin with a struggle between hero and villain that does not begin to resolve until a catalyst appears. Something or someone shifts the balance, and the hero begins to prevail. Who, or what, is the catalyst in your story? What people or actions will come along to break the deadlock and allow the desired outcome? How can the listener (or viewer) of the story be the catalyst or cause the catalyst to come about?

Using these basic elements, begin to craft a myth in your simplified world. Try telling it to a six-year-old as a fairy tale. Try it out in a Greek myth style. See which ways of telling the tale create an emotional response in you, and then test it on others. An effective story should immediately make you proud, again, of the work you are doing.

Elements of the new myth can be used effectively to inform your language in newsletters or in features on your Web site. Although you may never overtly tell your story as a myth, comparing the way you speak to the myth you have created and trying to draw from its emotional resonance will vastly increase your audience's participation and sense of inspiration.

CHAPTER 4

Mobile Phones

When Philippine activists wanted to topple the corrupt regime of then-president Joseph Estrada, they reached into their pockets and pulled out their mobile phones. They sent brief mobile-phone text messages to invite friends to Manila's People Power shrine, saying, "Wear red. Bring banners. Come now."[1]

Protesters amassed at the shrine throughout the day. Inspired by the enthusiasm of the crowd, new arrivals used text messaging to invite yet more friends. When more than seven hundred thousand people stood chanting at the shrine, Estrada resigned, turning power over to the crowd's choice for president, Gloria Arroyo. Estrada sullenly refers to his ouster as a "coup de text."[2]

Several years later, Gloria Arroyo was caught up in an election-rigging scandal. A former deputy wiretapped Arroyo allegedly making a pact with the election commissioner to overcount the vote in her favor. Arroyo denied that the voice on the recording was hers and made it illegal to broadcast or distribute the tape.

The scandal was mostly contained until the recording was leaked. TxtPower, a Philippine consumer advocacy group, turned the recording into a ringtone, the short sound clip that plays when you receive a call on your mobile phone. Millions of young people installed and played the ringtone.[3] Protests erupted within days, spurred in part by the widespread distribution of the recording enabled by mobile phones. Arroyo soon admitted that the voice on the tape was hers. She managed to quash subsequent impeachment attempts and remains in office, although she is a weakened and, some say, illegitimate president.

You can listen to the Arroyo ringtone on this book's Web site:

mobilizingyouth.org/resources/ringtones

The use of mobile phones in political movements took both politicians and activists by surprise. Many knew that phones had become a staple of youth life, but few imagined that they could be used to organize, mobilize, and lead to the overturn of governments. Following the Estrada protests, however, dozens of similar events unfolded around the world.

In the wake of these events, nonprofits and politicians started to explore ways to harness mobile phones to organize young people. Unlike a personal computer, they are so fundamental to youth lifestyle that few leave the house without one.[4] And they offer *immediacy*: at a coffee shop, concert, rally, or bus stop, a young person is instantly accessible.

So far, the most successful mobile-phone campaigns have relied on text messaging. A text message is a series of up to 160 characters, typed on the keypad of the sender's mobile phone, that travels through wireless networks and arrives on the screen of the recipient's mobile phone. The term *SMS* stands for "short messaging system" and is used interchangeably with "text messaging." You might also hear people refer to it as "texting" or just "text." The growth of text messaging has been explosive. In the United States, over 63 percent of mobile phone users send texts,[5] as compared to 90 percent in Germany, 83 percent in Spain, 85 percent in Britain, [6] and 65 percent on average across Australia, Hong Kong, Malaysia, China, Singapore, South Korea, and Taiwan.[7]

In many countries throughout the world, a significant majority of the population owns a mobile phone. An analyst from the market research firm Ipsos thinks that mobile phones could soon overtake personal computers as the primary means of accessing the Internet (via the phones' built-in Web browsers). [8] In sum, mobile phones are having a transformational effect on how people connect to one another and the Internet. They are ubiquitous devices capable of sending and receiving messages, taking photos, and browsing the Web. As such, mobile phones offer numerous opportunities to reach and organize supporters.

How Organizations Are Using Mobile Phones

Nonprofits and political campaigns use mobile phones in a variety of ways, but text messaging has shown consistent promise. It is being used to recruit supporters at events, deliver timely on-site information, and coordinate on-the-ground teams. Some recent experiments combining text messaging and interactive voice menus have delivered particularly positive results. After the Arroyo incident, ringtones have drawn prominent news headlines, but they are more difficult to use as a means of driving social change.

Recruiting at Events

The crowd simmers with excitement as the rock band U2 launches into its second set. Bono, the band's charismatic front man, tells the crowd to raise their mobile phones in the air. Thousands of little lights flicker in the night sky. An impassioned Bono describes the horrors of AIDS and poverty in Africa and says,

"Time to do a magic trick. These little devices—these cell phones— they can do all sorts of things."

The immense screen above the stage displays the phrase "UNITE. 86483." Bono asks the crowd to type their names, addresses, and the keyword "UNITE" into their cell phones and send it to the number on screen. As they text in, their names scroll across the giant display. By the end of the evening more than ten thousand people had joined Bono's cause. Over 250,000 had signed up by the end of his tour.[9]

It doesn't hurt to have an international superstar stump for your cause, but even if all you've got is a crowd of people, texting offers an inexpensive and effective method for gathering contact information. To use this method, you have to persuade people to send a text to what is known as a *shortcode*. A shortcode is a five- or six-digit number that works a lot like a Web address. Texts sent to it are routed to a computer that records the sender's phone number and whatever other information you've requested from him or her.

This initial "text-in" serves as your first point of contact. It's the beginning of a dialogue with a potential new supporter. Subsequently, you can send additional texts to request more information or direct the person to another medium, such as a standard voice-based phone call. We'll see examples of this type of redirection later in this chapter. One of the primary advantages of gathering contact information in this way is that it's instantly centralized and digitized. You don't have to transcribe names and numbers from a sign-up sheet; they're automatically stored in a spreadsheet-friendly format.

Bono promoted his shortcode with an announcement from stage and then reinforced the message on-screen. The common rules of advertising apply to shortcode marketing: for best results, show your message as often as possible and in as many different media as possible. Talk about it at events, print it on ads and fliers, and show it on computer screens.

Jed Alpert, the CEO of Mobile Commons, one of the leading text-messaging vendors, reports that live events frequently generate initial response rates in the 50 percent range; of these respondents, 20 to 40 percent typically provide additional information, such as an e-mail address. At events with substantial crowds, text messaging has the potential to serve as a highly efficient recruiting mechanism.

Petitioning

The International Fund for Animal Welfare ran an effective newspaper and texting campaign in support of its "Stop the Seal Hunt" initiative in the United Kingdom. The newspaper ad is pictured in Figure 4.1.

Text-Messaging "Keyword"

Most text-messaging campaigns make use of keywords, which are preselected words that identify a text message as belonging to a specific campaign. Thus it's possible to run several campaigns on a single shortcode.

For example, you could run one campaign using the following call to action, "Text 'VOTE' to 75444 for voter information," and another with "Text 'FISHINFO' to 75444 along with the name of a fish to discover its mercury levels."

These are two distinct campaigns using distinct keywords on the same shortcode. The software that receives the text message knows which text message response to send on the basis of the keyword. It sends voter info to the person who used the word VOTE and looks up and sends back mercury levels for the fish specified in the message using the FISHINFO keyword.

You can also use keywords to test various media *within* a campaign. You might promote the keyword "JOIN" on billboards and "SIGNUP" on flyers. You'll quickly be able to determine if billboards are more effective than flyers or vice versa. Combine this information with the date and time data that are automatically attached to each text message, and you'll have a trove of interesting numbers to crunch.

Note that if you have a shortcode all to yourself and don't want to do keyword-based tracking, there's no reason to use a keyword.

Figure 4.1. Newspaper Ad Incorporating Text Messaging

The ad pictures a cute furry seal next to a compelling call to action. According to organizers, the newspaper ad achieved a 0.5 percent response rate, which resulted in more than fifty thousand people texting in. When asked to reply with their names, 92 percent responded; when asked for their e-mail addresses, 68 percent responded. The names and e-mail addresses were then forwarded to the British Parliament.[10] These rates were much higher than similar advertisements for a different campaign in which organizers listed a Web site address alone.[11]

From a technical standpoint, the campaign is similar to the one led by Bono. It asks people to text in for a cause. The primary difference is that the strategy uses the familiar language and structure of a petition to recruit supporters. Because texting is still relatively new and exciting to use, it can help increase response rates. When people don't understand what will happen after texting in, however, they're less likely to participate. A charismatic superstar (like Bono) helps people overcome this obstacle, as does the familiar mechanism of a petition.

Delivering Timely, Relevant, and Personal Information

Young people live mobile lives. They're on the move between home, school, work, cafés, and friends' homes, among other places. Text campaigns work well when they deliver timely and personal information of value to someone who is on the go.

For example, Asthma U.K. recently launched a text-alerts campaign to warn asthma sufferers about high pollen days so that they can take extra precautions. The organization's Web site advertises the service and provides the forms necessary to sign up.

This campaign delivers time-sensitive and useful information to people who may not have had access to the information otherwise. It makes extremely good use of texting as a medium by addressing the needs of a mobile constituency. One problem with the campaign, however, is that asthma sufferers are required to sign up for the service on a Web site. The campaign takes advantage of texting to *push out* relevant information, but doesn't use the same model to *pull in* potential asthma sufferers. Asthma U.K. might increase its number of participants if it advertised its service outdoors, where people tend to experience asthma the most.

One of texting's primary benefits is that it can be inserted into a targeted, relevant place. The San Francisco Department of Public Health took advantage of this opportunity to deliver sexual health information through its "SexInfo" campaign (see Figure 4.2), which offered facts and resources about sexually transmitted diseases, condoms, and pregnancy.

Figure 4.2. SexInfo Ad

The campaign focused on privacy. The Department of Public Health understood that young people have few avenues for privately learning about sex. Mobile phones happen to be perfect devices for having private conversations. The campaign advertised the service at bus stops and on billboards around the city and enabled young people to request, read, and delete information on their terms. The program made optimal use of text messaging because it selected an appropriate place to promote the service and to deliver information.[12]

Conducting Advocacy . . . on Demand

As this book was going to press, the Blue Ocean Institute just launched a text-messaging campaign called "Fish Phone," which has subtle but important distinctions from the examples I've already described. The institute maintains a database of "ocean-friendly seafood," meaning that the fish is relatively abundant and harvested using environmentally responsible techniques. The group has now made its database accessible via text message.

Text the keyword FISH followed by the name of a fish to 30644, and you'll receive details about that species on your cell phone. For example, if you text "orange roughy," you'll learn that the fish is typically caught using habitat-damaging trawl gear and that fishing also catches threatened deep-sea sharks. Skipping orange roughy on the market shelf, you might then text "striped bass," which has a high rating on the ocean-friendly scorecard.

Like the asthma and SexInfo campaigns, this program delivers timely and relevant information. The key difference is that it's intended to be used as an ongoing, on-demand service. Whenever you're in the fish market, the institute wants you to remember to text in. Unfortunately, marketing this type of service is difficult. The best place to promote the service (at the market) is also the least likely to accept advertising. This program doesn't have the location advantages of the SexInfo campaign, or the ability to know when its information is relevant, as does the asthma campaign. It's a valuable service that will be challenging to promote effectively because it's reliant on the (unfortunately) imperfect human memory. However, at press time, the campaign is seeing an impressive average of seven hundred requests per day, five hundred of which are unique. Despite the difficulty in marketing this service, it appears to be filling a pressing need among concerned fish consumers.

Coordinating Protesters

Greenpeace Argentina recently won a campaign to save the Pizarro Reserve on behalf of the Wichi people, thanks to a campaign that used text messaging to coordinate activists. Situated in Argentina's northwest province of Salta, the reserve came under threat when the local government sold some of the Wichi's land without the tribe's consultation or approval.

Greenpeace gave mobile phones to Wichi leaders, instructing them to text Greenpeace organizers whenever the developers approached with their bulldozers. Once alerted, Greenpeace organizers would send texts en masse to their volunteers. Those who were available at the moment would hop on a motorbike, ride to the designated area, and chain themselves to the bulldozers. Others would arrive with video cameras to film the intervention. The activists would stay on the site until sentries at the park entrances alerted them that police were on the way. At this point, those with video footage would make a quick exit, leaving a small contingent behind to get arrested (for the sake of generating public sympathy).

Greenpeace was therefore able to deliver compelling and regular footage to supporters and the news media. After a twenty-month battle, the reserve regained its protected status. Oscar Soria, one of the Greenpeace leaders, says of the effort: "Using short message service [texting] to mobilize people on the ground, in the forests, and in the cities is an extremely powerful tool, because you are able to reach so many people in one moment."[13]

Texting enabled Greenpeace to coordinate a nimble team that stayed one step ahead of their antagonists. Activists across the world have used the same military-style tactics to evade police and organize flash mobs of protesters.

For more examples about text-message-based political movements and mobilizations, see

www.mobileactive.org

Mobilizing Crowds

This chapter's opening showed how texting played a role in a massive mobilization in the Philippines. Since the early 2000s, similar text-enabled political movements have erupted throughout the world. In 2002, text messaging was instrumental in the election of South Korean president Roh Moo-hyun. When election-day polls showed that Roh's opponent was winning, hundreds of thousands of Roh's supporters mobilized friends via text messaging. Roh edged out a victory.

After the 2004 bombings in Madrid, Spain, officials banned demonstrations in the twenty-four hours preceding the election. In defiance of the ban, Spanish citizens used text messaging to organize impromptu demonstrations against the government. Most believed that the government lied about key facts related to the bombing. Thousands arrived, and the incumbent, who had been ahead in the polls, lost the election.

Such spontaneous mobilizations are now recognized as a potent political force. Texting changes the dynamics of mass political movements; like a flock of birds synchronizing themselves through silent signals, crowds respond dynamically to compelling texts. They gather in a flash, disperse in an instant, and shift the balance of power.

These large-scale mobilizations are extraordinarily difficult to manufacture because they depend on a unique combination of political events and popular sentiment. However, organizers have taken advantage of texting to coordinate targeted smaller-scale mobilizations.

In 2006, I had the good fortune to partner with Working Assets, the student Public Interest Research Groups (PIRGs), and a team of academic researchers to conduct a campaign to test the effectiveness of text messaging in getting out the vote for the November elections.[14]

Leading up to the election, we registered young people to vote, online and on the ground. In addition to the standard information that the Federal Election Commission requires, we asked if registrants would mind receiving a text-message reminder to vote. We compiled a list of about twelve thousand phone numbers through this method. The day before Election Day, we sent text reminders to half of these numbers (leaving the other half to serve as the control group). The messages said,

> "A friendly reminder that TOMORROW is Election Day. Democracy depends on citizens like you – so please vote! –PIRG/TxtVoter.org."[15]

When the voter files later became available, the research team was able to see how many people voted in both the experimental and control groups. Text reminders increased an individual's likelihood to vote by 4 to 5 percentage points. As the first study of its kind, it showed that texting has a statistically significant effect on voter mobilization.

Text-messaging mobilization campaigns that don't require as much effort as getting voters to the polls have shown even higher participation rates. In late 2006, a number of bills were proposed in Congress. Working Assets (now Credo) felt that the passage of several of these bills was important to the organization, and set up a text campaign that was responsive to the unpredictable and time-sensitive nature of the legislative process.

When a high-priority bill came up for a vote, Working Assets sent a text message to its network of activists, containing a short note about the importance of the upcoming legislation as well as a phone number to call to take action. When supporters called the number, they heard a recorded message describing what was at stake in the legislation. Callers were then automatically transferred to their congressional representative's office.

Each time the messages went out, supporters responded enthusiastically: 28.8 percent responded to the first batch of messages, 31.4 percent to the second, and 18.3 percent to the third.[16] This campaign relied on the ability of text messaging to immediately mobilize a large group of people. It also shows how text messaging can be used as an initial hook—to route interested supporters to a more persuasive medium, such as voice.

Fundraising

A special type of text message, called premium short messaging service (PSMS), allows an organization to place a charge on a supporter's phone bill. The funds are then passed from the wireless carrier to the organization every month. PSMS holds great potential for fundraising, except for the fact that in the United States, carrier commissions range from 40 to 50 percent. Such high rates have significantly hampered the growth of text-based financial transactions.

Wireless Carrier or Operator

The business that sells wireless service to consumers, such as Sprint, T-Mobile, 02, Vodafone, or Rogers

At times, the wireless carriers have agreed to waive their fees. In the wake of Hurricane Katrina, for instance, the Red Cross conducted a campaign called "Text 2HELP," in which it asked supporters to text the keyword "HELP" to a shortcode (24357). After texting in, a $5 tax-deductible donation was charged to the supporter's phone bill and paid to the American Red Cross for disaster relief efforts. The carriers agreed to completely eliminate their commission, and the Red Cross raised over $100,000.

Until the carriers reduce their fees, fundraising via PSMS will probably not be cost-effective. Still, workarounds exist. The John Edwards 2008 presidential campaign sent text messages to supporters who had previously indicated an interest in receiving such messages (via Edwards's Web site). The texts asked supporters to call a number included in the message. When they called, they heard the following recorded message from Senator Edwards:

> "I'm calling to remind you that with just over a week before the end of the quarter, the time to act is now. I'm not asking you to help us outraise everyone else. I'm only asking you for what we need to get our message of real change out to voters in Iowa, New Hampshire, and other key states nationwide. Press 1 to be connected to an operator who is ready to take your credit card donation."[17]

About 10 percent of supporters responded to the initial text message, and 15 percent of these people donated.[18] Edwards's campaign avoided using the PSMS system, but it still incurred the expense of operating a call center. This method may work for campaigns with thousands of potential donors, but is ill suited for smaller campaigns with limited budgets. However, it shows a creative workaround to the carrier's hefty fees.

Acquiring Opt-In

According to carrier policy, a person must opt in to your mobile campaign before you can send him or her a single message. People can opt in through a form on a Web site or by sending a text message to your shortcode. The carriers also require that you provide a method for the person to opt out in the first message that you send to him or her—and that you make opting out available at any point in time. Here's an example of a carrier-approved first message: "Thanks for joining Mobile Voter's voter info text alerts program. You'll receive one pithy message every week. Reply 'Stop' to opt out at any time."

Conducting Ringtone Advocacy

Young people love ringtones—they've purchased over 520 million of them (at $1.00 to $2.50 each) since 2001. Most ringtones are short-ened versions of popular songs. For example, in 2006 rapper 50 Cent sold more than 1.9 million downloads of his hit tone "Candy Shop," a remix of his full-length song of the same name.[19] Young people use ringtones as they would a concert T-shirt to publicly declare their affiliation with an artist or genre of music.

The ringtone in the Philippines that demonstrated President Gloria Arroyo's vote-rigging activity showed how an expression of identity can also be used to convey solidarity and outrage. But the case may be unique to the Philippines, where a majority of the country's people own mobile phones but few own personal computers. When the government barred the mainstream press from distributing the audio file, there was only one other distribution mechanism: sending a ringtone from phone to phone. In countries where personal computers are prevalent, it's doubtful that a similar event would take place. Citizen-powered media hubs like YouTube offer a much more compelling option.

Ringtones can be used as an incentive for participation, however. Barack Obama's 2008 presidential campaign offers ringtones as a reward for supplying contact information. It's clear from the sales figures that young people are willing to pay a couple of dollars per ringtone. If you're giving one away, a young person may be interested in giving your organization an equivalent value in personal information. If you've got an exclusive remix of "Candy Shop," you can expect a successful campaign. If you're limited to a shoddy recording of your candidate talking about tax law, you may want to consider other options.

In a more compelling example, the International Fund for Animal Welfare (IFAW) offered to make ringtones for the winners of its Whale Remix Contest. The contest featured an online game that allowed Web site visitors to create a "mix" from a series of whale-song audio tracks. IFAW's panel of celebrity judges selected the winning mixes; winners were awarded prizes, and their remixes are now being sold as ringtones, with the proceeds going toward programs to protect whales.[20] The nonprofit promoted the campaign on its Web site, a blog, and MySpace. This is a good example of how an organization can use ringtones to support a broader campaign across multiple channels.

Deploying Citizen Journalists

In the European Union, almost 100 percent of the population owns a mobile phone; in the United Kingdom, 75 percent of these phones have cameras.[21] If you were to do something outlandish, illegal, funny, or otherwise of note in any British public space, you can assume that 75 percent of the strangers around you might see fit to document your performance photographically. The photo or video recording is minutes away from being uploaded to a Web site like Flickr or YouTube, where tens of thousands of eyes may see your gaff.

Mobile-phone cameras have dramatically limited our ability to maintain private lives. Every public space, and all but the most tightly controlled private spaces, have an unseen and potentially massive audience.[22] On one hand, this amplifies mistakes and lapses of judgment, while creating a permanent search-ready record for posterity. On the other hand, it raises the level of accountability among governments, politicians, police, celebrities, and average citizens.

Your organization or political campaign may be able to harness supporters' mobile phones to report via text, voice, photo, and video from almost any location. A mobile army of amateur citizen reporters is at your disposal. If your organization has an antagonist with secrets, the citizen journalist working on your behalf creates a powerful disincentive for misbehavior. From Ku Klux Klan meetings to toxic dumping, an event in which a supporter could surreptitiously record caught-in-the-act video becomes a source for citizen reporting. Your organization can use actual footage to exert pressure, or *just the threat* of publicizing actions that may be illegal, embarrassing, or unpopular.

Phones are not the exclusive device for capturing photos and video, of course, because many people use inexpensive digital cameras, but phones are the most widely used and available device.

How Mobile Phone Technologies Work

Most organizations and campaigns rely on text messaging exclusively or on a combination of text and voice. Here's a look at some of the possible configurations for a mobile-phone campaign.

Two-Way Texting

In this scenario, all interaction occurs via text messaging. It's a conversation between a supporter and text-enabled software that is configured to ask a series of short questions. Most event-based campaigns use this approach. The performer or speaker asks supporters to text in; the texting software receives the incoming texts, and replies with a preconfigured response, such as a request for additional information or a thank you message. This entire conversation is scripted beforehand.

Text Alerts

Text alerts are a series of recurring texts, used in a manner similar to that of a mailing list. Supporters first request to join the alerts campaign, either by texting in or by filling out a form on a Web site. The organization then decides when to send messages to the list. Asthma U.K. used this approach to send texts to its list whenever the pollen count exceeded a certain limit. Most texting software will allow you to segment your group according to demographic data, such as zip code, area code, or other information you have compiled about your supporters.

Text to Voice Broadcast

This method is similar to a text alert, except that instead of receiving a regular text message, your supporters receive regular voice messages. Supporters subscribe to the voice broadcast by texting in a request to join, and then you can push out a recording whenever you like. Companies such as SayNow.com offer this type of service and have had success using celebrity spokespeople.

Text to Voice

Using this tactic, you text a phone number to supporters, along with a compelling short message that encourages the receiver to call the number. In most cases, the number connects to a call center or an interactive voice response (IVR) system. IVRs are the systems that ask you to "Press 1 for x; press 2 for y." Alternatively, you can send a number that connects your supporter with a real person, such as a congressperson.

Intelligent Texting

In what I call "intelligent texting," text messages travel from mobile phones to software applications that process the messages and send replies relevant to the incoming text. In a sense, the text message functions as a computer mouse. Instead of clicking, however, the user is required to send a particular keyword. The keyword behaves as the click—it expresses interest in a particular subject area. In the Blue Ocean Institute campaign, for example, texting the name of a fish returns information about that fish.

Ringtones

Methods for installing ringtones vary widely among different types of mobile phones. Ringtone service providers have made a business of understanding the differences among handsets (particular models of mobile phone) and offering "universal" ringtone delivery services. If you want to offer ringtones to supporters, the easiest route is to hire one of these vendors to do it for you.

How to Get Started

You can start a text (or text and voice) campaign in four ways: by hiring a mobile application vendor, hiring a Web-based texting provider, setting up an account at an aggregator, or configuring mobile phone modem software on your computer. The field is quite new, so vendors and providers are still figuring out the balance between price, service, and features. Their offerings change frequently, so it's in your best interest to do some comparison-shopping.

Mobile Application Vendors

Hiring a mobile vendor that specializes in nonprofit and political work is the easiest way to set up a text campaign. These specialists can get a new campaign started in a couple of days. Most have built proprietary systems for managing incoming and outgoing messages. If you want a customized solution, these vendors can usually build it for you or help you configure a set of existing tools. They will offer you support, tracking, and strategic advice. Typically, they charge for setup, monthly usage, and per-message usage.

For a list of vendors specializing in text messaging, see

mobilizingyouth.org/resources/text_vendors

Web-Based Texting Providers

If you don't need a guide to walk you through the process of configuring a texting campaign, a Web-based provider may be the way to go. To get started, head to the provider's Web site, decide which of its plans works best for you, fill out a few forms, leave your credit card number, and you'll be up and running within several minutes. Most providers offer a wide variety of services, ranging from sending out a one-time message to a list of phone numbers, to integrating texting into a software application you may already own and operate.

Expect to pay a premium on the per-message fees, which is how these providers earn their money. Most make it easy to sign up, and charge little up front. If you plan to send a lot of messages, a text vendor may end up being less expensive because it's making its money on monthly fees instead of by the message.

Text Aggregators

A company that works with each of the carriers to centralize and coordinate sending and receiving text messages is called an aggregator. The carriers don't want to negotiate deals with thousands of small organizations, so they've chosen these companies to take on that responsibility. There are just over a dozen in the United States. Mobile application providers and Web-based texting providers send all their text messages through one or more aggregator.

If you've got a highly technical staff, ample financial resources, and long-term texting goals, building an in-house texting application using an aggregator will give you maximum control over functionality and cost. Be warned, however, that this route can be a trying experience. It requires

- Reserving a shortcode with the Common Shortcode Administration (www.usshortcodes.com). This process is similar to reserving a Web domain name, but a lot more expensive.

- Purchasing an account with an aggregator.

- Waiting two to six months for all the wireless carriers to approve your application.

- Coding of the software application that handles incoming and outgoing messages.

- Ongoing maintenance and actions required for compliance with carriers. (They change their rules frequently.)

Note that some aggregators are now offering services that mirror those of mobile application providers and Web-based texting providers. They realized that configuring a custom-built solution was more work than most organizations could handle. Thus the lines between aggregator and application provider are blurring.

Mobile Phone Modems

If you're on a tight budget and aren't expecting a lot of throughput, you can set up a texting system using your personal computer and a mobile phone or mobile phone modem. A mobile phone modem does not support voice calls and is designed to be controlled by computer software rather than by human hand. Software such as FrontlineSMS has been created to allow you to configure your own intelligent text-messaging system using either a modem or one of a limited number of mobile phone handsets.

This route is inexpensive, fast, and easy, but frowned upon by the carriers. They threaten to terminate service to your phone number if they discover that you're using one of these systems. However, unless you're sending an extraordinarily large number of text messages, there's little chance that they will find out.

Strategic Considerations

Put yourself in the shoes of a young person. Your phone stays close to your body, usually in a pocket, throughout most of the day. You use it to keep in touch with a close circle of your friends. Your phone is a *private* device that reflects your identity and facilitates your social life.

In this context, uninvited text messages are an intrusion of privacy.[23] Mobile phones don't have a "spam" button to send messages to a junk-mail folder. In fact, most young people pay a small fee to send and receive messages (currently about $0.05 to $0.10 per message). For your organization to operate in this environment, it needs to develop and maintain a trusted relationship with supporters. The following are some of the considerations in developing this relationship and conducting a successful campaign.

The Old Advertising Rules Still Apply

Each supporter needs to opt in to your campaign, according to carrier policies. This means that you'll need to promote your campaign widely in order to convince people to opt in. You might use announcements from stage and on event screens, Web site promotions, and newspaper and outdoor advertising. In all of these scenarios, the old rules of advertising apply. Higher frequency and greater reach result in better response rates. Promote your call to action far and wide.

Use a Trusted Messenger at Live Events

If your organization is not well known, you face an obstacle in persuading young people to text your shortcode, because most young people know that their numbers are captured when they text in. Ask someone who is known and trusted among your community of supporters to make the announcement. In trials of our texting software at events, we found that when a person unknown to the community asked people to text in, response rates were around 1 percent, but rates increased to 15 percent to 45 percent when a well-known person made the request.

To maintain this level of trust, you'll need to treat your supporters' personal information with respect, which means giving them an easy method for opting out of the text campaign and not selling their numbers to third parties, unless they grant you permission to do so.

Provide Incentives

What does a young person get in return for texting your shortcode and giving you their personal information? In the case of Bono's concerts, participants' names scrolled across a giant screen. Some organizations give away backstage passes, coupon codes, bumper stickers, or ringtones. If possible, devise incentives that support your cause while taking advantage of the immediacy made possible by mobile phones.

For example, San Francisco Health's SexInfo campaign offered valuable and confidential information in return for participating. The incentive was a relevant message at the location where the campaign was advertised.[24] Bono scrolled names across the screen immediately upon receiving the incoming text message. Connect the incentive to the participant's immediate location.

Ensure Timeliness and Relevance

Timeliness is counted in hours, not days. Relevance is measured in terms of the value of information *in a given place.*

Being timely is easy. Avoid sending messages that refer to events that occur in more than twenty-four hours.[25] Ask your supporters to make a call *now* or to come to an event in an hour. Don't tell them about a speech taking place the next evening. Text messages are ephemeral—take advantage of the near term.

Relevancy is a lot more difficult to achieve, because it depends largely on a supporter's location. If the person is at home and you send him or her information about environmentally friendly fish, the message is not very relevant. If the person is running errands, it's more relevant. And if the message is received while he or she is at the market, it's incredibly relevant. The best way to ensure relevance is to encourage your supporters to request information *from you* when they're at a location that fits your campaign.

Write Clear Texts

Confusing language hampers many texting campaigns; you've got to keep the message simple. With only 160 characters at their disposal, organizations use shortcuts and take numerous liberties with language. Consider this message from the Edwards campaign:

> "John Edward wants 2 talk 2 you! Hit Reply. Type 'CALL' & hit
> Send. John will call YOU right back! OR call 202-350-9749. txt
> STOP 2 unsub"

This call to action is a jumble of words and numbers—it's incredibly confusing. Follow the old K.I.S.S. adage (Keep It Simple Stupid). Here's a much simpler call to action from SexInfo:

> "no matter if it's ur b-friend g-friend uncle neighbor, u don't deserve 2B hurt or touched how u don't want 24/7 sexual abuse resource center 206-8386"

Use Texting as an Initial Hook

Texting is great for reaching a large number of people in an instant. It also works well in situations where you want many people to be able to reach you simultaneously, such as at a concert. But texting is a shallow medium. If your campaign isn't suited to delivering extremely valuable information in the space of 160 characters, consider moving the supporter to a more immersive medium, such as voice. Use texting for its strengths: immediacy, timeliness, and ubiquity.

Support a Broader Campaign

Integrate texting, ringtones, and mobile photos into your campaign. In its effort to save the whales, IFAW used ringtones to support a broader story, which culminated with a contest to create the best whale song remixes; this coordinated approach was a much more compelling strategy than simply offering whale song ringtones for download on the IFAW Web site.

Challenges and Opportunities

As one of the primary communication devices for young people around the world, mobile phones offer a wide array of opportunities. However, mobile phone campaigns suffer from a structural problem that is unique among the technologies discussed in this book: a small number of powerful businesses own the wireless networks. In the United States, the vast majority of voice calls and text messages pass through the proprietary cables, towers, and transmitters of four companies:

Cingular/AT&T, Verizon, Sprint/Nextel, and T-Mobile. Unlike data that flow freely across the Internet, these four businesses exert strict control over the terms of data transmission.

Recently, Verizon barred the abortion rights group NARAL from sending messages related to reproductive rights to its members. Verizon said its policy prohibits "highly controversial" and potentially "unsavory" messages from being distributed on its network. After activists protested, Verizon reversed its decision.[26] Some carriers require that campaigns filter all text messages through a "bad words" list that disallows such words as "prostitute." Other carriers block what they consider "spam," without notifying the sender. Carriers can revoke your ability to use a shortcode with no advance warning, and they can block traffic from your server without giving a reason.

At press time, Google has upturned the mobile industry by proposing a more open mobile phone operating system called Android and by stating its intention to bid on a portion of the wireless spectrum. If successful in this bid, Google may force the industry to adopt more transparent and open standards. However, these changes are several years away.

Today, you'll have to navigate restrictive usage policies and the carriers' definitions of decency. If you can do so, the mobile phone holds tremendous promise as a tool for recruiting, advocacy, mobilization, and providing information for young people. Few other technologies have such wide reach and deep integration into the social fabric of young lives. The rate of use of text messaging will continue to climb, and advanced mobile technologies will work their way down to less expensive handsets.

Many phones now ship with full-featured Web browsers that let you surf the Web just as you would on a personal computer. The screen is smaller, connections aren't as fast, and typing is often laborious, but the technology is also improving rapidly. Connection speeds are rising, and handset manufacturers are inventing speedier methods for entering text.[27] Such innovations as fold-up and rollout screens may further boost the comfort of browsing the Web on mobile phones.

And in contrast to personal computers, the mobile phone is *aware of its location*. When you travel with it from home to the office, it knows where you are and where you've been. It obtains your coordinates either from an embedded global positioning chip (GPS) or by triangulating your position relative to cell towers.[28] Applications that use these data are called location-based services (LBS).

Businesses are already making mobile search engines that automatically return results based on your current location. Weight-monitoring applications track the number of steps you've walked and calories burned. Dating applications detect if there are people who share your interests in the vicinity. The phone is becoming a context-sensitive device. Using this technology, the Blue Ocean Institute wouldn't need to advertise its service at a fish market. It could enter the locations of all fish markets in a given city into its database and send a text whenever you approach one.

Note that carriers have not yet made the built-in triangulation data available on the majority of handsets. They cite legal and privacy concerns. Instead, software developers must rely on coordinates from embedded GPS chips. These chips are currently very expensive and only available on high-end phone models. Thus, widespread availability of location sensitive mobile applications is still years away.

As mobile Web browsers become more powerful and location-based services more widely available, social interactions will become more fluid as the phone's limited address book becomes more like a social networking application. Imagine that as you walk down the street your phone tells you which friends are close by. You tell it that you'd like to eat lunch, and it gives you a list of nearby restaurants that match your preferences. You pick one, and the phone texts a lunch invitation to your nearest friends, along with your estimated time of arrival.

Political campaigns and nonprofits could also develop novel applications. Imagine a political-friending application that tells you which people in a given room share your political views, or a volunteer-coordination service that gives you a list of nonprofits in your immediate vicinity that would benefit from thirty minutes of your time. Mobile phones will bring the power of social computing to real-world spaces. They will create opportunities for supporters to meet, discuss, and mobilize *offline*. In the hands, pockets, and purses of a majority of the world's population, these diminutive devices are redefining what it means to be connected to the Internet and to each other.

Endnotes

1. Note that by now the details of this event are shrouded in myth. Different people tell different versions of the story. Thus, the gist of this anecdote is factually correct, but the details are a matter of clouded historical memory.

2. www.washingtonpost.com/wp-dyn/content/article/2006/08/24/AR2006082401379.html

3. See scandal time line at http://en.wikipedia.org/wiki/Timeline_of_Hello_Garci_scandal and at http://en.wikipedia.org/wiki/Hello_Garci_scandal.

4. www.marketingcharts.com/interactive/mobile-phone-penetration-84-wireless-revenue-155b-by-years-end-1371

5. This statistic is from a Telephia report: www.slideshare.net/pacificleo/mobile-content-market-size-slides-q1-07.

6. www.mmetrics.com/press/PressRelease.aspx?article=20061003-sms-shorttext

7. www.teleclick.ca/2006/03/sms-text-messaging-keeps-strong-edge-in-asia-pacific

8. http://www.ipsos-na.com/news/pressrelease.cfm?id=3049

9. Bono's campaign has been widely criticized for gathering this contact information and then failing to take any further action. Additional details about Bono's text-messaging efforts can be found here: www.networkworld.com/weblogs/layer8/008985.html.

10. www.youngvoterstrategies.org/index.php?tg=articles&idx=More&topics=35&article=184

    www.rights-group.com/case_seal.html

11. Information from this campaign was provided verbally by Jed Alpert of Mobile Commons, the vendor that operated this campaign.

12. Note that this advertisement asks MetroPCS users to text their request to a standard number. Many prepaid phone services, such as MetroPCS, do *not* allow their subscribers to text to a shortcode. This is a serious limiting factor for campaigns operating among lower-income populations where many mobile phone accounts use the prepaid system. Information about this campaign can be found at www.sextextsf.org/news.html.

13. www.personaldemocracy.com/node/756

14. The full study is here: www.newvotersproject.org/uploads/jX/a4/jXa4y7Q3JFWhnPsmdQcGfw/Youth-Vote-and-Text-Messaging.pdf.

15. TxtVoter was the name of our 2006 campaign. The name of the organization that registered the individual was attached to the end of each message.

16. This anecdote and data were provided by Mobile Commons.

17. http://techpresident.com/node/1220

18. Information from this campaign was provided by Jed Alpert of Mobile Commons, the vendor that operated this campaign.

19. www.usatoday.com/life/music/news/2006-01-25-ringtones_x.htm

20. www.capecodtoday.com/news412.htm

21. www.cellular-news.com/story/24603.php

22. For an interesting article about how mobile phone cameras are making private events public, with dramatic worldwide consequences, see www2.enn.ie/frontpage/news-9866790.html about the hanging of Saddam Hussein.

23. My organization had the unfortunate experience of sending texts to another organization's list of supposedly opted-in recipients. They turned out only to have opted into receiving e-mail updates. We spent several days on the phone with angry recipients and representatives from their wireless carriers.

24. The location was, of course, public, but it was private in the sense that it was not mediated by adults. Ironically, a bus stop crowded with strangers can be one of the most private places in urban areas.

25. The astute reader will note that the author's own texting campaign asked voters to vote "tomorrow," and the campaign delivered positive results. We made this decision in response to the unreliable nature of wireless networks. They go down with some frequency. We didn't want to rely on the networks to send messages on Election Day. By sending them the day before, we gave ourselves a one-day buffer. If the networks went down the day before, we'd try on Election Day.

26. www.nytimes.com/2007/09/27/business/27cnd-verizon.html?ex=1348545600&en=be862e29bc5b54e9&ei=5088&partner=rssnyt&emc=rss

27. Apple's iPhone uses a new technology called "multitap" to enable faster touch-screen typing.

28. Some systems even use other known transmissions, such as television signals!

THE BIG PICTURE

Permission Politicking

Essay by Seth Godin

Seth Godin is the author of nine books about marketing, including such bestsellers as *Permission Marketing, Unleashing the Ideavirus,* and *Purple Cow.* He writes a popular marketing blog (http://sethgodin.typepad.com) and is the founder of Squidoo, a fast-growing recommendation Web site. Seth is one of those rare people who can condense complicated ideas into a few sentences that give you an "Aha" moment.

When the Web started rolling out ten years ago, there was a lot of excitement from politicians. What candidates used to do to get elected was yell at strangers. Campaigns would buy TV commercials, hope that people would see them and, if enough people saw them, that they would send money. Then the Web came along, and campaigns thought: look at all these people! And it's nearly free! We'll build a Web site or buy an e-mail list, and we can just yell at everybody!

But within a couple of years, it became clear that this is the worst medium ever for yelling at people—because they can ignore you. Think about the last time you were on a Web site that had ads. Can you remember even one of the ads? Of course not, because it's so easy to ignore them.

So the lesson from the first generation of the Internet was that no one wants to hear from you *unless he or she gives you permission.* It's like dating. You can yell at me all you want, but we're not going to go out unless I say yes.

Once I give a candidate my e-mail address and I look forward to hearing from him or her, that candidate's building an asset. And that's what I call permission: it's delivering anticipated, personal, and relevant messages to people who actually want to get them.

People in the political sphere don't get this. *Acquiring* my e-mail address is irrelevant. Lots of people on both sides of the aisle are doing it exactly wrong. You can't keep yelling at people, because they're going to go away. The core of a campaign can't be built around saying, "How do we raise more money to yell at more people?" It has to be, "How do we make something that people want to talk about?"

And now we have Web 2.0. What Web 2.0 means is that you can go to people with whom you have permission and *they can talk about you.* And that becomes really fascinating, because it's viral. So if your candidates or ideas are remarkable, people will choose to talk about them.

The future of the Web is going to be about empowering your biggest fans and your best supporters. You'll give them the tools to talk about you, and they will do that, not because you've yelled at them, but because you've created something that they want to talk about.

THE BIG PICTURE

How to Really "Get" the Internet

Essay by Zack Exley

Zack Exley is a correspondent for the *Huffington Post,* an adviser to the Off the Bus project, and a founder and president of the New Organizing Institute. He directed the online campaign for the British Labor Party's 2005 reelection, and was director of online organizing and communications at Kerry-Edwards 2004. Before that, he served as organizing director at MoveOn.org and was an adviser to the early Dean campaign. Zack has a knack for peering past the less important details on which many of us get stuck, in order to see problems from a big-picture perspective.

I joined the labor movement right out of college in 1993. The AFL-CIO had a training program that foreshadowed the elimination reality shows of today. It was like *America's Next Top Union Organizer.* In my class, they pitted thirty recent college grads against each other on a three-week internship to compete for three available apprenticeship slots.

Each day we had one simple task: get in the car and visit as many workers as possible. We started each day with twenty-five workers' addresses and a big county map. If we could track down and visit with just eight workers, it would be considered a very successful day. Six was the minimum acceptable number.

On the first night, we all came back with nothing. This of course was before GPS navigation or Google maps on your cell phone, so just finding the addresses was hard enough. But finding workers at home was even harder.

I figured out that there was a county dispatcher who helped ambulances and fire trucks find even the most off-the-grid addresses. He spent most of his time sitting around doing nothing, and was perfectly willing to help me find the addresses that didn't appear even in the map book.

The greater challenge, though, was catching people at home, as most of these folks worked two jobs. I developed a system: I frantically cycled through as many addresses as I could, over and over. And I made a chart of the times I tried each house. Each day I'd switch up the order, and eventually I found each worker's one-hour window between shifts.

Being a good union organizer was about a whole lot more than finding people at home. Once you found them, could you inspire them? Could you get them over their fears? Could you coax them to make a commitment to get involved? Actually *moving* people was the more rich and important part of the job. I was terrible at it! But if you couldn't master the technique of simply finding people, then nothing else mattered. So the AFL took a chance on me and gave me an apprenticeship position.

All organizing involves technique. And all technique is based on tiny, mundane details that you can see only when you're there on the ground in person.

If you're trying to reach young voters, it doesn't matter how perfectly you've focus-grouped your message. It doesn't matter how many celebrities you have involved. Nothing matters if your base-level technique is not working to reach the people you're trying to reach.

In the 2004 campaign, I saw $100 million voter-contact efforts in which technique was handled so badly that volunteers were coming back at the end of long days having seen only one or two voters—or none. Some phone-banking operations were based on such low-quality lists that volunteers would walk out discouraged after an hour of reaching no one but wrong numbers, Republicans, and dead people. "Robocalls" were waking people up at three in the morning, and probably doing more harm than good even when they reached people in the daytime.

Technique always matters. But it seems as though much of the progressive and Democratic establishment—and perhaps our whole culture—is mired in a crisis of incompetence when it comes to technique.

A Silver Bullet?

One thing is clear: campaigns and organizations of all political persuasions are looking toward technology and the Internet, not as tools that can help them better master the technique involved in voter contact, but instead as a magical escape from the need for technique altogether. The Internet is seen as a brand-new mystical realm in which method and details don't matter. If you have a powerful message or a really cool "creative," then you need only put it on the Internet, on a social network, on a user-generated-content site—and it will go *viral*. Or if you want to reach young voters, then you need only to pay someone to send out your message using the technologies that young people love—like text messaging, MySpace, and instant messaging.

An army of consultants—backed by an evangelistic corps of academics—is pushing that idea on campaign managers. But we can't blame consultants and academics for doing their job, which is to dream, to experiment, and to get wildly and prematurely excited about new technologies.

Instead, we have to blame campaign managers for failing to do *their* job, which is to obsessively pay attention to technique. It is their responsibility to determine whether good technique is being practiced inside their campaign, judging on the basis of whether results are being achieved.

The real problem is that, as long as they refuse to personally immerse themselves in the use of the Internet, campaign managers will not do what only they are suited to do properly: separate sense from nonsense, results from hype, and organizing from experimentation.

Top campaign managers can start by ending the practice of putting "Internet guys" in charge of Internet programs. Because this sphere is still so misunderstood and misused, and becoming so much more important with every cycle, campaign managers need to take personal responsibility for it, even more than they do for the traditional campaign departments.

There is still a huge role for the enthusiastic Internet consultants: they should sit right outside the campaign managers' office. They should propose experiments and execute the ones they can justify to good, skeptical managers. And those campaign managers need to hold them rigidly accountable for results exactly the same way they do with every other department—even more so because, in working in a new field, there is just so much bullshit to cut through.

If that could happen, then over time the campaign world will integrate the Internet right alongside other fields of campaigning.

CHAPTER 5

Wikis

If you've searched the Web, there's a good chance that you've encountered Wikipedia, the ubiquitous online encyclopedia with over 7.5 million articles in 250 languages. Each day, the English-language version alone gains over seventeen hundred new articles.[1] As its content has grown, so has its readership. Wikipedia consistently ranks in the top ten most trafficked Web sites.[2] Compared with Encyclopedia Britannica, the erstwhile leader in the field, Wikipedia is twenty times larger and receives about 450 times more Web traffic.[3]

Wikipedia has become the world's foremost wiki, but it was not the first. In 1994, a software developer named Ward Cunningham appropriated the Hawaiian term *wiki*, which means "fast," to refer to his new Web publishing system, which he called WikiWikiWeb. This system dispensed with editorial hierarchy, turning every reader into a potential editor. On each page, he placed an "edit" button, which allowed readers to modify the page at will. So if you were reading an article about the causes of youth asthma, for example, and you caught an error or omission, you could make immediate changes and republish the page for the benefit of all readers. Cunningham also made it easy to add new pages. While reading about youth asthma, you could quickly create and link to a new page about asthma rates in your town. Cunningham believed that his system would facilitate collaboration and the exchange of ideas.[4]

The software attracted widespread attention beginning in 2001 through the success of Wikipedia. The encyclopedia's rapid adoption showed that a group of decentralized and unpaid volunteers could create a professional body of work that dwarfed prior efforts. Wikipedia's success proved one of the central tenets of Web 2.0: "the wisdom of crowds." This principle states that a large, distributed, and loosely associated network of individuals can accomplish more than a tightly managed, hierarchical team. Such groups benefit from faster cognition (speedier and more reliable decision making), optimized coordination (people unconsciously move in sync, as do pedestrians on a sidewalk), and augmented cooperation (peer approval guides good behavior).[5] Wikipedia's dramatic proof of the "wisdom of crowds" theory took the world by surprise.

Skeptics claimed that Wikipedia's content couldn't match the work of professional editors. But in a 2005 side-by-side test, the journal *Nature* determined that Britannica and Wikipedia had essentially the same level of accuracy.[6]

Many organizations have attempted to replicate Wikipedia's success, using wikis in a similar fashion to build encyclopedic knowledge around specific topic areas. Others have explored the potential of wikis to build community, advocate for social change, and make their workplaces more efficient. Most find that creating a successful wiki requires extensive planning, dedicated training sessions, and ongoing management.

How Organizations Are Using Wikis

For the purposes of this book, we're interested in how wikis have enabled nonprofits and political campaigns to recruit, organize, and engage youth. Although young people appear to be the primary contributors to Wikipedia[7] and several other popular wikis, political and nonprofit uses are rare. Businesses and ad hoc civic groups have taken a leading role in using the software. In the examples that follow, we'll move between the public and private sectors, teasing out the opportunities and pitfalls.

Capturing Enthusiasm and Creating a Resource

The most common types of wikis form around affinity groups. These wikis allow aficionados to deconstruct and document the minute details about their favorite things. Topics run the gamut of human interest from sports to religion. Many of these fan wikis engage young audiences, such as the eWrestling Encyclopedia, Halopedia (a wiki about the video game *Halo*), the Transformers wiki (about robot cartoon characters), and the Harry Potter wiki. Several of the most popular appeal to slightly older audiences, such as the Marvel Comics wiki, Star Wars wiki, Wookiepedia (another Star Wars wiki), 24 (a popular television show), and Memory Alpha (a Star Trek wiki).

Fans create these wikis for fellow fans. The opening paragraph to the Transformers wiki reads "Welcome to Teletraan-1: The Transformers Wiki, the fan-maintained database of Transformers knowledge that anyone can edit." The home page lists the following categories: characters, factions, toys, franchises, locations, stories, media, fandom, creators, and merchandise.

Although the more general Wikipedia also maintains several entries about the Transformers, this specialized wiki provides a more focused topical discussion: every click leads to more Transformers' information. The same body of content would have been lost within the massive Wikipedia. The Transformers wiki also serves as a central location for fans to share their interests, discuss current events, and debate the best ways to present information. On most modern wikis, in addition to the "edit" button, there is a "discussion" button. Clicking this button opens a page where people can discuss the current page and propose edits before making changes. On the day I visited the Transformers wiki, several people discussed the possibility of swapping the photo of Megatron on the home page for one of Optimus Prime.

The wiki format provides fans with a public space to meet like-minded individuals and to explore their topic of choice. These wikis are vibrant online spaces that feature constant activity about a *narrowly defined* subject matter. The key to their success lies in the selection of a limited topic around which there's considerable passion. It's important to note, however, that even the most vital of these wiki communities have many fewer contributors and articles than Wikipedia. Wookiepedia, the largest of the wikis mentioned here, includes 51,000 articles (versus 7.5 million articles on Wikipedia). The Transformers wiki consists of 4,666 articles and seventy-seven active contributors. The Harry Potter wiki has just 1,200 articles.[8]

To complicate matters, several wikis exist for each of these topic areas. Another Star Wars wiki contains 14,752 articles. An alternate Harry Potter wiki features yet another 1,400 pages. With the exception of Wikipedia, most wikis are supported by small groups of people, made smaller because of competition. A wiki can harness the energies of people who are passionate about a topic, but organizations should not expect to repeat Wikipedia's dramatic growth.

Examples from the nonprofit and political realms are few, but the success of these fan wikis leads me to believe that similar not-for-profit successes may be possible. One of the most promising is YouthRights.net. Sponsored by the National Youth Rights Association, this wiki offers numerous references to youth rights literature, discusses important issues, and provides a collection of how-to articles, such as the "Teenagers Guide to Financial Independence." Although it has only a handful of frequent contributors, the wiki is well organized and delivers a unique collection of valuable content.

Wiki Gardener

This term refers to a person who keeps a wiki organized. Without gardening, wikis tend to grow into an unmanageable tangle of incomplete paragraphs, odd formatting, and links to nowhere. Gardeners also keep out such pests as spammers, who post false entries with links to their own Web sites in order to increase their search engine rankings.

Without the enthusiasm and almost manic attention to detail of a community like Transformers fans, the wiki will have difficulty remaining useful. Recently, the National Youth Rights Association invited CommonAction, another youth rights nonprofit, to become the wiki's sponsor and administrator. CommonAction plans to promote the wiki on its Web site and during its in-person workshops around the country. The nonprofit's wiki will need this kind of attention to fulfill its promise.

Building and Supporting a Community

In the case of fan wikis, communities form as a by-product of an intense interest in a narrow topic. Some organizations take the inverse approach: they start with a community and build content around its interests. For example, the Autism wiki aims to give people with autism and their caretakers a place to share stories and offer knowledge. Its contributors have created pages about recent scientific studies, definitions, interventions, medications, and therapies. One area of the wiki features stories from people who live with the condition.

A twenty-four-year-old named Guillermo shares his story of coping with the syndrome throughout his life, touching on such topics as dating, sports, and work. Guillermo frequently offers recommendations for others with autism, as well as their parents, including the following note:

> "Sooner or later, a kid with AS is going to know that he has it. He's also going to learn whether it's a good thing or a bad thing. When you tell your kid about what he has, make sure you say it doesn't mean you love him any less. You're just curious about why he behaves unusually, especially if he is unable to give a good answer. Emphasize his good qualities, but don't be too hard on him for his bad ones."

Unfortunately, like the wide majority of wikis and despite its compelling efforts to build community, the Autism wiki suffers from a dearth of contributions. There are only five other featured stories, and some provide only sparse detail. Several core contributors make changes and additions to the wiki's 163 articles on a near-daily basis, but a critical mass of participants does not exist. The wiki represents a sincere effort by a small group of passionate individuals, but it lacks breadth and vitality.

Using wikis to support communities has a great deal of potential, but the strategy requires the commitment and attention of a critical mass. Wikis increase in value as more people use them; in order to generate the wisdom of crowds (or in this case, the support of crowds), you need to form a crowd in the first place. A great way to boost wiki usage is to launch it among an existing group of supporters. The Autism wiki could benefit from promotion among an autism-related parent's group, a learning differences school, or an advocacy group.

Conducting Advocacy

The Student Global AIDS Campaign (SGAC) created a wiki for the single purpose of putting pressure on Abbott Laboratories to provide its Kaletra drug to people living with HIV/AIDS in Thailand. Abbott produces one of the most popular HIV management drugs, and the only one that works in hot climates, but the company drew the ire of worldwide health groups in 2007 when it refused to sell Kaletra in Thailand. (Abbott took this action after Thai officials refused to grant patent protection for the drug.[9])

Outraged that the company would put profits over lives, the campaign leaped into action. It started a wiki (abbottsgreed.com) that asked supporters to post photos, stories, and any information that would pressure Abbott to sell Kaletra in Thailand. The site offers a time line of Abbott's actions, information about HIV/AIDS medications, a review of Thai law, demands for Abbott, and a list of recommended actions for activists, students, and doctors.

The tactic worked. Within five months, Abbott agreed to sell the drug in Thailand. The wiki wasn't the only source of advocacy, but it served as a focal point for coordinated group action and documentation. Since the victory, SGAC has expanded the scope of the wiki, putting pressure on Abbott to offer the drug in more countries at lower prices.

Whatever your perspective on the politics and business of health, this example demonstrates the effective use of a wiki for an extremely targeted purpose. Within a short time frame and using limited resources, the campaign encouraged widespread participation and resulted in a convincing show of community support. As a testament to its success, the Web site is mentioned in almost every mainstream article about the topic.

It remains to be seen if this wiki will continue to be effective after the initial objectives of the campaign have been achieved. In fact, its main value may have been as an influencer of the mainstream press. With the momentum generated by its success, however, SGAC has a good opportunity to turn the wiki into a gathering point for a much broader community.

Enhancing an Existing Service

In the examples I've described, organizers put 100 percent of their Web efforts into wikis. But as we've seen, it's difficult to develop and maintain participation in wikis over time. Many sites witness a flurry of initial activity followed by slow atrophy. The enthusiasm of the founders typically dies when Web traffic does not grow to Wikipedia levels. The successes we've seen so far require either a highly energetic community or a short-term objective. Can wikis work over the long term with less effort?

We find an affirmative answer in the world of Web music. LastFM is one of the world's largest music-focused social networks. As you rate and listen to music, LastFM learns about your musical preferences. Each time you use the service, it offers recommendations based on this preference profile. Most of the Web site's features focus on recommendations and networking with people who share your interests.

LastFM's fifty-person staff designs and edits most of the site's content. However, musicians' biographies, event listings, and photos are presented in wiki format. An "edit" button on each page allows fans to contribute and edit information about their favorite artists. On the events page, for example, LastFM asks, "Know something we don't? Add an event for this artist."

LastFM determined that the aggregate knowledge of its users would exceed the capabilities of its small staff. The company took a risk in ceding control to its community, but the bet paid off. The site now has over fifteen million registered users, and CBS Interactive purchased it in 2007 for $280 million. The wiki didn't drive the site's success, but it expanded its ability to deliver relevant and comprehensive information. Perhaps more important, it demonstrated trust and a reliance on its community, two qualities that resonate with young audiences.

The LastFM example shows that wikis can work well as a supplement to an existing Web site. This approach mitigates the risk of low participation. If no one provides biographical information for an artist (or even for any of the artists), the site still contains enough additional content to maintain interest. Unlike the majority of organizations that use wikis, LastFM doesn't rely on the wiki as its primary means of engaging users.

Other Uses for Wikis

Some of the most interesting ways to use wikis are not related to recruiting, organizing, or engaging youth. However, they're worth noting, as they may be of use in your organization, professional career, or personal life:

- **Conference documentation.** Many conferences document the proceedings on a wiki. A designated person posts notes to the wiki at the end of each session. Usually a wiki gardener cleans up the notes at the end of each day, while the ideas are still fresh.

- **Improving internal coordination.** Many organizations use wikis to coordinate internal teams and projects. The wiki offers an easy way to track to-do lists, decisions, meeting notes, and reference materials. Using a wiki can also cut down on e-mail. Most organizations find that a designated wiki facilitator is crucial.

- **Personal thinking space.** Some people find that a wiki helps organize their thoughts. They write notes, upload photos and documents, and use it like an online notepad. The advantage of the wiki over a pad of paper is that it's shareable, searchable, and difficult to lose.

How Wikis Work

A wiki fuses three functions: it's a Web site, a system for editing pages on that Web site, and a system for discussing the site. Using Figures 5.1 through 5.4, let's take a look at how a wiki works.

Figure 5.1. Typical Wiki Page

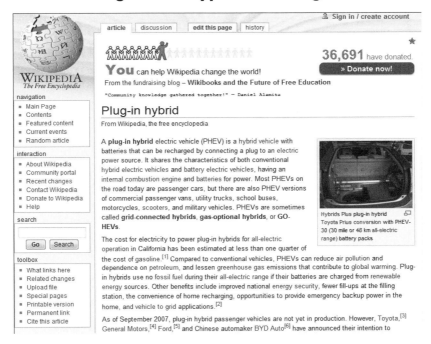

This is a typical wiki page as it would appear to a first-time reader. Note the "discussion," "edit this page," and "history" buttons at top.

How to Get Started

Starting a wiki is easy. The next sections describe the necessary steps.

Research Software Packages

Wiki software is available from a variety of vendors. Visit this book's Web site for a list of such vendors (see URL following the list). Use the following criteria to compare and evaluate options:

Figure 5.2. Wiki Page in Editing Mode

This is the same page as the one shown in Figure 5.1, but after "edit this page" has been clicked.

- **Cost.** Prices range from free to thousands of dollars per month. For example, the software that Wikipedia uses is open source and available at no charge. It's called MediaWiki and requires a fair bit of technical knowledge to get up and running. SocialText offers a full-featured wiki package that doesn't require any technical know-how, but it costs much more.

- **Editing tools.** Some wikis offer basic editing tools (bold, italic, different typefaces); others provide a wider range of user-friendly options.

- **Content.** Wikis can support non-Roman languages, audio, video, RSS (feeds), and a host of other content types and features. If you have a specific need, make sure that your wiki supports it.

Figure 5.3. Wiki Page in Discussion Mode

the practice is actually used in real life. I don't have the time nor inclination to do that research at this time. Perhaps someday once BEVs and PHEVs are common place and companies are willing to offer battery leasing contracts and swapping service stations, but that's all speculation at this point. --D0li0 16:48, 10 May 2007 (UTC)

Conversion and Patents sections need to be improved [edit]

~~The bullet items in the 2006-present section need to be converted to paragraph (at least two sentences each) and reference citation format. *James S.* 22:31, 19 April 2007 (UTC)~~ Done. *James S.* 13:28, 20 April 2007 (UTC)

~~Also many if not most of the external links and see alsos need to be moved up into the article. *James S.* 14:15, 18 April 2007 (UTC)~~ Done. *James S.* 13:28, 20 April 2007 (UTC)

the intro's whitespace needs to be removed ... intro consolidated J. D. Redding 03:00, 19 April 2007 (UTC)

Actually, if you look at WP:LEAD, an article of more than 30 kB is supposed to have three or four paragraphs for the intro. Thank you for your great help otherwise. *James S.* 03:17, 19 April 2007 (UTC)

And the Conversion and Patent sections need to be converted to standard reference format. *James S.* 01:23, 20 April 2007 (UTC)

Should we have the PHEV-(miles) designation in the intro? [edit]

I think so. *James S.* 21:47, 19 April 2007 (UTC)

Well, with the effort you put into the article today ⅇ who am I to argue? Great job! You too Jack! The only sticky point is whether the designation represents miles or kilometers... One might assume that any vehicles in the states without a m/km were in miles while vehicles from elsewhere would use km by default. Perhaps we should head that issue off right now by using, especially in the introduction for example, PHEV-20m which would be equal to PHEV-32km? I imagine that the All-electric range article can go into more details and perhaps describe future regulations as they come into effect. --D0li0 10:45, 20 April 2007 (UTC)

I've only ever seen PHEV-x referring to miles, and never with m or km suffixes. However, Google led me to this report 📄 which suggests to me that PHEV(x)km means kilometers and PHEV-(x) means miles. *James S.* 11:07, 20 April 2007 (UTC)

Note that some lines have been crossed out, presumably after the issue listed was addressed and no longer relevant. Most wikis allow people to discuss potential changes. This feature has been the primary force driving the formation of wiki communities—groups of people who socialize around the editing of a wiki.

- **Design.** Design has been a critical historical failing of wikis. Navigational systems are especially confusing and are not built to support thousands of pages. Some newer packages allow enhanced control of the look and feel. Choose a wiki with as much design control as you can afford.

Figure 5.4. Wiki Page in History Mode

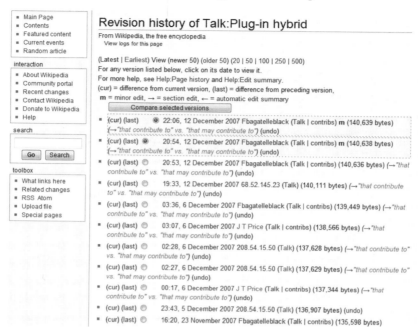

The history page lists edits to a page by author and date. A new version is saved after each change (no matter how small), and previous versions are viewable at any time. This feature adds a critical degree of accountability and creates an incentive for people to act as good citizens in order to ensure continued community approval.

- **Permissions.** When you set up your wiki, you'll determine who can edit, delete, and create pages. Some wikis allow you to configure permissions per author and per page; others give you less refined controls.

- **Ads.** Many of the free wikis put ads on your pages; others allow you to insert your own ads.[10]

For up-to-date information on wiki software
providers and other resources, head to
mobilizingyouth.org/resources/wikis

Select a Hosted Service or Install on Your Server

Most wiki software is available using the "hosted service" model. This means that you pay a company to install and manage the software on their computers. You don't have to worry about system failures, upgrades, or server overload. You pay the wiki vendor to deal with these issues for you. Most nonprofits and political campaigns can benefit by outsourcing the technical resources required to manage a wiki.

If your organization has technical resources and wants a greater degree of control, you can download and install wiki software onto your own servers. The primary advantage to this route is that you can modify the way the software works and more easily integrate the wiki into other parts of your Web site.

Create an Entry on Wikipedia

Tens of thousands of people each day visit Wikipedia. It's a great place to put information about your cause or organization. If there's an existing page about your organization, make sure that it's accurate. Several politicians recently discovered that their detractors wrote misleading information about their issue positions. If there isn't a page, create one. It's free promotion.

Develop Community Guidelines

Early wikis allowed everyone to edit. Unfortunately, people took advantage of these completely open systems. Cases of vandalism—deleted pages, deliberately false information, and scrawled obscenities across pages—have long been common. Spammers submit links to their own Web pages (usually pornographic), in the hopes of luring new visitors. Most modern wikis have established procedures that require contributors to sign in and identify themselves publicly. Some wikis allow a small number of anonymous edits, after which subsequent contributions are sent to a moderator. Your policies will be partly shaped by the capabilities of your software package, so make sure that you either pick the software before you set policies or first find software that aligns with your guidelines.

Strategic Considerations

Managing a successful wiki requires skills in a wide variety of areas, including design, group facilitation, individual psychology, and information management. A wiki's ease of use belies its inherent complexity. If you're considering starting a wiki, first explore the following questions and issues.

Management Resources

Wikis need time—a lot of it. You'll need a dedicated person or team to generate enthusiasm, clean up misformatted writings, and keep a vigilant eye on spammers and vandals. As mentioned earlier, this person is often called a wiki gardener, and spends most of the day tending to the wiki, weeding out inappropriate content, and providing sustenance to contributors. Ensure that this person has enough time to garden every day.

Characteristics of Contributors and Subject Matter

Who are your wiki's core users? Are they passionate about the subject matter that you want to address? If so, perhaps there's a preexisting group or individual that you can convince to lead your wiki effort. Wikis often work best among small groups of known individuals. For this reason, corporate wikis are becoming popular.

Rewards and Group Dynamics

Set up the wiki so that it rewards people for sharing their knowledge. Contributors are motivated by social reinforcement: they want to know that their contributions are read and valued. Be clear about how contributors will be recognized. Consider setting up a prominent wiki page that features contributors, with links to their writings. Your wiki gardener can manage this process.

Also ask yourself how you are going to handle disagreements or fights between contributors. Make clear from the start the rules governing how differences of opinion will be resolved. You may also consider designating someone as a greeter or mentor. This person welcomes new contributors or guides their efforts over time.

Competition

What benefit will your wiki provide over Wikipedia? Are you offering depth in a niche subject area? Are there competing wikis in this area? Unless you've got a preexisting group of people dedicated to your wiki, it may be difficult to drive traffic to it. Without traffic and constant activity, a wiki appears listless and uninteresting.

Vandalism and Spam

Develop a strategically aligned spam and vandalism plan. The creators of abbottsgreed.com didn't want anyone from Abbott Laboratories to weaken the language of their claims, and so used a strict user account mechanism. All contributors need to be approved by the wiki gardener. The Autism wiki, in contrast, allows anyone to edit. The creators want to encourage participation and are less concerned about vandals.

Cultural Fit

Are people in your organization comfortable editing a public document? Many organizations launch their wiki only to find that employees are wary of communicating in an unpolished format. Contributing to your organization's wiki may require a shift in the structure of work, as participation cuts across the existing hierarchy. Is your organization comfortable with these changes? Think about appointing an evangelist to promote wiki usage and to train new users. Most people will not understand how to use a wiki or maintain it. They will need hand holding.[11]

Information Design

Poor information design is the number one wiki killer. Out of the box, most wiki software sets you up for failure. The navigational structure of a wiki is determined, in part, by contributors, and these people are not students of library sciences. They don't know how to create clear, consistent, and intuitive navigation from one piece of information to another. The result is a tangle of pages, links, and dead ends.

You have two options for addressing the problem. (1) Train your wiki gardener in information design. A wizened and attentive gardener can solve a lot of problems that contributors create. (2) Choose the software that offers the best user experience. You'll get an instant sense of a system's ease of use as you explore a few examples of wikis made with your software of choice. Visit this book's Web site to see several examples. A wiki that confuses you or obscures your information will fulfill few of your objectives.

> To learn more about wiki tactics and strategies, turn to
> ### www.wikipatterns.com

Vitality

Unused wikis sink quickly into obscurity. Many of the problems I've already outlined lead to disuse: poor design, too much spam, lack of maintenance, lack of community support, and too little social reinforcement. If you address these issues effectively, you'll stand a much better chance of creating a vibrant, frequently used, and valuable wiki.

To give your wiki a boost, incorporate it into your broader organizational activities. Create an outreach or advertising campaign to drive traffic to it. Invite community members to become contributors.

Alternatively, you might not want to make a wiki the focus of your Web efforts. Follow the example of LastFM and use it in a limited fashion. This approach mitigates risk while taking advantage of the wiki's ability to aggregate community knowledge and expand organizational reach.

Challenges and Opportunities

As a child, I was reprimanded for writing in my library books. I can recall the librarian's stern warning that "books are for reading, not for writing." Today's young people are learning a dramatically different way of relating to their reading materials, and wikis are one of the primary technologies driving this change. Wikis are Web sites for read-ing, writing, and discussing topics of intense interest. They are designed for collaborating with friends and strangers, building community, and advocating for a cause. In short, wikis have changed the experience of interacting with online content—every reader has the potential to be-come a writer.

This prospect has generated as much exasperation as it has enthusiasm. Wikipedia, in particular, has been called the "cult of the amateur," the product of a "hive mind," and even a form of "Digital Maoism." These critics rightly lament the declining role of the professional editor, writer, and researcher. We need the experience and expertise of these profes-sionals. However, they have too long been the exclusive source of con-sumable information. Wikis and other people-powered social media are bringing many more voices to the fore. They empower a seventeen-year-old in her living room to directly debate a *New York Times* journal-ist. This young woman has the potential to offer an underrepresented perspective and insight absent from traditional media. The democratiz-ing effect of this shift is not perfect, but it is real and valuable.

Wikis have also been accused of representing the interests of a narrow group of people. Like blogs and every other form of Internet medium, wikis are created by people with Internet access. Anyone can click "edit," but in reality, this capability is available only to those who have access to a computer. Wikis do not solve this problem. It remains an impor-tant limitation of Internet media.

The third main criticism of wikis is that thousands of collaborative edits sap the personality and individualism from the writing. Aggrega-tion and averages squelch the poetry of human expression. This gripe ignores how wiki pages are actually created. On a micro level, each page is the product of discussion, social pressure, squabbling, and rep-utation. The writing is less an aggregation than a considered patchwork of individual expression. The wiki system may not lead to poetry or even to a complete replacement of the Encyclopedia Britannica, but it offers a viable alternative for creating and distributing information.[12]

Even if you are a wiki believer, the path to creating a successful one is not easy. Although setting up the software is relatively simple, building a community-driven resource requires ongoing effort and a strategic approach. It's every bit as complex as organizing a group of people on the ground.

If you can overcome these challenges, wikis offer numerous opportunities. They create a nexus for collaboration, production, and community building. In the best cases, wikis fulfill the promise of the "wisdom of crowds" theory. A large, diverse, independent, and decentralized group of people, connected by the Internet, really can achieve a collective ability that exceeds the average of its members. These groups of ordinary people can accomplish feats equal to those achieved by a group of specialists, as exemplified by the story of Wikipedia.

For organizations operating on thin budgets and tight time frames, wikis can help maximize use of limited resources. When the Student Global AIDS Campaign needed to create a Web site, for example, it put up a wiki and a call to supporters. Within weeks, volunteers had built a Web site complete with personal stories, action lists, news articles, photos, and up-to-the-minute bulletins. By relaxing the controls over content production and quality assurance, and by relying on volunteers, organizations can extend their productive capacities in this manner.

Crowdsourcing

A neologism for outsourcing a task to a large group of people via the Internet

In the process of building a wiki, contributors discuss, debate, and deliberate. They find others who are interested in exploring the minutia of a given topic. In this sense, the wiki becomes much more than an accumulation of work; it serves as a common ground for like-minded people. Across the Internet, clusters of people passionately discuss issues close to their hearts. Organizations are likewise discovering new ways to support and create these budding online communities.

In the future, the Web will start to look more like a wiki. Web sites and services will encourage visitors to participate and collaborate. We may also see the wiki concept being applied to other creative endeavors.

Media analyst Douglass Rushkoff posits that the "collective is nowhere near being able to compose a symphony or write a novel,"[13] but I wouldn't be so sure. Ten years ago, it would have seemed preposterous that a motley group of amateur and unpaid strangers could create a reference to rival Britannica.

Endnotes

1. www.alexa.com/site/ds/top_sites?ts_mode=global&lang=none&page=1

2. http://en.wikipedia.org/wiki/History_of_Wikipedia

3. Yes, it's telling that this information is found on Wikipedia: http://en.wikipedia.org/wiki/Encyclop%C3%A6dia_Britannica#Internet_encyclopedias.

4. http://en.wikipedia.org/wiki/WikiWikiWeb

5. http://en.wikipedia.org/wiki/The_Wisdom_of_Crowds

6. http://news.com/Study+Wikipedia+as+accurate+as+Britannica/2100-1038_3-5997332.html

7. No one is sure exactly how old contributors are, although in one survey, most reported being born in the 1980s: www.nytimes.com/2007/07/01/magazine/01WIKIPEDIA-t.html?pagewanted=2&ei=5088&en=cc8a71cf15fcaff4&ex=1340942400&partner=rssnyt&emc=rss and http://meta.wikimedia.org/wiki/List_of_Wikimedians_by_age

8. www.wikia.com/wiki/Most_active_communities

9. www.pharmalot.com/2007/03/abbott_plans_its_own_coup_in_t

10. Thanks to www.wikihow.com/Choose-a-Wiki-Package for much of this guidance.

11. www.km4dev.org/journal/index.php/km4dj/article/viewFile/99/225

12. See a fascinating discussion of these issues at www.edge.org/discourse/digital_maoism.html.

13. www.edge.org/discourse/digital_maoism.html

THE BIG PICTURE

Harnessing the Power of Networks for Social Change

Essay by Martin Kearns

Martin Kearns is an innovator in the field of "netcentric" campaigns and advocacy. These are initiatives that rely on the Internet to connect, organize, and motivate people to take action. He is cofounder and executive director of Green Media Toolshed. As I interviewed people to write this book, I heard one question a lot: "Well, have you read Martin Kearns's work?" Thankfully I had, and now you can get a sampling of it here.

Can activists use the power of network culture? Some are already trying. Last year, Josh Marshall's TalkingPointsMemo.com asked the site's readers to get their members of Congress on record about whether they supported Bush's plans to privatize Social Security. A traditional organization would have needed a large, expensive staff to make the thousands of necessary calls—if they could have gotten responses at all as nonconstituents. But by working together in a mass electronic barn-raising, Marshall's thousands of readers got this critical information quickly and easily. Moreover, they had fun doing it.

A similar dynamic is creating new forms of journalism. Jay Rosen's NewAssignment .Net hopes to cultivate a pool of volunteers able to, for instance, check for voting irregularities in every precinct in America. And Trevor Paglen and A. C. Thompson, the authors of *Torture Taxi: On the Trail of the CIA's Rendition Flights,* worked with a network of amateur plane spotters to track secret flights around the world. As Paglen recently said, "When the plane-spotter community and journalists came together, it became one of the few ways to see the outlines of this program."

These are great, innovative examples, but they involve a challenge for tomorrow's leaders: Are you approaching networked culture in a systematic way? Are you planning sustained action on projects that demonstrate the full potential of networked volunteers?

Networks of Volunteers

Information is surprisingly "expensive"—that is, gathering accurate data requires enormous amounts of time and effort. For instance, as anyone knows who's ever done press, huge amounts of energy are required to keep track of the reporters and producers out there. It's almost impossible. And although there are commercial, national media directories, subscriptions might cost $10,000, beyond the reach of all but the best funded. Thus everyone doing progressive PR is forced to reinvent the wheel separately across the country on a daily basis.

But many hands make light work. If a database requires twenty-five thousand hours of effort, it could be produced by a staff of thirteen working full-time for a year—or by 125,000 volunteers working just twelve minutes each.

This type of volunteering holds special promise. There's an enormous, positive pool of energy for change in America, but potential activists have few ways to dip their toes in the water. Yes, it's now easier than ever to give money, but past a certain point, everyone resents being treated just as an ATM. And there are always far more people who might get involved than have the resources to contribute. Yet often the only other option that seems meaningful is for volunteers to dive in completely and spend dozens of hours a week on their chosen cause. As much as we might wish, most won't do this, at least initially.

However, asking volunteers to spend ten to thirty minutes of their time as part of a project that's truly meaningful will get a far greater response rate (as Amnesty International consistently shows with its letter-writing campaigns). Moreover, for some significant percentage of people, this small measure of involvement will act as a gateway to greater activism. Few things keep people coming back for more than a sense of actually accomplishing something.

The Time to Start Is Now

Five years from now, imagine a nation of networked volunteers—where a lawyer working late in Manhattan takes a fifteen-minute break in her fortieth-floor office to volunteer for the environmental movement working to save her favorite river. Her work is cross-checked by a nurse sitting in a San Diego library who got involved via her union, while a bright twelve-year-old in Tennessee digs up information that's checked by a marketing director in Iowa City who just joined the ACLU. It's all part of an Internet bucket brigade thousands of links long, doing work that before could only have been accomplished by corporations or governments.

This is an exciting time for progressives. Although we can't deny that the present is dark, the future may be bright if we turn potential into reality. Robert F. Kennedy spoke of individuals sending out tiny ripples of hope, "crossing each other from a million different centers of energy" to "build a current that can sweep down the mightiest wall." What he didn't realize is that these ripples might well travel via your Internet connection.

CHAPTER 6

Maps

As you turn on your computer, the earth materializes, rotating majestically on your screen. The atmosphere's thin haze illuminates the planet against a pitch-black, star-speckled sky. With a flick of your mouse, the globe spins toward Africa. You watch rivers wind their way through valleys far below. As you approach Sudan, something reddish-yellow catches your eye. It's fire.

You move in for a closer look and see icons that depict flames covering nearly every square inch of Darfur, Sudan. Yellow flame represents a damaged village; red indicates total destruction. The icons scattered everywhere depict utter devastation (Figure 6.1). You move across the landscape from village to village, seeing vivid satellite imagery of the cracked yellow earth. Only charred thatched huts remain. You click on additional icons that show photos, videos, and written testimonies. You read survivors' stories of death, destruction, and endurance. You click a link titled "How Can I Help?" and the United States Holocaust Memorial Museum gives you five steps for taking action.[1]

This is the new face of advocacy, à la Google Earth. The stunningly realistic, freely downloadable mapping software creates a seamless patchwork of satellite and aerial photography that gives you the visceral experience of manipulating and navigating a three-dimensional (3D) world. It makes the Sudanese refugee seem as close as a neighbor. As you peer down on the planet, staring at actual photographs of the earth's surface, you can't help but feel closer to the world's crisis points.

Google offers Earth as a canvas. Organizations like the Holocaust Museum paint this canvas with what are called *layers*, which mapmakers use to thematically organize information, such as images, icons, graphs, charts, and text.[2] The Holocaust Museum created several layers to tell the story of Darfur, assembling photos in one layer, icons of damaged villages in another, and a 3D chart showing displaced people in yet another. The power of mapping lies in giving spatial context to this kind of data. A disembodied statistic—the number of destroyed villages—comes to life when you see the icons spread across the terrain. A video in which a man describes the murder of his parents is made more shocking because we can see the location where the brutality occurred.

By arranging layers in combination, the mapmaker conveys a narrative. Seeing both the destroyed villages and refugee camp layers at the same time gives a sense of the scale of human displacement in Darfur. The mapmaker could have told a different story by including a layer about ethnic groups and religious populations. Likewise, layers about population density, water levels, or UN peacekeeping forces would have led us to a different set of conclusions about the nature of the conflict.

Over the past several years, mapmaking has undergone a dramatic transformation. Internet-based tools have put mapmaking, once the domain of skilled cartographers, and the distribution of maps within the reach of nonprofessionals. Organizations like the Holocaust Museum can now use the language of cartography to weave a story. Realizing the power of maps to sway hearts and minds, nonprofits have seized the opportunity to engage potential supporters through this medium. They are utilizing maps to understand complex issues, document the impact of their programs, provide community services, bring transparency to obscure information, conduct advocacy, and connect activists.

Figure 6.1. The Holocaust Museum's Darfur Layer

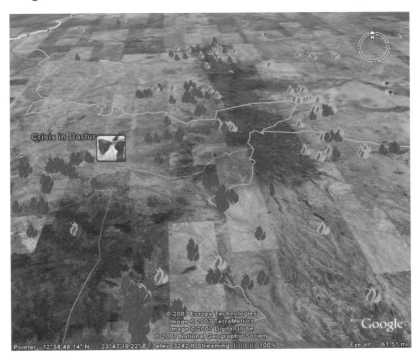

Fire icons indicate destroyed Sudanese villages in Google Earth.

How Organizations Are Using Maps

From 1996 to approximately 2004, maps were used primarily to provide online driving directions. In 2005, Google launched two products that would change the course of mapping history. The Google Earth and Google Maps products enabled people with moderate technical skills to create and distribute customized maps.

Because it requires a download and a relatively fast computer to run the software application, Google Earth is not as widely used as Google Maps. Google Maps features more traditional maps that are viewable from within a Web page, just like other graphics, such as photographs or logos. Google dominates online mapping, but does not hold a monopoly. Microsoft and Yahoo! offer compelling competing products (see Figure 6.2). In the examples that follow, we'll explore ways in which nonprofits are using mapping products to engage new and existing supporters.

Figure 6.2. Yahoo! Map Embedded in a Web Page

This map is almost identical to those offered by Google and Microsoft.

Geographic Information Systems (GIS)

GIS refers to the data, software, and techniques used to generate useful information about location, usually in the form of maps or charts. GIS professionals are modern-day mapmakers. We'll scratch the surface of GIS capabilities in this chapter, focusing on online mapping tools that are commonly available to nonprofessionals.

> To learn about intriguing GIS possibilities that require higher levels of expertise and resources, refer to
>
> **mobilizingyouth.org/gis_pro**

Enabling Access to Community Resources

In low-income neighborhoods, fast-food franchises dot the landscape, selling fattening fare at low cost. Fresh produce and nutritious groceries are difficult to find and usually more expensive. The combination of

Pins, Placemarks, and Balloons

On paper maps, people often use pins to mark places. Digital mapmakers have appropriated the term and concept. Digital representations of pins are used to indicate locations that match a search result or a place of interest. Clicking the pin usually brings up a balloon, or a small window that contains additional information about the location, such as text, imagery, or video. In Google Earth, a pin is called a placemark.

Figures 6.2 and 6.3 show two maps containing pins and balloons. Note that the design of pins and balloons differs. Google, Microsoft, and Yahoo! use unique designs. The mapmaker also has the option to specify a custom design.

these factors contributes to malnutrition and obesity. The New York City Coalition Against Hunger (NYCCAH) aims to give low-income families tools to find affordable, healthy food. Mapping plays a central role in their efforts.

In summer 2007, NYCCAH launched a service to help youth under twenty find healthy free meals in their neighborhood. The Summer Meals Finder is an online tool that shows a map of New York City. After the user enters a zip code or selects a borough, the map refreshes to show participating food kitchens. Green pins indicate kitchens that serve lunch; blue pins show locations that serve all meals. In a few seconds, young people can find a square meal with "no restrictions [and] no paperwork."[3]

This map serves a double purpose. In addition to helping young people find meals, it helps NYCCAH advocate for its cause. When the organization shows the map to city officials, NYCCAH adds layers showing fast-food restaurants, large supermarkets, farmers' markets, and food assistance agencies. Patterns emerge to reveal gaps in access to healthy foods. The more comprehensive map demonstrates the size and complexity of the problem alongside NYCCAH's efforts to combat it. In fact, this advocacy role may be the map's primary value. As a community service, its use is limited—low-income families are the least likely population to own personal computers. Although the map serves a pressing need, barriers to Internet access may reduce the effectiveness of this tool for nonadvocacy purposes.

In a future version, NYCCAH would be wise to make its maps and service available to mobile phone users. Most low-income youth own a mobile phone and would be able to use it to discover healthy food locations.

Visualizing Hard-to-Find Information

Some organizations use maps to represent relationships among data. Planet Hazard mapped pollution and population data from the U.S. Environmental Protection Agency, U.S. Census Bureau, and U.S. Geological Survey. Its Web site contains hundreds of preassembled maps that reveal specific emissions for over eighty-six thousand companies, as well as their proximity to local schools.

For example, you can view the top ten polluters by nation, state, county, or city. Pulling up the top ten for my hometown, Philadelphia, lists an assortment of businesses represented by charcoal-colored pins. The worst of the bunch appears to be Sunoco, with thirty-seven pollutants and over twenty million pounds of emissions per year. These emissions are broken down by chemical compound: sulfur dioxide, nitrogen oxides, primary PM10, and many others. Clicking "map nearby schools" brings up an array of bright blue pins, which surround the polluter's charcoal pin (see Figure 6.3).

Seeing the polluter's location only blocks away from schools impels us to consider the health of our children or children we know. Most people who see the map will tend to view Sunoco less favorably.

Planet Hazard takes several clear steps toward framing the issue of pollution and population, but stops short of making an explicit statement. It doesn't complete the story that it begins to tell and doesn't provide enough detail to help us make sense of the argument. The site states that Sunoco has "Total Emissions: 20,083,015.51," but doesn't give us enough context to understand this figure, nor does Planet Hazard suggest a path toward advocacy. The organization has gone halfway toward

Figure 6.3. Sunoco Surrounded by Schools at PlanetHazard.com

using maps and commonly available government data to make a compelling argument for social change.

The city of Portland, Oregon, takes a similar approach in making government data more accessible. Unlike Planet Hazard, PortlandMaps refrains from framing the data around a particular issue. This neutral approach allows map viewers to formulate their own questions and answers about Portland. The maps offer a wide variety of layers, such as those related to crime, elevation, parks, transit, schools, sewage, natural resources, and zoning. Provided with a comprehensive data set with easy-to-understand figures, the viewer can easily gain insight into city life.

For example, I am interested in the relationship between green space and crime: Do neighborhoods with more natural vegetation experience less crime? With a couple of clicks, I see that in downtown Portland, there is a clear relationship in this direction. Of course, I'll need to do a lot more research to determine the nature of the relationship, but PortlandMaps has achieved its mission by empowering me to quickly glean answers from government data.

PortlandMaps is one of the few examples in this chapter that doesn't use Google Maps. It uses a professional GIS (see definition earlier in this chapter) to create map imagery, which facilitates the behind-the-scenes processes of turning data into maps, but results in a clunky and unresponsive user interface. It doesn't feature many of the niceties that are now standard in online mapping.

Advocating for Change

ILoveMountains uses mapping to explicitly frame an issue and deliver a call to action. The organization is a coalition of nonprofit groups that seek to stop mountaintop coal mining in Appalachia. It uses Google Earth, video, audio, and a Web site to weave a compelling story about the devastation there.

Mountaintop miners blow up mountains from the top down in order to access veins of coal. The method requires many fewer employees and is far less hazardous to workers than the traditional tunneling technique. In the process, however, mountain landscapes are transformed, and tons of debris are pushed into the valley floor. Local residents must contend with constant noise, increased flooding, and contaminated drinking water.

The coalition uses Google Earth to humanize the issue. It has created a layer that leads you through the process of mountaintop mining, providing in-depth stories about twenty-two destroyed mountaintops and the communities that surround them. Via embedded video and text, local residents describe life adjacent to the mines. Stray boulders flatten houses. Flash floods wash away small towns and take lives. Coal sludge escapes containment walls and contaminates local water supplies. The stories overlay Google Earth's satellite imagery of each location. You travel across Appalachia listening to people talk about their lives, viewing the destruction, and learning about mountaintop mining. Throughout the tour, the coalition encourages you to write a letter to Congress and to donate money.

By the end, you feel that you've visited Appalachia firsthand. The coalition succeeds in crafting a powerful argument against mountaintop mining, as well as in converting empathy into action. Each personal story leads naturally into an opportunity for participation.

ILoveMountains deserves recognition for creating this engaging campaign. To a certain degree, however, Google Earth earns a lot of the credit for having set the stage for a new kind of interactive online experience. It has created a representation of the planet that is a virtual world in every sense of the phrase. In some ways, it's a more compelling environment for social change than many other popular virtual worlds (see Chapter Seven for a discussion of these spaces). Through an exact representation of earth, it delivers an unparalleled sense of place and connection. Of course, because it's displayed on a computer screen, Google Earth is an artifice. However, it *feels* real. Flying over the Appalachians in Google Earth feels as it might if you were in a small airplane. The addition of photos, video, and audio enhances the sensation of reality. The task of advocacy thereby becomes much easier, because the organization has allowed you to see and feel its issue.

Recruiting Supporters

ILoveMountains spent a lot of time and effort to build its mountain tour layer. Several nonprofits have created much simpler Google Earth layers to achieve more limited goals. For example, the Earthwatch Institute produced a basic series of balloons with the intention of recruiting people to join one of their real-life trips.

Earthwatch aims to engage people in scientific field research and education to promote sustainable environmental policies. It offers a series of 140 expeditions around the world; these are hands-on vacations in which "volunteers" pay about $2,000 per week to assist scientists in their efforts to protect endangered habitats.

Earthwatch's Google Earth layer places a logo marker at each of the locations. When clicked, the marker brings up a simple balloon with a photo, a text description, and a call to action. For example, if you click on the marker located at Madagascar, the balloon shows a photo of a leaping, catlike creature. The text describes a project in which three scientists monitor the size and density of the carnivore population on the island. Highlighted at the bottom of the balloon is a box that reads, "Want more than just a vacation? Volunteer to work on this research project." Clicking the box takes you to the expedition booking page on Earthwatch's Web site. You can spin the globe and view all of Earthwatch's markers. Each one brings up a similarly formatted balloon.

Connecting People

Blogs, virtual worlds, social networks, wikis, and many of the other Web 2.0 technologies bring people together. They are spaces for conversation, debate, fun, and group participation. Organizations are just starting to incorporate these social features into their mapping applications.

Idealist.org is a large social network that aims to connect the world's activists. Its Web site lists nonprofit jobs, volunteer opportunities, internships, and many other resources for people seeking to make a difference in their community. One part of the site features a Google Map that displays recent comments from members. Pins appear at locations around the world. Clicking on a pin brings up a balloon with the comment. For example, Jamie from Munich, Germany, says, "I can see so many people who are able to share so many constructive and amazing skills to make this world a better place."

The map visually connects Idealist's members. It shrinks the distance that separates this diverse group of like-minded individuals and also demonstrates global activity. Unfortunately, there's no mechanism to contact someone on the basis of his or her comment. The addition of such a mechanism would capitalize on the connections that the map makes. Nonetheless, the map adds value to Idealist's Web site with very little investment of time or resources.

Harnessing Collective Action

One of the most exciting developments in online mapping is the ability for the viewer to supply the data used to generate a map. This approach allows the mapmaker to define a framework and the community to provide the details. For example, ReformBallot.org aimed to influence the Philadelphia mayoral election by delivering a community-supported reform agenda to the candidates. The organization created a wiki that outlined its set of agenda items. Anyone with Internet access and a Philadelphia address could edit the existing items or add new ones to the list. When the editing period was over, participants voted for the items that would appear in the final agenda.

ReformBallot.org then created a map layer that showed the distribution of participants over the city of Philadelphia. Although the actual number of participants was small (around 570), the visual representation of those individuals on the map was powerful. ReformBallot.org delivered the twenty-four-point agenda and corresponding map to all mayoral candidates, and a majority of them responded to each of the points.

This example shows how the combination of online collaborative tools (map and wiki) can help the citizenry shape political agendas. In fact, the map may have amplified the campaign's impact, because it obscured the small number of participants. The map showed colored shapes representing supporters across a majority of Philadelphia. However, many of these expansive shapes represented only one supporter.

At the Tuck School of Business at Dartmouth, research fellow Quintus Jett used collaborative mapping to build a community resource in the wake of Hurricane Katrina. He designed a mapping system to track and accelerate rebuilding efforts in the heavily damaged Gentilly district of New Orleans. During spring 2007, he led a team of Dartmouth student volunteers on a block-by-block information-gathering effort. With the assistance of local residents, they classified each building into one of several categories: heavily damaged, under construction, renovated, or vacant. The students also encouraged local residents to use a Web site to submit block-specific information, which the team incorporated into the map. Using this information, restoration teams could better prepare to meet the specific needs of each street. In addition, residents could track the ongoing restoration of their neighborhood, upload photos, post stories, and communicate with neighbors.[4]

This project shows how mapping can be used to focus and organize group efforts. The map serves as a visual representation of progress, similar to the classic thermometer goal in fundraising. It also functions

as a virtual base camp for neighbors, enabling conversation, documentation, and coordination of support services. Nonprofits and politicians
can use the technique more generally to coordinate any offline action
that has a geographical focus. For example, it could be of particular
benefit to an organization operating youth street teams.

How Mapping Technology Works

Professional mapmakers spend their careers developing techniques,
learning the technology, and telling stories with maps. We're concerned,
however, with the much smaller field of online mapping tools that are
accessible to average people and organizations. Following are a few of
the key mapping concepts.

Geographic Identifiers

In order to know where to put something on a map, you need a system
for identifying geographical locations. The most commonly used iden-
tifier is latitude and longitude. This system precisely identifies a given
point on the surface of the earth. More complex systems add elevation,
which enables you to specify a point above or below another point on
the earth's surface.

Geocoding

This term refers to turning addresses into latitudinal and longitudinal
coordinates. Many mapping services have built-in geocoders into
which you can feed addresses (from your database or spreadsheet).
However, you'll need to make sure that the addresses are as precise
as possible. If you're missing a small bit of data from an address, the
geocoder may mistakenly locate it.

Geotagging

This term refers to the practice of adding a geocode to a piece of information, such as a photo. It identifies that piece of information as belonging to a particular location.

Overlays

An overlay is an object associated with a given map coordinate. These objects can be custom icons, lines, polygons, or images (such as the flames in the Darfur example). Most online mapping applications also provide the capability to create a pop-up balloon or information window.

Thematic Layers

These are the containers into which the mapmaker puts a collection of overlays. Mapmakers determine which layers are turned on by default, and can also give the map viewer controls to manipulate layers.

Zoom Levels

The zoom level indicates map magnification. Most mapping applications will allow you to specify different overlays for each zoom level, in order to avoid visual clutter when the map is in its least magnified state.

Data Sources

Most organizations create layers from a data source that specifies a collection of geographic identifiers, overlay object types, and other relevant information. For example, in the opening Darfur example, the data source for the villages' layer contains one entry for each camp; the entry includes

- The geographical location of the village

- An icon type: partially or completely destroyed

- The name of the village

- A URL to display in the balloon that pops up when the icon is clicked

You can store data in a spreadsheet or database. Depending on the type of map that you are creating, the data will be precompiled into the map layer or retrieved on demand from a server. Using the on-demand method, you can frequently update your data set.

3D Mapping Applications

These applications drape satellite and aerial imagery over a model of the earth. We've discussed Google Earth; other 3D mapping applications include Microsoft's Virtual Earth 3D and NASA's World Wind. Each of these applications has methods that allow you to add your own content to the map.

For example, in Google Earth, you create layers using a markup language called Keyhole Markup Language (KML). It's the equivalent of HTML for Web pages. A Keyhole Markup Zipped (KMZ) file is a compressed collection of KML files and supporting imagery. Clicking a link to a KMZ file from a Web page will launch Google Earth with the contents of the KMZ file turned on.

Web-Embeddable Mapping Applications

Maps that can be viewed from within Web pages are called "Web embeddable." Google, Yahoo!, and Microsoft are the leading vendors of Web-embeddable mapping tools. Each provides methods for placing custom layers and for annotating and sharing maps. They also include various built-in functions, such as driving directions and traffic overlays.

How to Get Started

The obvious place to start is to explore a few different mapping applications. Visit Web sites that use maps. Download Google Earth and Virtual Earth 3D, and experiment with the various controls. Pay attention to layers and custom overlays. Recently, map enthusiasts have created Web sites to aggregate and showcase interesting uses of online mapping.

For links to map resources and showcases, go to

mobilizingyouth.org/maps/resources

Mapmaking Services

A crop of new services enable you to create a map in a matter of minutes. They provide easy-to-use tools for selecting a region, uploading photos, writing text, and placing pins. When you're finished, you can save the map and add it to your Web site or e-mail it to friends. Using these services is the easiest way to get started mapping. However, they offer only a limited set of capabilities—they currently permit only one layer, for instance. It would be difficult to tell a story using these services, as they're intended primarily for personal and small business use. But for a quick introduction to online mapping, it's worth giving them a try.

> For a list of mapmaking services, go to
> **mobilizingyouth.org/resources/mapping_easy**

Choosing a Mapping Provider and API

To take full advantage of the evolutionary trends in online mapping, you'll need a Web programmer. Each mapping service (Google Earth, Google Maps, Microsoft Live, Yahoo!) allows you to create custom maps through the use of an *application programming interface* (API). Each provider's API will offer slightly different features and possibilities for map customization. A web programmer will understand how to write software that makes use of these APIs. API refers to the method by which a software application can be controlled by an external script or software application. Although the term sounds extremely technical, in practice, using an API is one of the easier programming tasks. Someone who is moderately familiar with JavaScript and HTML will be able to create a custom map. To create maps that pull live data from databases, you'll need a little more technical expertise.

To select a mapping provider, research the options that the various APIs make available. One of the best ways to make a comparison is simply to look at maps from each provider. You'll get a sense of what's possible without having to read the technical specifications. Frequent Web users are probably already familiar with Google Maps' interface, due to its ubiquity. They understand how to pan, zoom, and navigate Google's controls. This advantage makes a compelling case for sticking with Google, but some open-source mapping tools offer more advanced querying and analysis tools, such as Mapbuilder and Mapserver. These advanced tools enable you to develop more detailed and complex maps.

For more information about mapping providers, see

mobilizingyouth.org/resources/mapping_providers

Strategic Considerations

If your organization's work is tied to specific geographical locations, maps may be a powerful tool to bridge the gap between the digital and physical worlds. Before you dive in, however, you may want to consider the following questions and issues.

Tell a Story

Maps tell stories in many ways. They juxtapose data from one source with data from another and connect it to a physical location. Before creating a map, design your story using the range of elements made available by your mapping provider of choice. Determine how you will build the strongest narrative in support of your cause. Video and photo enhance the reality of the viewing experience.

Does your story expose inequality? Consider overlaying demographic information, which can be specific down to several city blocks and is freely available from the U.S. Census Bureau. Is access to resources an issue? How are interests vested in this location? Layers of information that identify ownership, political jurisdiction, and physical proximity may illustrate a problem and provide insight on how to change it.

Alternatively, map information may remain agnostic by simply providing a series of layers from which people can draw their own conclusions and make their own discoveries.

Think About Computer Experience and Access

To whom are you trying to tell your story? If they have fast computers, are Web savvy, and can download and install applications with ease, Google Earth may be an appropriate option. If not, Google Earth may be too intimidating. Does your audience have ready access to computers? In the NYCCAH case, the organization created online maps to help its audience find food kitchens, but this audience is unlikely to be able to get online to see the maps (except perhaps at a public library).

Use Good Information Design

As Edward R. Tufte wrote in his landmark book *Envisioning Information,* "To envision information . . . is to work at the intersection of image, word, number, art. The instruments are those of writing and typography, of managing large data sets and statistical analysis, of line and layout and color. And the standards of quality are those derived from visual principles that tell us how to put the right mark in the right place."[5]

Tufte describes data visualization as an art form that merges design and statistics. He might be appalled at many of today's online maps. As mentioned earlier, mapping providers offer a standard set of mapping tools, such as pins, balloons, and graphics, that make it easy to overload a map with confusing graphical elements. Apply the same design principles to mapmaking as you would to writing an essay or designing a brochure. Use good design to tell a compelling story.

Plan Your Data Sources

Maps elucidate data. What data sources support your story? How can a map help crystallize facts that are difficult to understand without visualization? Are the data publicly available, or will you have to purchase the information? Will you need to build a database to house your data?

Many of the most popular maps pull data from public sources, such as feeds (see Chapter One for an introduction to feeds). Look for feeds that meet your data needs. Perhaps you won't have to do the work of compiling and managing data. Maps that pull data from various feeds are called mashups (see Chapter Three for a note about mashups). Think about becoming an innovative assembler, rather than a creator, of data. You may find it less expensive in terms of money and time.

Make Use of Public Data

Counties, cities, and government agencies are often rich with data. You may be able to download layers from their Web site (San Francisco, for example, has a page where you can download a host of different layers) or request them. Reusing existing data may save hours of time-consuming gathering, sorting, and cleaning of your own data sets.

Socialize and Collaborate

Can you build social features into your mapping application? Some of the most successful Web 2.0 efforts rely on their users to create dynamic and useful services. Think about what your supporters can offer to one another in a map-based environment.

For example, I recently consulted with the California Dance Network (californiadancenetwork.org) on the creation of its new Web site. The network's primary goals were to connect members of the California dance community with each other and to show the breadth of dance across the state. My suggestion was to build a map that allowed members to place themselves on it, along with tags describing the nature of their work. Now, any member of the dance community (or other Web visitor) can quickly find like-minded and closely located dancers, performance spaces, promoters, and dance companies. Simple messaging and commenting tools allow dancers to connect with one another. The map is a collaborative effort that has enabled the dance community to visually materialize itself online. The site is launching at press time—head to the aforementioned URL to see if it's working.

Develop a Marketing Plan

If no one sees it, even a great map is a failure. You've got to ensure that your supporters know about and use your map.

Your choice of mapping service may affect your marketing options. If you are accepted into Google Earth's "Global Awareness" program, for example, you'll have a head start. Google operates this program to showcase nonprofits in Google Earth. ILoveMountains and the Darfur layers are both part of this program. It gives them a tremendous boost in traffic.

Otherwise, you'll have to promote your map like any other Web site. Write about it on your blog, buy ads, request reciprocal links, send e-mails to your list. Map marketing becomes especially important in the case of maps that depend on participation of users to build the map content, such as the California Dance Network map. Heavily utilized maps will attract increasing usage. Unused maps will seem lifeless and devoid of useful content. In the case of California Dance, the group is working within a known community, has an extensive e-mail list, and is providing definite value to dancers (free promotion).

Be Aware of Biases

The Mercator projection, developed in Germany in 1569, is the most common map used in U.S. schools. It places Germany at its center, despite the fact that the country is in the northern quadrant of the earth.[6] This design decision focuses importance on Europe while diminishing the relative sizes of countries in the Southern Hemisphere. Greenland looks comparable to Africa even though it is only one-fourteenth the size. The map reflects the perspective of European expansionists from centuries ago.

These intentional and even unintentional biases are not always evident. Does the mapping software that you're using or the layer that you've created introduce mapping biases? Consider implicit assumptions as you craft your story. If you're presenting several data points, ask what you're leaving out. If you're graphically representing data, think through the ways in which that graphic may be interpreted. ReformBallot.org effectively overstated participation in its political effort through a misleading graphical overlay. This decision may or may not have been intentional, but it surely affected interpretation of the map. You might find it helpful to dedicate time periodically to looking for areas of potential bias.

Fulfill Broader Objectives

Determine how your mapping project fits into your broader strategic goals. Are you creating an experience aimed at delivering emotional impact? Are you creating a visual story for the press? Or are you offering a community service? The answers to these types of questions will guide you toward selecting relevant data, mapping tools, and graphical elements.

Challenges and Opportunities

I've gone to a few online mapping conferences over the past year. A palpable enthusiasm and energy radiate from attendees and speakers. They feel that their work is about to radically change our lives. I think they're right.

Although the technology is still in its early stages, it's already simple and inexpensive enough for organizations to benefit from. Maps make data real. They connect us to familiar physical locations, grounding us so that we can better understand stories about our lives. On a Web page, a video showing a man speaking about murder in his village is upsetting. When we see this video alongside satellite imagery of the burned village—when we stand in the man's shoes, looking at the contours of his land—the video becomes heartbreaking. The map contextualizes the video data in a way that elicits our empathy.

Maps also highlight patterns that are evident only from a bird's-eye view. We see rhythm, density, proximity, and juxtaposition. The mapmaker draws these patterns from intangible columns of numbers and information. When we place a city's park inventory over a layer that shows income levels, an ordinary person immediately understands a relationship that was previously evident only to a skilled statistician.

Of course, similar mapping capabilities have been available to cartographers for centuries. The key difference today is that technologists are putting these tools into *our* hands. We have access to over fourteen petabytes (one petabyte equals one million gigabytes) of imagery running on more than nine hundred servers, shot from billion-dollar satellites and hundreds of airplanes, and compiled over several years.[7] These data and the software that turns them into a usable map are ours for free. We can use it to craft stories and reveal patterns that address the issues we care about.

The technology is free in dollar terms, but it comes at the cost of lost privacy and of dependence on the large mapping companies that have made these vast investments. California's mosquito surveillance program now uses Google's satellite imagery to identify homeowners who have neglected to clean their backyard pools. Enforcement officials pay a visit to these infrequent swimmers with orders to clean up. In 2007, Google launched yet another innovative mapping product called Street View. It provides 360-degree, panoramic, street-level photography of major U.S. cities. Among other daily scenes, it shows someone leaving a strip club, protesters at an abortion clinic, and a man scaling a locked fence door. Google has thus far responded quickly to requests to remove offending photos, but our private lives are much less concealed. We've received the gift of geographical language and lost some of our ability to remain discreet. We have (so far) ceded important decisions about our personal lives to a handful of multinational corporations.

In the upcoming years, maps will play a much larger role in the way that we consume and create information on the Internet. At the moment, 3D maps like Google Earth are static places. Most of the text and images were created months before we access it. But maps are becoming much more dynamic. Layers show live traffic patterns. Millions of people now geotag their photos, which enables us to travel across a map, viewing the world through the camera lens of friends and strangers.

New applications, such as Everyscape, turn geocoded snapshots into navigable 3D spaces. Most Wikipedia entries are geocoded. Turn on Wikipedia's layer in Google Earth, and you can read collaboratively created reference materials about millions of places on earth. Discussion groups are embedded at geographical locations. Want to discuss the effects of new construction on river quality in Poughkeepsie, New York? Go there on Google Earth, view images of the building sites, and speak in real time with fellow water-quality allies.

Recently, Google launched Sky and Moon, 3D map models that allow us to explore celestial objects using imagery from lunar landings and the Hubble telescope. While Google models the heavens, Microsoft has been creating more realistic versions of our world on a micro level. It has recently erected billboards within Virtual Earth, bringing the mapped world ever closer to real life. It may not be long before representations of ourselves wander down photo-real streets, or across craters on the moon, interacting with each other, purchasing products, listening to lectures, and organizing protests.[8]

Endnotes

1. Some of the language of these paragraphs intentionally mirrors a passage from *Snow Crash,* the sci-fi novel by Neal Stephenson from which Google Earth's founders drew inspiration.

2. In GIS terminology, maps consist of points, lines, polygons, and images.

3. www.nyccah.org/maps/schoolfood.php

4. http://icpd.dartmouth.edu/viewer.php and http://mba.tuck .dartmouth.edu/digital/Research/ResearchProjects/GentillyAprilMay Report.pdf. This project uses ArcIMS for mapping; see www.esri.com/ software/arcgis/arcims/index.html for more information about ArcIMS.

5. Tufte, Edward R., *Envisioning Information*, Cheshire, Conn.: Graphics Press, 1980, p. 9.

6. www.rethinkingschools.org/archive/15_03/Map153.shtml

7. This information is from "The World on Your Desktop," *Economist Technology Quarterly,* Sept. 8, 2007, p. 18. A scan of this article is located at: www.galdosinc.com/wp-content/uploads/2007/10/ TheEconomist_2007-09_TheWorldOnYourDesktop_Google.pdf. The original is in print only.

8. In Chapter Seven, you'll read about virtual worlds. They are just such places, but they are also fantastical. I'd be willing to bet that the virtual worlds of our future will look a lot more like Google Earth.

THE BIG PICTURE

Getting Things Done

Interview with Jason Fried

Jason Fried is cofounder and CEO of 37 Signals, a Web application company that is defining and practicing many of the guiding principles of the Web 2.0 movement. The company's project management software, BaseCamp, has been adopted by hundreds of nonprofit organizations because of its ease of use and simplicity—and, in particular, because it allows its users to invent their own uses for it. It's a prime example of software that allows what I've described in this book as *emergent behaviors*. I interviewed Jason in summer 2007. He talks primarily about business, but the ideas apply to any organization designing and operating a campaign for social change. An edited portion of the transcript is presented here.

A lot of what's going on today in organizations is being done by small teams. The traditional business process is just way too complex. People are saying, "Look, we need to get something done quickly. If we make some mistakes, we'll just fix them along the way. No big deal. We don't need to plan everything out ahead of time."

I'm seeing more and more companies and groups do that. It's just an easier, simpler, and faster way to get things done.

At Google, they're a big company made up of small teams. At Amazon, Jeff Bezos has this thing about the "two pizza team." If two pizzas can't feed a team, the team's too big. When things really need to get done, and they're really important, companies tend to reduce the head count. Not only that, but they put those people aside from those who could bother them.

The traditional method is where you write functional documents, and you have a lot of meetings about something that is going to happen in the future. At 37 Signals, we're not smart enough to know what's going to happen. We're better off diving in. You're always going to know more about something as you're doing it. You can ride a bike better three months in. You can drive better three months in. Everything you're going to do, you're going to do better after you've started doing it.

We don't try to think about all the things we think we know. The idea is to learn on the fly, adjust on the fly, and be agile enough to change if you see something that needs to be changed.

The Art of Decision Making

Typically we do that by making very small decisions. Instead of making three huge decisions, we make a lot of small decisions about whatever it is that we might be doing: a piece of functionality or an interface design idea, for instance. That way, anything we get wrong, it's not a big deal to rewrite. It's just another extra day or two to fix the things that went wrong, unlike if you have three months invested in something, and lots of meetings, politics, and resources, and you see that it's wrong. When you make a lot of small decisions, it's OK to get one wrong. The solution's very quick, as well.

The best decision you can make right now is better than the decision that you either can't make for various reasons or a decision that you decided on three months ago because you thought you knew what was going to happen. You're much better off making a decision right now, based on the current situation and circumstances. If it's wrong, it's not a big deal.

In making decisions, we usually just ask ourselves, "Does this change behavior?" So if there's some new fancy animation thing you can do, we'll ask ourselves, "Does this actually matter? Does this actually change your behavior? If someone has this, will the experience really be that much better, or will it just be cool?"

I think the trick is not to confuse enthusiasm with priority. It's really easy to get totally pumped about a new technology. The fun stuff is good to do on the side, or with a new project, but constantly retrofitting what you have to make it cooler is a recipe for misplaced priorities.

The Near-View Mirror

We also don't have a strategy document. We basically look out thirty, sixty, ninety days max, and we don't write it down. Sometimes we'll make a list, perhaps, but usually it's just, "Here are the things we want to take care of; let's start working on this one." When it's done, we'll say, "OK, what's the next most important thing?" And if we can't remember those other things that were supposed to be so important, then they weren't so important. And new things probably came up in the past two months that we hadn't thought about two months ago.

I think the problem is that if you start making this long list, and set out to say, "Over the next five years, we're going to be doing this," then you miss a lot of opportunities, and you're not really paying attention to what's going on. You're just doing something that you made the plan for five years ago, and you're not really paying attention to what's going on today. We're very much into paying attention to what's going on today.

CHAPTER 7

Virtual Worlds

Ailin Graef earns millions of dollars speculating in real estate. She grew up in Hubei, China, and in the mid-1990s, moved with her husband to Germany, where she took odd jobs teaching English, Chinese, and German. By 2004, Graef had saved enough money to purchase and develop a small plot of land. Although she hadn't trained as an architect or urban planner, she believed that she could build a space that would focus on community. The landscaping and flow of movement through the complex would encourage chance encounters and social interaction.

Her architectural formula was an instant hit. Graef sold her property and reinvested the profits in a larger plot of land. Within a few years, she had built an empire. Today she owns close to one thousand acres on which she operates shopping malls, chain stores, and themed residential complexes. Her office employs over sixty staff members and operates branches in Germany and China. Her rags-to-riches success story has been featured on CNN and in the pages of *Fortune, BusinessWeek,* the *Financial Times,* and *Der Spiegel.* In August 2007, Graef fulfilled a longtime wish to become a philanthropist by donating a small business center to the Nonprofit Commons, which will use the space to hold meetings and community events and to house the offices of its thirty-two member organizations.

215

Avatar

term

Most worlds allow "residents" to select a graphical self-representation, which is called an *avatar*. Residents move their avatar through the world and interact with other avatars.

The word avatar is borrowed from Sanskrit, in which it refers to the incarnate form of a deity who has descended to earth—usually referring to Buddha, an avatar of the god Vishnu. Use of the word to describe a virtual body was popularized by Neal Stephenson in *Snow Crash*, his seminal book about virtual worlds. Stephenson undoubtedly used the term to imply a sense of hubris in his fictional sci-fi world.

This story is true, but Graef's properties are virtual. They're made of pixels in the three-dimensional (3D) world called Second Life. It's a downloadable software application in which people create avatars and experience a virtual existence with all the trappings and problems of modern life, including property ownership, artistic expression, social clubs, vandalism, and theft.

Most people I've met have never visited a virtual world, and their typical reaction ranges from skeptical to dismissive. These overwhelmingly negative impressions seem to result from a tendency to conflate "virtual" with "fake." Many people cannot imagine that someone could derive value out of spending hours each day in a simulated world in which buildings are made from digital bricks and people adopt fantastical forms.

What may be hard to fathom is that although Ailin Graef's buildings exist in a virtual world, her profits, employees, and recognition are real. Graef's initial investment was $9.95. Today, her holdings are valued at more than one million *real dollars.* Real estate and digital objects in Second Life can be bought and sold using either Linden Dollars (the currency named for the company that operates Second Life) or U.S. dollars. At press time, the exchange rate is L$265 to US$1. The space Graef has donated to the Nonprofit Commons, although virtual, will host real conversations among activists making real-life social change (see Figure 7.1).

Figure 7.1. Activists Sitting Around a Campfire at the Nonprofit Commons in Second Life

This world is virtual, but it's not fake, nor is it a game. Its residents make, buy, and sell goods. They meet, marry, discuss, fight, steal, and advocate for causes. Their world comprises the range of human emotion and endeavor.

Virtual life (also known as VL) is not, however, an exact duplicate of real life (RL).[1] It is shaped by unique attributes that affect the nature of communication, the demographic makeup of the community, and ways in which it can be used to drive social change.

Second Life is the virtual world that dominates the news headlines, but many others exist. Active Worlds models real-world countries. Doppelganger offers music-themed spaces and events. Club Penguin targets the under-thirteen crowd with friendly-looking penguin avatars and extensive parental controls. Whyville encourages hands-on educational experiences for preteens. MTV's Laguna Beach simulates the California beach culture of the popular television series of the same name. Second Life currently boasts over 11 million residents—1.4 million of whom have logged in over the past month. When combined with the populations from other virtual worlds, total virtual world inhabitation rivals that of the planet's largest cities.

Virtual worlds vary widely in their appearance and functionality, but they share several defining characteristics:[2]

- *Shared space.* Many people can participate at the same time in the same common space.

- *Immediacy.* Interaction takes place in real time. For example, when you walk forward, the people with whom you are interacting will see you walk forward at the same time.

- *Immersive visual environments.* Worlds depict physical space, ranging in style from two-dimensional "cartoon" imagery to more immersive 3D environments. Many of the popular virtual worlds simulate some aspects of real life, such as gravity, topography, and architecture.

- *Personalization.* People can alter, develop, build, or submit customized objects that are seen or used in the world.

- *Persistence.* Life in these worlds continues regardless of whether or not individual users are logged in.

- *Socialization and community.* Worlds allow and encourage the formation of in-world social groups—teams, guilds, clubs, cliques, housemates, and neighborhoods.

Most worlds allow "residents" to select an avatar. The most popular worlds permit property ownership; allow users to build and sell objects, such as clothes and residences; feature a form of currency; and have many ties to real life. For instance, in a virtual world you can purchase a T-shirt from a real-world store and have it sent to your real home address. These connections are becoming increasingly seamless; eventually, interacting with a virtual world will become as easy as surfing the Web.

On average, virtual world residents are well educated and affluent. The average age is twenty-six. (In Second Life, the average age is thirty-three.) In the average virtual world, a quarter of the residents are teenagers, and a third are students.[3] Young people constitute a sizeable and active contingent, but they do not dominate. Older and wealthier people are more likely to own state-of-the-art computers and therefore constitute a majority of the population. Although virtual worlds are likely to become more accessible in the future, at present they are inhabited by a relatively privileged class.

Second Life is a free software application that you download and install on your personal computer. Get the software at **www.secondlife.com**

How Organizations Are Inhabiting Virtual Worlds

[Other forms of online media] lack the physicality, immediacy, and nuance of Second Life. Using those tools, you can't whisper to your neighbor, show loyalty (or pique) by hunkering down in one part of the room or another. Second Life's combination of real-time interaction and physical embodiment create[s] a space unlike anything else online.
—Nancy Scola, Institute for Politics, Democracy, and the Internet[4]

Despite hosting an exclusive population, virtual worlds provide a fertile ground for recruiting, engaging, and activating young people. They offer rich environments for experiential learning, forging personal connections, and creating change beyond virtual borders. If none of the technologies described in this book were familiar to you before you turned the first page, virtual worlds may be the easiest to conceive of in practice. The reason is that they closely mirror the real world. Tactics that work in real life tend to work in virtual life. Organizations give away tchotchkes, conduct outreach events, and attempt to generate media hits. Many of the examples that follow are not particularly innovative; they simply seek to copy successful real-world initiatives.

Conducting Outreach Events and Giveaways

To attract new listeners, BBC Radio organized a two-day music festival in Second Life to coincide with a real-world event in Dundee, Scotland. The organization rented a tropical island in Second Life and built a sound stage on a grassy hill. Above the stage was a giant screen that simulcast performances direct from the Scottish event. BBC Radio planned promotional activities, such as dance contests and balloon rides. Staffers wandered through the online crowd to distribute free virtual radios, which played recordings after the event. Organizers hoped that residents would carry the radios around in Second Life and thereby promote the BBC long after the event was over.[5]

The BBC ran radio and print ads to promote the festival. By final count, about thirty thousand people attended the real-life show in Scotland, six thousand visited the Second Life event, and twelve thousand digital radios were given away.[6] The vendor that designed the virtual space for the BBC called it "a defining moment for new media."[7]

Unfortunately, the BBC didn't provide any data beyond attendance figures. If the moment defined something, it's tough to know what that was. We don't know how many of these people were listeners previously, how many new enthusiasts tuned in, or how often they listened to their radios after the event. Many organizations with deep pockets have constructed similarly elaborate events. Pontiac built a "Motorati Island" featuring virtual performances and car races. Starwood Hotels threw a chic party featuring a live appearance by popular singer Ben Folds.[8] It's unclear if any of these events succeeded in recruiting new customers or supporters.

Earning Media Recognition

What is clear, however, is that these events generated a massive amount of press coverage. Music festivals happen every week. Virtual world music festivals are new phenomena. For a *limited time*, the mainstream media will chronicle every virtual world "first" as if it were the virgin flight of the *Hindenburg*.

In fact, when discussing the ROI of opening a Second Life outpost, some analysts point to press coverage as the prime benefit.[9] Ten thousand people may visit your virtual world location, but one million may read about it in newspapers and blogs. Each of these impressions has the potential to attract a new supporter to your organization or cause. From an investment standpoint, it may cost less to build a virtual world presence than to conduct a traditional marketing or public relations effort.

Press mentions may be the prime benefit of these campaigns because it's inordinately difficult to attract visitors to any given virtual world location. Worlds such as Second Life are so vast that its population is spread exceedingly thin. Except in the case of major media events like the BBC music festival, visitors to virtual locations are sparse. Thus far, the VL headquarters of Sears, Sun Microsystems, Dell, Coca-Cola, Reebok, Coldwell Banker, and Calvin Klein have attracted fewer than five hundred avatars per week.[10] After obtaining the initial media hit, American Apparel closed its Second Life location, as it faced high upkeep expenses and infrequent traffic.[11]

Creating Immersive Educational Experiences

Despite the difficulty of driving people to your virtual world location, once they've arrived, worlds offer compelling tools for creating an experience around your organization or issue. These experiences combine the benefits of personal proximity with absolute environmental control. Unbound by many of real life's limitations, you can educate, involve, and connect young people in ways not previously possible.

Psychologists believe that on a neurological level, humans are unable to distinguish between virtual and real experiences. Our brains process cues from virtual worlds the same way they would those from the real world.[12] Whereas this fact leads to uncharted territory in many areas, such as law and relationships, it presents a remarkable educational opportunity. Organizations can make someone *feel* the effects of an action or event that he or she experiences virtually. Experiential learning has proved to be one of the most effective methods for teaching youth.[13]

UC Davis medical staff created a space in Second Life that simulates the audiovisual hallucinations associated with schizophrenia. On your journey through a psychiatric ward, voices tell you that you are worthless and fat, and that you should kill yourself. Bagpipe music begins and abruptly ends. A reflection stares back at you from a mirror and whispers, "You're dead. You're dead."

The designers of Schizophrenia House say that the environment helps people understand the disease by allowing them to experience it personally. The doctors are using the virtual world to educate patients' families and caregivers and to train medical students and hospital staff. In the future, the UC scientists plan to explore immersive environments such as those enabled by Second Life as a form of therapy for afflicted patients.[14]

Like UC Davis psychologists, scientists at the National Oceanic and Atmospheric Administration (NOAA) used Second Life to provide visitors with unusual experiences. The agency created an island where you can fly through a hurricane, explore underwater habitats, and watch glaciers melt into the sea. The glacier exhibit demonstrates how the sea level is rising as a result of climate collapse (see Figure 7.2). A tsunami exhibit teaches visitors about the warning signs and shows the resulting destruction.[15] The director of NOAA's program says that the island serves both outreach and educational functions. A third of the visitors had never heard of NOAA, and many found the exhibits "totally engrossing."[16]

Both examples show how virtual worlds can be used to create compelling learning environments. They are real enough to give a person a sense of what it's like to experience schizophrenia or to feel the force of a giant wave. They offer the entertainment value of amusement-park rides and deliver the educational value of the classroom.

Connecting and Engaging Supporters

In an effort to involve youth on a recurring basis, Global Kids developed a dedicated space in Teen Second Life, a version of Second Life with more parental controls. Global Kids is a nonprofit based in New York City that seeks to encourage at-risk urban youth to become com-

Figure 7.2. NOAA Global Warming Exhibit

Image on the left shows an avatar standing before glaciers as they're seen today. Image on the right shows the rising sea level after glaciers have melted (note that the dock is submerged).

munity leaders. The group used the space to conduct a variety of teen-focused programs.

In summer 2006, for example, Global Kids organized an intensive three-week Global Leadership Summer Camp in this virtual world. Youth involved in the program participated in daily workshops about a range of global issues. During the course, participants identified child sex trafficking as the most critical issue facing worldwide youth. They invited and welcomed guest speakers, such as MIT professor Henry Jenkins and actress-activist Mia Farrow, who arrived (virtually) to speak on this issue.

As their final project, the participants collaboratively constructed a maze to educate their peers about child sex trafficking and to raise money for the Polaris Project, an antislavery organization. Wandering through the maze, visitors are presented with "fact cards" that deliver compelling information about child slavery. At the conclusion of the maze, the visitor is given a quiz, asked to donate money, and put into a communal space to discuss the issue with other maze visitors. More than twenty-five hundred teens visited the maze in its first ten weeks, and 20 percent made a small donation. Youth involved in the program blogged daily about their experiences. It's clear from their posts that they became deeply engrossed in the subject matter, connected to their fellow campers, and grew proud of their final project. You can feel their excitement when visitors from around the world start to arrive at the maze and converse about the issues that these youth framed in a space they had built.[17]

Extending Traditional Media

Tessa and Rocky go everywhere together in Laguna Beach. So when Tessa's ex-friend Kyndra invited her for coffee, Rocky assumed that he was invited too. "Big mistake," says the promo for MTV's third season of the hit television show *Laguna Beach*.[18]

MTV uses a custom-built virtual world to continue the drama that builds in its on-air television show. In Virtual Laguna Beach, participants can hang out at the beach, shop at a surf store, and experience life in Orange County as it's depicted in the show. The show's actors make virtual cameos, controlling avatars that look just like their television personalities. Events and objects in-world are designed to generate engagement with the on-air content. When the winter formal approaches, virtual residents can look for a date, try on a tux or prom dress, and presumably experience the excitement of the event, just as the on-air characters do.[19]

MTV registered six hundred thousand users in its first six months. The median age was twenty, 85 percent were female, and 64 percent returned for multiple visits.[20] The effort was so successful that MTV built several additional virtual worlds: Virtual Lower East Side, Virtual Cribs, Virtual Pimp My Ride, and Virtual The Hills. MTV actively pursues product placement within these worlds (which must account for its ability to open so many new worlds), and they have become hot spots for upcoming DJs and musicians.[21] MTV has even launched a "mixed-reality" fashion label. Lauren from Virtual Laguna Beach designs and tests the clothes in the virtual world, and the most popular outfits are produced in real life.[22]

By building its own world, MTV was able to tightly control events, the economy that developed around them, and the structure of social interaction. This high level of control enabled MTV to earn handsome prof-its from deeply integrated product placements and to create seamless ties between offline and online content. A similar level of investment and risk, however, would be daunting for most nonprofits and political campaigns. For this reason, the majority of examples in this chapter en-tail building a virtual world outpost within an *existing* world, primarily within Second Life because of its popularity and extensively customiz-able controls. Still, the MTV example demonstrates that with the right combination of investment, marketing, story, and audience, custom building a virtual world can succeed in engaging youth on a long-term basis.

Organizing Meetups

The 2004 Howard Dean presidential campaign popularized the *meetup*, a term that refers to a group of people who meet online and then coor-dinate a face-to-face meeting. Analysts credit meetups with driving grassroots support for the candidate, calling it the "backbone of Dean's surprising early success."[23] Meetups combined the connective power of the Internet with the motivational qualities of real-life interaction.

Meetups' primary strength, connecting neighbors with one another, is also a weakness. Because of their physical proximity, meetup partici-pants tend to be demographically homogenous and therefore less ef-fective at spreading support outside their own community.[24] Virtual worlds enable organizers to coordinate meetups that attract a more diverse group of people.

RootsCamp.org organizes monthly meetups for the progressive com-munity in major cities around the United States. Until it constructed a Roots Camp Second Life, activists who lived far from these cities were unable to attend. Now, Roots Camp hosts weekly meetings in Second Life that are usually attended by about forty avatars. They sit in a circle and discuss such issues as the genocide in Darfur, antiwar protest plans, and strategies for upcoming elections.[25] Organizers say that "relative to other online community toolsets, the experience of interacting with others in Second Life . . . more closely approximates real offline face-to-face interaction."

The current Second Life demographic precludes real diversity, but these virtual meetups allow an approximation of in-person participation across great distances. Environmental activists are particularly excited about this capability, because it allows people to reduce transportation emissions. However, some environmentalists question the real savings by estimating that, at present, one avatar consumes approximately 1,752 kilowatt-hours per year, which is about the same as driving an SUV twenty-three hundred miles.[26] Although a virtual world meetup may not be as environmentally friendly as it appears to be at first glance, it does provide an opportunity to involve people who are isolated by geographic barriers or distances.

Selling Virtual Objects for Charity

The U.K.-based charity Save the Children developed a "Yak Shack" campaign that sold virtual yaks for about US$3.50 (see Figure 7.3). New yak owners could ride the yak around Second Life, knit a sweater from her fur, and fill a bucket with her milk. The campaign sought to raise funds and garner attention to the group's Tibetan yak-purchasing program. In Tibet, families rely on yaks for nutritious milk, wool for knitting, and plowing.[27] All the profits from virtual world sales go toward purchasing yaks for needy Tibetan families.

Save the Children sold over two hundred yaks online, raising about $800. Clearly, the campaign didn't earn a lot of money, but it did generate a good deal of media attention and encouraged youth to play an active role in supporting a cause.[28] Friends of the Urban Forest ran a similar campaign in which it planted a real tree in an urban neighborhood for every virtual tree it sold. Since the program debuted, 125 virtual trees have been sold. For a small nonprofit, this level of sales is significant. It represents about 10 percent of all trees that the group has planted in a year.[29]

It's clear that participation in these programs can encourage offline action. In a survey by USC's Annenberg School, 20 percent of people participated in an offline endeavor that matched their online activities. Nearly two-thirds of online community members who were involved in a cause learned about it through their in-world participation, and

Figure 7.3. Save the Children's Virtual Yak

almost half reported becoming more politically active since joining an online community.[30]

Conducting Pledge Drives

In one of the most successful Second Life campaigns to date, the American Cancer Society raised over $75,000 through a Virtual Relay for Life. On January 27 and 28, 2007, participants' avatars walked around a custom-built track. Over thirty volunteers constructed the track, which featured such entertaining diversions as lighting virtual luminaria and making skydiving excursions. Walkers were encouraged to camp out before the event and to sell digital items to other residents. Donations were accepted through in-world ATMs and by filling out pledge cards.[31]

The organization started Relay for Life events in 1985. Today it conducts events in forty-six hundred communities in the United States and in twenty-three countries worldwide. The Society has raised more than $1.5 billion in the fight against cancer.[32] It applied these years of organizational experience to create and operate a successful Second Life initiative, demonstrating that real-life expertise can be effectively applied to virtual world initiatives.

How Virtual Worlds Work

Virtual worlds operate either within your Web browser or as a software application on your computer. Web-browser-based worlds are created with Adobe Flash, a browser add-on that is installed on about 98 percent of computers.[33] Downloadable software is usually proprietary and graphically richer. Second Life, for instance, requires a download, as it's too complex for modern browsers to display reliably. The following sections give an overview of important virtual world concepts.

Virtual Worlds Versus Games

Many people conflate virtual worlds with video games. Games have a beginning and ending point and, usually, an overarching objective. Some games are less directive than others, but from a conceptual standpoint, they lead a *player* through a series of tasks. Virtual worlds, in contrast, create a space for *residents* to engage in social experiences. They don't have a story line that unfolds in a linear way. Some virtual worlds have built-in games. As in real life, you can play these games in the course of your virtual life. Your virtual life, however, is not a game.

Avatars and Digital Objects

Virtual worlds offer widely varying capabilities to customize avatars and create digital objects. For example, in Club Penguin, avatar customization options are limited. You can change your penguin's color and dress him up with a few accessories, such as sunglasses. Second Life, Virtual Laguna Beach, and Kaneva provide residents with sophisticated 3D modeling tools that enable an almost infinite number of avatar permutations. Some worlds permit advanced object scripting—that is, you can encode an object with a given behavior. For example, you can create a piano and use the computer-coding language to define what happens when it is played. Figure 7.4 shows avatars from popular virtual worlds.

Figure 7.4. Avatars from Habbo Hotel, MTV's Virtual The Hills, Second Life, and Club Penguin

Economies and Property Ownership

Most virtual worlds have a currency system that allows for buying, selling, trading, or accumulating virtual property and commodities. One of Second Life's primary innovations was that it allowed residents to own their own digital goods. This structural decision led to a financial system that is becoming as complex as those that support real-world economies. Virtual banks offer interest-bearing loans, and virtual money can be exchanged for real-world dollars. People create, buy, and sell digital objects. Simpler worlds, such as Club Penguin, use a system of redeemable points. You earn points as you explore the world, which can be exchanged for a limited set of premade objects, such as penguin clothing.

Mixed Reality

Some virtual worlds represent objects or events that occur both in the virtual world and in real life. For example, proprietors set up virtual shops that sell real-world goods. You can purchase these goods with a credit card, just as if you were using a standard Web site, and they will be shipped to your real-world address. The BBC example described earlier demonstrated a mixed-reality event in which a concert took place both in Second Life and the real world.

Augmented Reality

Cousin to virtual reality, augmented reality software is intended to super-impose computer graphics over the real world. Imagine driving directions projected onto your windshield in real time, or glasses that identify the person with whom you are speaking and project information about him or her, such as the person's C.V., in the space next to his or her body. Envision visiting a clothing store that allows you to virtually try on an outfit while peering into an augmented reality mirror. These technologies exist, although they are years away from mass production, due to expense.[34]

Connections to Other Internet Services

Many worlds feature connections to Web sites and other Internet-enabled devices. For example, from within a virtual world, you can send a text message to real-world mobile phones, watch videos from such Web sites as YouTube, look at photos from Flickr, or listen to live music from online music services, such as Shoutcase or Icecast. Most complex virtual worlds are enabling an increasing number of connections to other Internet services so that the world becomes your gateway to using the Internet.

Conversations and Messaging

Residents converse with one another using built-in chat and messaging tools. In most worlds, chatting is embedded directly into the scene—you type a message, and it appears in a talk bubble next to your avatar. Voice-based conversations are becoming more prevalent as well, allowing you to use your computer's microphone to broadcast your voice in-world.

Some worlds also feature in-world messaging, which works a lot like Web-based e-mail. You send a message, and it is sent to the recipient's inbox.

Movement

Complex 3D worlds enable a wide range of avatar movement. In Second Life, for example, avatars can dance, fly, sit, point, and move in a variety of other ways. Adults-only virtual worlds, such as Red Light Center, offer a range of movement conducive to avatar sex. In the much simpler Habbo Hotel, Lego-like avatars shuffle from one point to another.

Second Life Facts

- Second Life has 11,454,669 residents, 1.5 million of whom have logged on in the past sixty days. They spend about US$9 million per month on virtual land, products, and services.[35]

- Reuters has opened a branch office in Second Life where its dedicated correspondent, Adam Pasik, reports news and has interviewed such luminaries as Archbishop Desmond Tutu, eBay CEO Meg Whitman, *New York Times* editor Bill Keller, blogger Arianna Huffington, singer Peter Gabriel, and San Francisco mayor Gavin Newsom.

- In spring 2007, Harvard University taught its first semester-long class in Second Life, titled "CyberOne: Law in the Court of Public Opinion." Over 125 colleges and universities have followed suit.[36]

- As mentioned earlier, the American Cancer Society raised $75,000 on a virtual Relay for Life on a track in Second Life.

- Toyota, GM, and Pontiac have opened virtual dealerships where they offer test drives and celebrity appearances.

- In May 2007, the National Basketball Association launched a virtual headquarters in Second Life where it sells merchandise and invites fans to play a variety of basketball games.[37]

- Sweden established diplomatic relations by opening an embassy in Second Life on May 30, 2007. Carl Bildt, Sweden's foreign minister, cut the virtual ribbon.[38]

- Several of the 2008 candidates for president have opened campaign headquarters in Second Life. One of these was vandalized on opening day.

How to Get Started

For most organizations, the largest expenditure in building a virtual presence is time. Virtual construction requires learning a new and complex toolset and committing to ongoing management. The investment is considerably higher than an equivalent effort on a social networking site, for example.

Before you attempt to construct a virtual world location, it makes sense to sign up and log in to an array of virtual worlds. Second Life is the obvious first choice. It's the dominant virtual world today and plays host to a wide variety of nonprofit and political initiatives. Many sites compile lists of direct links to Second Life locations, which are called "SLurls" or Second Life URLs. Jumping straight to a location can save hours of wandering.

> Get a sense of the lay of the land in Second Life
> at this Google Maps–Second Life mashup:
> **slurl.com**

After exploring (and inhabiting) Second Life and other virtual worlds of interest, if you determine that your organization can benefit from a virtual world presence, you have three options. The first and least time-consuming option is to join an existing virtual world community. Use your avatar as a representative of your organization and promote your issues on a one-to-one basis. You can find new supporters and collaborators by shaking hands, entering discussions, and participating in group meetings. This route won't generate any news headlines, but it will provide an introduction to virtual worlds and new supporters with a minimum level of commitment.

> For an extensive list of virtual worlds, see
> **mobilizingyouth.org/vworlds**

The second option is to build a virtual world outpost. After understanding the culture and community of your virtual world of choice and formulating a plan that supports your organizational objectives, you can purchase virtual land and begin to construct your base. Alternatively, you can hire a virtual world vendor to help strategize and build a base for you. At present, virtual vendors are rare, which keeps prices high. A less expensive route is to collaborate with a similar organization. The Nonprofit Commons mentioned at the beginning of this chapter may be a good place to find like-minded organizations.

If you work for an organization with a well-known brand, a dedicated audience, and significant resources, you might consider option three: building your own virtual world. Creating the software from scratch is beyond the scope of all but the most technically savvy organizations, but an alternative exists. Several virtual world providers faltered in their efforts to build thriving communities. Instead of going out of business, though, they decided to offer "white-label" versions of their technology for others to license and brand. MTV didn't build its own software to support Virtual Laguna Beach; it licensed it from Makena Technologies, the company that created There.com. For its latest virtual world, MTV licensed the software from Doppelganger, the world that specializes in music experiences. In addition to the licensing fee, managing a successful virtual world requires a major commitment to marketing and ongoing maintenance.

Strategic Considerations

Conducting a virtual world campaign is necessarily an experiment. You should set your expectations accordingly. At this point, virtual world strategy is inchoate (thus the brevity of this section). It primarily involves balancing the need for direct and tangible results against the benefits of experimentation. The following issues and questions can help focus your efforts.

Develop and Align Objectives

What are you trying to achieve with your virtual world campaign? Many organizations established virtual world outposts simply to say that they had done it. Most are reconsidering this strategy because it didn't deliver any clear result.[39] Prepare a list of campaign objectives and expected results. Identify objectives that are aligned with virtual world attributes. For example, virtual worlds are well suited to conveying a sense for space and environment, as well as facilitating lifelike personal interactions. If you find that your objectives don't rely on attributes specific to virtual worlds, ask if other media might be better suited to your campaign.

Consider the Opportunity Cost

Operating a virtual world is rarely inexpensive. You may want to hire a virtual world specialist to help you construct avatars and buildings and to guide you in the intricacies of a particular world. Alternatively, you can spend time learning the tools and social conventions. In both cases, you'll face a considerable learning curve and no guarantee that your campaign will attract supporters or achieve its objectives. Before beginning a virtual world campaign, chart the time and money you expect to spend on the project and ask if this expenditure makes sense for your organization. If you're operating on a tight budget and need measurable results, your resources might be better used elsewhere.

Make Partnerships

Instead of buying your own land and constructing buildings, you can save time and effort by partnering with like-minded organizations that already have a virtual world presence. Nonprofits interested in Second Life should contact the Nonprofit Commons (http://secondlife .techsoup.org); you may be able to lease an office or hold meetings with little investment.

Future-Proof Your Offering

Some virtual world platforms use proprietary software, and others are moving down the path toward more open-source strategies. Building an outpost in a proprietary virtual world means that your investment lies in the hands of a for-profit business. That company can change the rules—or go out of business—at any time, which is particularly common in the volatile realm of virtual world software. Be sure to investigate the company behind a virtual world before making an investment of time or resources, and to understand their software licensing options and future plans.

Challenges and Opportunities

The improbable visions of science fiction writers are now becoming reality. We're witnessing the rise of parallel worlds composed of pixels and avatars. The audacity of these efforts—their unapologetic attempt to re-create life as we know it—and the colorfulness of their first residents make for great news. Almost every week, journalists publish sensational stories about happenings in virtual worlds. They write about bizarre mixed-reality love triangles, a cadre of young people spending their lives in-world, billions of dollars in virtual transactions, and the changing face of business in a world where physical distances are nonexistent.

To say that virtual worlds are overhyped is an understatement. We've seen a range of examples that demonstrate the difficulty of achieving mission-related objectives in virtual worlds. The software is largely unstable (it crashes often), worlds are sparsely populated (when compared to the Web as a whole), and campaigns require a large investment of time and money just to get started. In addition, virtual world inhabitants consist of the top tier of computer users: those who are relatively wealthy and endowed with the latest computer equipment. Some notable campaigns have achieved positive results, but these are exceptions. Media attention has been one of the primary benefits thus far, and it's already starting to fade as the novelty diminishes. For these reasons, skeptics dismiss virtual worlds as a fad.

Virtual worlds are certainly embryonic, but they're not ephemeral. Existing user interfaces are too complex, integration into standard web browsing is too uneven, and the time required for meaningful participation is too high. However, the virtual worlds of today show real promise for the future of business and social enterprise. The benefits are too compelling to ignore.

Costs are high because these worlds are relatively empty. However, improvements in the software will allow more people to experience virtual life. The time required for meaningful participation will shrink as the worlds become integrated more smoothly into the flow of everyday Web browsing. We'll reach a tipping point where there are enough people inhabiting these worlds to justify businesses on a massive scale. In the next several years, virtual worlds will become an integrated part of our Web-browsing experience. Linden Labs, the creators of Second Life, along with a variety of leading businesses, such as IBM and Google, are actively working on open-source programs that will lead to the creation of avatars and digital objects you can carry across the Internet. You might use the same avatar to interact with friends on your MySpace page or to visit a location in Google Earth. The avatar and your objects will become your portable Internet identity.

Consumers and activists will stream down virtual sidewalks and congregate in popular meeting spots. Cities akin to London, Paris, and New York will rise up—but they'll be accessible to anyone in any location with an Internet connection. Imagine standing in a virtual Times Square and being able to instantly locate every individual who supports your cause, then giving them the option to teleport to a private meeting space where you can persuade them to join your effort. Instead of showing photos or handing out fliers, you can change the very structure of their environment. You can explain glacial melting by putting a person on a glacier and applying heat. You can teach someone about schizophrenia by turning his or her world inside out.

The virtual worlds of tomorrow will not look exactly like they do today, but these are not science fiction fantasies. They're evolving realities. For organizations that can afford to experiment, the effort will build a framework for understanding the Internet of tomorrow. If this sort of experimentation is beyond your organizational budget, at least explore a virtual world. Spending even a few hours controlling an avatar in one of the top virtual worlds will inform your understanding of the present and your vision for the future.

Endnotes

1. These terms are used often to distinguish virtual life from that which most people call "real life." However, I make the case that there is no distinction. VL is a form of RL. It's one way of experiencing RL.

2. Most of this excellent list of virtual world characteristics comes from http://virtualworldsreview.com/info/whatis.shtml.

3. www.tnl.net/blog/2006/08/05/characteristics-of-virtual-world-users

4. www.ipdi.org/UploadedFiles/Avatar%20Politics.pdf

5. http://news.bbc.co.uk/2/hi/technology/4766755.stm

6. I'm assuming that people took more than one radio, but can't find any data on how the BBC gave away a larger number of radios than there were people who visited.

7. www.spacethinkdream.com/bigweekend.php

   www.spacethinkdream.com/files/BBC_R1.pdf

8. www.adweek.com/aw/iq_interactive/article_display.jsp?vnu_content_id=1003286949

9. www.hhcc.com/?p=269

10. http://gigaom.com/2007/05/24/virtual-world-marketing-lots-of-companies-few-visitors-so-far

11. American Apparel's press release about closing their Second Life location: http://americanapparel.net/presscenter/secondlife

    An article about Second Life's "honeymoon" being over: http://adverlab.blogspot.com/2007/07/media-pendulum-swings-on-second-life.html

12. Alter, Alexandra, "Is This Man Cheating on His Wife?" *Wall Street Journal*, Aug. 10, 2007. http://online.wsj.com/public/article/SB118670164592393622.html?mod=blog. The personal histories described in this article offer another argument for the case that virtual experiences are in fact real and that there is little effective difference.

13. http://en.wikipedia.org/wiki/Experiential_learning

14. www.ucdmc.ucdavis.edu/psychiatry/research/virtual.html

15. www.publicaffairs.noaa.gov/releases2007/apr07/noaa07-023.html

    www.esrl.noaa.gov/outreach/sl

    http://slurl.com/secondlife/Meteora/177/161/27

16. www.secondlifeinsider.com/2006/08/18/noaa-comes-to-second-life

17. http://leestone.newsvine.com/_news/2006/08/07/316231-second
    -life-educates-about-trafficking

    www.holymeatballs.org/teen_posts.htm

18. www.mtv.com/ontv/dyn/laguna_beach/series.jhtml#bio

19. http://news.com.com/8301-10784_3-6117738-7.html

20. http://mmopub.com/2007/03/28/mtv-announces-virtual-cribs
    -vlb-usage-no%e2%80%99s

21. http://mmopub.com/2007/06/13/mtv%e2%80%99s-virtual-lower
    -east-side-takes-shape

22. http://mmopub.com/2007/03/09/mtv-launching-mixed-reality
    -fashion-line

23. www.cbsnews.com/stories/2003/06/04/politics/main557004.shtml

24. www.washingtonpost.com/ac2/wp-dyn?pagename=article&node=
    &contentId=A10736-2003Jul4&notFound=true

25. www.slnn.com/index.php/article/about/rootscampsl.html

    www.rootscamp.org/RootsCampSLBackground

26. www.roughtype.com/archives/2006/12/avatars_consume.php

27. http://savethechildren.sandbag.uk.com/Store/
    DII-4—a+hairy+yak+.html

28. www.darrenbarefoot.com/archives/2007/08/my-gnomedex
    -talk-1100-stacies.html

29. www.nrdc.org/onearth/07spr/livgreen.asp

30. www.nrdc.org/onearth/07spr/livgreen.asp

www.digitalcenter.org/pdf/2007-Digital-Future-Report-Press-Release-112906.pdf

31. www.cancer.org/docroot/GI/content/GI_1_8_Second_Life_Relay.asp

http://slrfl.org/?page_id=16

32. http://slrfl.org/?page_id=2

33. www.adobe.com/products/player_census/flashplayer/version_penetration.html

34. "Reality, Only Better," *Economist Technology Quarterly,* Dec. 8, 2007.

35. www.businessweek.com/magazine/content/06_48/b4011413.htm

36. www.computerworld.com/blogs/node/5553

37. www.nba.com/news/second_life_070501.html

38. www.sweden.se/templates/cs/Article____16345.aspx

39. www.reuters.com/article/internetNews/idUSN1028324920071011?pageNumber=1

THE BIG PICTURE

The Future of Web 2.0

Interview with Mitch Kapor

Mitch Kapor is widely known as founder of Lotus Development Corporation and the designer of Lotus 1-2-3, the "killer application" that made the personal computer ubiquitous in the business world in the 1980s. Since that early success, he's had a long career in technological innovation and social change. He's currently chair of the Open Source Applications Foundation; he created and endowed the Mitchell Kapor Foundation; he was founding chair of the Mozilla Foundation and is a trustee of the Level Playing Field Institute. He was a founding investor in Second Life and continues to influence entrepreneurs and social change makers alike, with his frequent writings and active participation in the community of technology and philanthropy. In this interview conducted in summer 2007, Mitch reflects on three factors that are important to organizations thinking about how to use technology in their campaigns now and in the future. An edited portion of the transcript is presented here.

Web 2.0, Nonprofits, and Open Source

Web 2.0 is a convenient catchall to talk about the latest and greatest. It means so many different things to different people, but the latest generation of things you can do on the Web is much more participatory. They rely a lot more on users generating and sharing content with each other. They're much more media rich.

Web 2.0 is built on open-source software components, so the cost of development has dropped dramatically. Many more people are able to develop things much less expensively, especially people in college or right out of college. That's never been the case before.

It's always been a bit ironic that nonprofits have, on average, often been technological laggards rather than early adopters. Nonprofits are mission driven: they're trying in one fashion or another to improve the world. And that is very much at the heart of open-source values.

It is strategic for a nonprofit to leverage itself technologically. It really can't afford not to. And high leverage typically comes from using open-source and open-content tools. So if an organization is not equipped to do that, then it calls for a commitment to organizational change.

Virtual Worlds

Virtual worlds will undergo explosive growth in the next generation, in the same way that the first modern PC did over a little less than a human generation. Virtual worlds will become as widespread as the PC and the Web. The whole category is going to be the next major platform.

I would say that the comparable points in time are with the personal computer in the late 1970s or the early 1980s. It's certainly the DOS era, not the Windows era, for virtual worlds. In their current form, it's not a mass market with a billion people. It's a phenomenon, but it's getting there.

If you think that the Web is a platform for social change, you should be thinking about how virtual worlds are going to be an even more powerful platform for social change. And you should be learning now, by participation and experimentation in the early-adopter years, how those new dynamics work—and inventing the dynamics by which they work.

Social Features in Technology

It may be that one day almost everything you do online will have a social networking component. How that sorts itself out will be critical: How many networks are you going to belong to? Is your identity transferable? Why is this social network separate from that one? I don't know the answers to these questions, and I'm not sure that anyone else does. But this idea that you stay more actively connected with a community of people with whom you feel you have real relationships and interact with on-line is a very powerful one, and we're still in the early stages.

I'm on Facebook very frequently. It's like a news feed of what the people in my network are doing. For me, the social network is an enhancement of my real-world relationships. That's one model. Then there are other models, such as people in a World of Warcraft guild—that's their relationship with one another.

Social networking is an emerging phenomenon, and it hasn't taken its grown-up form yet. We'd like to believe that we know what's coming, but I think we just have to be prepared to move with it as it happens. As Alan Kay said, "The best way to predict the future is to invent it."

THE BIG PICTURE

Web 2.0, the Connected Generation, and the Future of Organizations

Essay by Katrin Verclas

Katrin Verclas has a long history working with technology and nonprofits. Most recently she was executive director of the Nonprofit Technology Network (NTEN). Prior to that, she codirected Aspiration, a nonprofit focused on providing software-related services to social sector organizations. Currently, Katrin is ramping up MobileActive.org, the network of activists making social change with mobile phones. In addition to being an incredibly sharp thinker with a voluminous memory and an intuitive strategic vision, she has been a dynamic force as board member to my nonprofit, Mobile Voter.

If nonprofit organizations want to survive, they'll need to adapt to a Web 2.0 world.

Web 2.0 describes a participatory, bottom-up, decentralized world full of individual expression where people have direct access to one another and enjoy an unprecedented ability to organize, meet, and coordinate without centralized control or traditional hierarchies.

People everywhere are expressing themselves online, bloggers are raising thousands of dollars for causes often not associated with established organizations, and members of nonprofit organizations have successfully and critically challenged old organizational orthodoxies. Wherever you look, there is a healthy skepticism toward "corporate-speak" and a digitally empowered activism that knows few sacred cows.

For young people in particular, the most profound change, and one that is often hard for adults to understand, is the pervasive *connectedness* of this new world—the constant access to friends and peers. As Tomi Ahonen and Allan Moore write in "Communities Dominate Brands," "Our communities, which previously only existed at given points in time, now become ever present. . . . In the connected age modern people are able to draw on the community for assistance, information, and support. We learn to search, share, and interact in a new way."

This Generation C—the "connected" generation—is more aware, more critical, and more skeptical of marketing messages. They are used to immediate feedback, quick to share, and always part of a multiplicity of fluid networks. Technology has made this generation possible.

Meanwhile, a wave of innovation has disrupted major industries, including the telephone, music, travel, and media businesses, to name just a few. It stands to reason that these disruptions will shake up nonprofit organizations as well.

So far for the typical organization, the disruption caused by what Web 2.0 embodies has not made organizational hierarchy and politics go away. The lowly member of a nonprofit or the frontline worker doesn't have as much power as the executive director, even if both can rant online. Organizations are essentially the same as they have been for the last fifty years.

Yet there is change in the air. The confluence of disruptive technology, highly connected young people, and the shifts we have seen in the commercial sphere are harbingers of an upcoming disruption in the third sector. Could it be that we are seeing the beginnings of a postorganizational society where, because we can connect and organize in so many new ways, we do not need the professionalized, advocating-on-our-behalf organizations that have dominated American civic life since the 1960s?

In an article in the *American Prospect* in 2004, the sociologist Theda Skocpol writes,

> Coming together in trade unions and farmers' associations, fraternal chapters and veterans' organizations, women's groups and public-reform crusades, Americans more than a century ago created a raucous democracy in which citizens from all walks of life could be leaders and help to shape community life and public agendas. But U.S. civic life has changed fundamentally in recent decades. Popular membership groups have faded while professionally managed groups have proliferated. Ordinary

citizens today have fewer opportunities for active civic participation. . . . Not coincidentally, public agendas are skewed toward issues and values that matter most to the highly educated and the wealthy.

More tellingly, she explains:

Today's advocacy groups are also less likely than traditional membership federations to entice masses of Americans indirectly into democratic politics. In the past, ordinary Americans joined voluntary membership federations not only for political reasons but also in search of sociability, recreation, cultural expression, and social assistance. Recruitment occurred through peer networks, and people usually had a mix of reasons for joining. Men and women could be drawn in initially for nonpolitical reasons, yet later end up learning about public issues or picking up skills or contacts that could be relevant to legislative campaigns, electoral politics, or community projects.

Does this not sound a lot like what happens today on sites like Facebook or Idealist.org?

It's easy, of course, to be hyperoptimistic and predict that the days of the dreary, checkbook-membership, top-down organizations as we know them are numbered. In the years following the Wright brothers' first flight, optimists predicted that because people couldn't see national borders from an aircraft, nationalism and war would disappear. Clearly, that did not happen.

However, it is safe to say that nonprofits, like companies, will have to change in order to survive this seismic shift in expectations and cultural assumptions. The shift is being driven by a generation that is experiencing an unprecedented degree of connectedness, community, and collective potential.

And although you can enhance your Web site with nice-looking gadgets all you want, in the end this is about a fundamental and even radical organizational change—because the world itself is irrevocably changing.

CONCLUSION

We're living in an age in which science fiction is becoming reality.

You can view the earth from space, spin it on command, and peer down at the rooftops below. A Sudanese refugee can speak to you as if he were your neighbor. News is no longer the exclusive domain of newspapers and television networks, but rather the product of millions of us writing in our blogs, uploading our videos to YouTube, and sharing our photographs on Flickr. Our body of knowledge is expanding exponentially through collaborative wikis. And wherever we go, we are within reach of a text message.

The scope and complexity of these changes may seem overwhelming, but through the examples in this book, we've seen how many organizations and campaigns are attempting to navigate the intricacies of Web 2.0 technologies and the associated shifts in our cultural landscape. At times, the technologies enable organizations to dramatically expand their reach, channel collective energy, empower supporters, and create new avenues for conversation and persuasion. Using Web 2.0 tools, some organizations have fulfilled their missions more effectively and at lower cost.

Others, however, seem adrift in the realm of possibility. They spend countless hours and dollars only to realize a lackluster return on their investment.

Do proven *formulas* for success exist? Unfortunately, no. Unlike such time-tested tactics as door-to-door canvassing, phone campaigning, and even e-mail marketing, Web 2.0 approaches have not been thoroughly researched. I've gathered anecdotal evidence from a wide array of sources for this book, but making social change with Web 2.0 technologies is still experimental. Can we observe *trends* among organizations that have conducted successful experiments? Thankfully, yes.

Factors Common to Successful Campaigns

In the process of writing this book over the past year, I've looked at hundreds of examples of nonprofit and political organizations that are using Web 2.0 technologies to support their missions or candidates. Four interrelated factors are common to some of the most effective efforts.

An Understanding of How People Use Technology

In the early years of the Web, circa 1995, many organizations created Web sites by scanning their brochures and putting them up on a Web page. This approach now seems quaint, because it barely scratches the surface of the Web's capabilities. Yet history is repeating itself as people yet again repurpose old tactics in a new context. One of the most common examples of this approach is using blogs and social networks to broadcast traditional advertising messages, instead of employing them as a jumping-off point for conversations and personal interactions. This type of repurposed advertising is typically ignored at best, ridiculed at worst.

To use Web 2.0 tools effectively, you have to know how they work and how people are using them. For example, blogging culture suggests that you write in a personal tone and respond quickly to comments. Text messages on mobile phones must be relevant to a person's physical location while delivering timely and useful information. Online maps ground people in a physical place, while revealing unseen patterns and associations. Social networks are akin to public spaces where people hang out, so traditional one-to-one organizing techniques work well.

Video can be used as much to have a conversation as to tell a story. People are making these tools their own, and they are often using them in ways you might not expect.

Adequate Resources

Most nonprofits and political campaigns are cash-strapped, understaffed, and short on time. Taking a risk on unproven technologies may seem unwise and unnecessary. In fact, it's likely that you can ignore Web 2.0 advances with few immediate negative consequences. Your old techniques will continue to work: the mainstream press is far from dead; television is still the fastest way to influence the largest number of people; young people will still respond to advertising.

However, as we've seen throughout this book, Web 2.0 technologies offer substantially new opportunities. Television may influence a vast number of people, but it's expensive—out of reach for all but the most well funded organizations. Online video, in contrast, makes visual communication accessible to almost anyone . . . and adds the element of conversation. Wikis enable organizations to quickly build vast resources by relying on supporters. In short, Web 2.0 technologies allow organizations to do more with less. Ignoring them would be a missed opportunity.

However, Web 2.0 tools are not magical—they don't simply work by themselves. You have to dedicate time and resources to making them work.

There are a few ways to begin using Web 2.0 tools. The first approach is low effort and low cost: you can experiment with building social networking profiles, reading blogs, uploading photos and videos, and designing a virtual world avatar. These efforts build familiarity with the tools and the social contexts that surround them, a necessary first step.

Once you've become familiar with the technical and cultural landscape, you may decide to take a more committed approach. In this case, you'll need to build, maintain, and integrate your Web 2.0 components. It's unrealistic to expect that simply putting up a social networking profile, for example, will achieve significant results without further effort. You'll have to spend time making friends, responding to messages, building widgets, and tying your efforts into a broader campaign. Being effective requires taking the time to understand the tools and then dedicating resources to make use of them.

A People-Centric Approach

It's exhilarating when you first fly through Second Life or crisscross the planet on Google Earth. However, there's a danger in fixating on the technology alone. If your supporters are highly technical, these applications may offer fertile ground for recruiting, organizing, and engaging them. However, most people, even youth, won't take the time to download, install, and learn technologies that are not already central to their social lives. Effective campaigns use technologies that are relevant and appropriate to the people they're intending to influence.

Online organizing is a lot like offline organizing: it's about people. This point should be reassuring, because it implies that successfully using Web 2.0 technologies relies on strengths and expertise common to many nonprofit and political organizations. Online organizing depends on the same principles that activists have refined throughout the last century: show people why they should act to change their world and then give them the tools to do it. Of course, some of the tools available now are relatively new, but people's motivations, incentives, and behaviors remain the same.

For example, to truly reach people, you need one of the oldest tools available: a good story. Author Ursula K. Le Guin has said, "The story . . . is one of the basic tools invented by the human mind for the purpose of understanding. There have been great societies that did not use the wheel, but there have been no societies that did not tell stories."[1] We use storytelling to convey emotion, elicit empathy, and generate action. Web 2.0 technologies can help by enabling richer, more vivid storytelling and by involving supporters in the telling.

Saving the Whales with a People-Centric Campaign

Here's how one organization successfully used technology to operate a campaign that focused on people. Greenpeace aimed to persuade Gorton's, a century-old seafood supplier, and their parent company, Nissui, to withdraw their support for Japanese whaling. Greenpeace's campaign story would start with a small hook, build to a moment of high drama (a so-called story arc), and then result in a successful action. But it wasn't a story that Greenpeace would tell alone—it would ask supporters to play a role in the telling of it.

The campaign began with an e-mail asking for a small donation to support Nathan Santry, a Greenpeace team member, on his voyage to find the Japanese whaling fleet in the Southern Ocean. Members who responded were directed to Santry's blog, where he posted frequent personal stories about his childhood, life on the open ocean, and his motivations for saving the whales. Over the course of several weeks, supporters developed a relationship with the campaigner, giving him encouragement in their blog comments. Greenpeace then made a slightly higher donation request around the winter holidays in order to keep Santry out on the water.

Santry found the whalers in January, and Greenpeace sent out a breaking news alert e-mail that linked to online video showing Santry's engagement with the Japanese fleet. With excitement running high, Greenpeace asked supporters to make their biggest contribution yet by hosting a house party to save the whales; 140 people agreed. Several weeks later, the parties took place across the country. The highlight was a conference call in which Santry answered questions via a satellite phone from the Southern Ocean. After Santry's call, Greenpeace reports that supporters were "fired up." At this high-energy moment, an organizer asked partygoers to spend the next thirty minutes making a plan for petitioning supermarkets where Gorton's products were sold.

Over the next month, supporters demonstrated in front of dozens of markets and gathered thousands of signatures on petitions. In the process, Greenpeace met a seventeen-year-old activist named Alexandra who lived in Boston, close to Gorton's headquarters. Organizers knew that if positioned cleverly, Alexandra would seize the attention of the *Boston Globe*, a newspaper that was likely to be read by Gorton's leadership and people in their social circles. On Valentine's Day weekend, Greenpeace's action team and Alexandra delivered the petitions to Gorton's along with a candy heart that read, "Have a heart, get out of the whaling business." They invited a *Boston Globe* journalist, and he wrote the story the following Monday. A few weeks later, Gorton's announced that its parent company agreed to divest from whale-hunting operations.

This fine-tuned campaign brought supporters on a journey from the Southern Ocean to Boston. It asked them to become progressively more involved along with the arc of the story, using blogs and online video to enliven the drama. Although Greenpeace organizers were extremely Web 2.0 savvy, they carefully chose only those technologies with maximum strategic value. The blog quickly created a strong personal connection between Santry and supporters that would keep them engaged and interested over the long term. Video delivered vibrant realism at a key point in the story's drama. Using Web 2.0 technologies to cultivate supporter enthusiasm, Greenpeace was able to drive *offline* action, a result that was critically important to achieving the campaign's objectives.

Campaigns that use Web 2.0 tools don't have to use these tools *exclusively*. Effective strategies often use the technologies as part of a broader campaign that centers on the motivations of people and involves them in a compelling story.

A Willingness to Embrace the Web 2.0 Ethos

The popularity of Web 2.0 technologies has been driven, in part, by a reaction to mainstream media. Blogs became widely read because they offered an authentic and personal alternative to traditional media outlets—newspapers, magazines, and television. The popularity of online video surged because it provided a forum in which viewers could respond. This is not to say that the mainstream media don't appeal anymore—far from it—it's just that Web 2.0 content commonly offers a more genuine and conversational alternative.

To be effective in the Web 2.0 environment, to some extent you have to adopt this more personal and transparent approach, while letting go of control and handing it over to your supporters. Successful organizations tend to value the contributions of their supporters, encourage individual leadership and decentralized action, de-emphasize hierarchy, share liberally, and create opportunities for supporters to interact with one another.

In the Greenpeace example described earlier, the blog became a place for supporters to interact with a staff member. This conversation was beyond the control of "branding" or "messaging." Supporters could say anything; Nathan Santry could say anything. Whaling proponents could have posted defamatory comments. There wasn't a marketing manager vetting the flow of information. Instead, Greenpeace trusted that this authentic dialogue would lead to its desired result.

This model of interaction represents a dramatic shift in how organizations typically operate. It allows supporters to help guide the direction of a campaign, suggesting that effective organizations will serve a role that is closer to that of a guide than that of a primary actor. They will find meaningful ways for volunteers to engage with a cause. They will nurture networks of individuals by providing resources, information, and expertise. And they will listen to supporters and adapt to what they hear.

Nonprofits and politicians stand to benefit from these changes by developing deeper relationships with supporters and making more efficient use of limited resources. We've seen dozens of examples throughout this book, such as Congressmen George Miller's substantive video-based dialogues with constituents and Ned Lamont's reliance on supporters to create campaign propaganda, the Student Global AIDS Campaign's use of a wiki to harness the energies of young activists to create a persuasive Web site, and Causes' Facebook fundraising tools, which allowed young people to raise significant sums.

The Next Wave of Innovation

New technologies are on the horizon that will complement those discussed in this book. One of the most promising emerging areas for social change is, believe it or not, online gaming. We're far from the days of shoot-'em-ups and Pac-Man, however. For example, with financial backing by MTV, several USC students have created a game called *Darfur Is Dying* that puts the player in the role of a Sudanese refugee. It raises awareness about the dangers facing children in this war-torn country and also asks for support. So far, the game has been played over 2.4 million times and has generated tens of thousands of dollars in donations and numerous mainstream media articles.

Currently the price of creating games prevents nonprofits, politicians, and average people from making extensive use of them. However, costs are falling quickly, and game-making tools are becoming less technical. Like that for online mapping, the technology may soon become simple enough that most people will be able to build games that tell stories and advocate for causes.

What else is coming? One of the biggest concepts that may well define the next evolution of the Internet is called the *Semantic Web*. Currently, Web pages are designed to be read by humans. For example, we can easily distinguish a blog post about global warming from a sales pitch for a toaster oven that warms bread and is sold globally. Computers cannot easily make this distinction without human assistance.

The Semantic Web movement aims to make the entirety of the Internet's information understandable to computers. If this vision becomes reality, you'll be able to query the Web as if it were a database. For example, you might write a query to find everything on the Web about global warming that was written by an accredited university professor and focuses on the impact on poor populations in coastal areas. When computers can make sense of the Internet's data like this, those data become infinitely more useful to humans.

Nonprofits and political campaigns stand to benefit not only from a higher degree of access to information but also from a freeing of internal information from existing data silos. One of the top complaints among social change organizations is that many software applications don't communicate with each other. Data are trapped in proprietary systems. The Semantic Web promises to alleviate this common problem—allowing organizations to put more attention toward making social change.

The Future of the Web 2.0 Movement

It's clear that tectonic shifts are well under way. Alternative media are flourishing. It's easier to communicate with close friends and distant relations alike, which is strengthening the wide diversity of social bonds. The range of information available to average people is growing rapidly. Significant hurdles and limitations exist, of course, such as a lack of access to computing resources among many of the world's poorest populations. However, on the whole, these changes are improving our quality of life and engendering a more vital, engaged, and democratic citizenry.

Still unclear is whether such optimistic trends will continue unfettered. Both radio and television once offered similar opportunities for individual expression and authentic dialogue, but established interests took control of the technologies and quashed these opportunities within a period of about twenty-five years. The Internet-enabled society of the future should continue to empower *both* business and the individual.

The time is right for politicians and nonprofits to take a leadership role in the development of Internet technologies. Social change organizations and political campaigns offer expertise, resources, and strategic insight that can positively guide the evolution of the dramatic shifts ahead, while ensuring that structural problems, such as lack of access, are addressed.

Every few generations, the ties that bind our society are shaken loose, and we're able to reshape facets of our lives. We can repair past in- equalities, redefine citizenship, and reframe the terms of economic success. We're in the midst of such a moment now. As social change makers and politicians, we have the opportunity to guide these forces toward the greater good.

Endnote

1. This quotation is widely attributed to Le Guin. It seems that it may have first been attributed to her in a "Dear Abby" column.